CW01368565

A–Z
of
Goldwork
with
Silk Embroidery

SEARCH PRESS

Contents

3 Brief history of goldwork
From the early beginnings

8 Before you begin
Get to know your threads and supplies
   8   equipment
   11 fabrics
   12 materials
   13 metal threads
   16 embellishment

17 Preparing for embroidery
Good preparation is the job half done
   17 transfer methods
   19 preparing the fabrics
   20 framing up
   22 finishing work

24 Starting and finishing
Good beginnings are happy endings
   24 appliqué
   27 applying padding
   32 securing threads

36 Goldwork stitches and techniques
Every step you need to know
   36   basic couching
   47   laid work
   64   couching over padding
   72   filling patterns
   80   pearl purl
   86   plate
   89   purl
   104 sequins and spangles

111 Silk embroidery
For extra colour and embellishment
   112 silk embroidery stitches

124 Design gallery
Exquisite goldwork projects
   124 butterfly
   128 strawberry pincushion
   131 rosehip
   134 flower border
   138 golden reticella
   141 autumn gold
   144 fleur de lys
   146 lyre

149 Patterns

153 Acknowledgements

154 Index

A small child finds a shiny pebble in a riverbed and the world is introduced to the glory of gold.

Brief history of goldwork

Throughout history, goldwork embroidery has been a symbol of opulence and distinction. It has been used to decorate the robes of emperors and kings, the ceremonial dress of military and clergy, and adorn the costume of the wealthy.

Goldwork refers to all embroidery worked with metallic threads regardless of the colour of the thread. The attraction is not just the colour, but the different textures of the threads and the interesting play of light created when altering the direction of the laid threads, or stitching over padding.

Court robe. Chinese before 1820.

Discovered in London antique shop 1964. Overall design in laid goldwork forming scrolling clouds and dragons.

Collection of Embroiderers Guild of America.

In the beginning

It is believed that gold embroidery originated in China and spread to the West with the silk merchants. In China, where strict rules dictated the use of colours and materials, gold embroidery was restricted to ceremonial and imperial dress, such as robes and rank badges. The gold threads were couched in coiling patterns to embroider five-clawed dragons, birds and beasts, or in laid pairs in fine lines for stylised clouds or to accentuate silk embroidery.

The art of gold embroidery travelled through West Asia to the Middle East and the ancient civilisations of Egypt, Assyria and Babylonia.

As the making of gold thread involved the manufacturing of both gold sheets and silk threads, the Jewish monopoly over both is likely to have extended to embroidered textiles. No embroidered pieces have survived, but a late 15th century painting shows Salome wearing a gown with floral motifs lavishly embroidered in gold thread.

Passages in the Old Testament describe strips of gold being worked onto a linen ground. After the birth of Christ, the techniques used for gold embroidery became widespread throughout the Middle East for both court and ceremonial ornamentation. Tyre, now Beirut, became the centre for gold embroidery and trade, both controlled by the Byzantines.

From the Mediterranean, gold embroidery spread to North Africa, through Spain into Italy and on to Western Europe, the British Isles, Scandinavia and North America.

Middle ages
English work ~ opus anglicanum

As the popularity of goldwork embroideries grew within both the church and the aristocracy throughout Europe, workmanship and opulence reached new heights during the Middle Ages and the Renaissance.

The term opus anglicanum means 'English work' and is thought to have derived from the inventories of noble households and churches of the period. It refers to embroideries, particularly ecclesiastical vestments, produced in England in the period from the 12th to the 15th century.

Book binding, opus anglicanum, 16th century. Restored late 19th century.

Worked on linen, the main characteristics of opus anglicanum are the figurative religious scenes, worked largely in split stitch, using coloured silks as well as the extensive use of underside couching for the background. This first appeared around the second half of the 12th century. The technique involves pulling the laid threads to the back with the couching thread so that no stitch is visible on the front. Stitches were placed in intricate patterns and as the couching threads were kept on the back of the work, the shadows created allowed the patterns to show up very clearly. Another advantage of using this couching method was that it allowed the garments to flow more freely.

The earliest examples of English goldwork in existence are fragments of a chasuble, which are kept in Maaseik, Belgium. Dating from the second half of the 9th century and in poor condition, these pieces show a linen fabric covered with embroidery worked in coloured silks, surface couched gold thread and pearl embellishment. The gold thread used for these pieces was made by wrapping pure gold strips around a single strand of animal hair.

The oldest, best-preserved pieces of opus anglicanum are the stole and maniple of St Cuthbert, dated 901 to 916, on display in the Durham Cathedral library. Both pieces have inscriptions on the back, stating they were embroidered at the request of Queen Aelfflaed as a gift to the bishop of Winchester. The figures, foliage and lettering are embroidered in fine silk. The background and haloes are filled with laid gold threads, couched five to the millimetre, in different geometric patterns, using coloured silk.

Opus anglicanum reached its peak between 1250 and 1350. Its reputation being such that simply stating a piece was worked by English hands was sufficient to prove its value. Much sought after on the continent, an inventory from the Vatican, dated 1295, lists over 110 opus anglicanum embroideries.

Royal and aristocratic costume and furnishings of opus anglicanum were also produced, but very few examples are still in existence. However, fine ecclesiastical pieces have survived and can be found throughout Europe. The best known is the Syon cope, late 13th to early 14th century, now in the Victoria and Albert Museum, London. Here the figures and rows of interlocking quatrefoils are worked in gold thread on velvet.

Towards the end of the period, robes were being made from luxurious silks and velvets and the characteristic dense embroidery of opus anglicanum was restricted to decorative bands and the shield-like hoods on the back of copes.

The specialised skill needed to work metal thread embroidery was highly prized and handed down through generations. Some ecclesiastical goldwork was made in convents, however much work was produced in professional workrooms with the designs most likely drawn by artists. The magnificent pieces were extremely costly. Records of payments for an alter frontal from Westminster Abbey, dated 1271, detail £36 in wages for four women working for 3½ years and more than £220 for the gold and silk threads, pearls and precious stones.

To maintain a high standard of workmanship, strict conditions were in place to control the embroiderers. Work could only be carried out after completion of an enforced 8 to 10 year apprenticeship. Embroidery could only be done by daylight, not candlelight and to ensure proper training; workshop owners were only allowed a limited number of apprentices. The quality of the gold was closely scrutinised and workers risked having their work destroyed if inferior metal was used.

Or nué ~ shaded gold

Towards the end of the 14th century, English work was in decline and spectacular embroideries were being produced in Italy, France and Flanders. Also known as Italian shading or shaded gold, or nué was developed in the early 15th century and soon surpassed other goldwork techniques throughout Europe.

Pairs of gold thread were laid and couched in place with coloured silks to create intricate pictures. The impression of depth, light and shadow was created using tonal values in the silks and varying the spacing of the stitches. Or nué is by far the most time consuming goldwork technique, but for the first time, embroiderers were able to imitate painted pictures. Italian embroidery became prominent, with such important artists as Raphael being commissioned to create embroidery designs.

The most exquisite surviving example of medieval or nué is the set of vestments for the 'Order of the Golden Fleece', which can be seen at the Treasury in Hofburg in Vienna. The faces and hands of the figures are embroidered in the finest silk thread and the robes and backgrounds worked in or nué.

Secular goldwork
16th to 19th centuries

The era of great English ecclesiastical embroidery came to an abrupt end when Henry VIII cut ties with the Catholic Church during the English Reformation. Large numbers of vestments were destroyed and the focus of professional workrooms shifted to domestic costume and furnishings. Knowledge of the precious pieces from this period comes largely from paintings as very few examples have survived. Most were unpicked and the metals and precious stones reused.

The exaggerated splendour of the Elizabethan court in the second half of the 16th century led to even more extravagant decoration of textiles with breathtaking gold embroidery, pearls, lace made from gold thread and

One of the vestments of the Order of the Golden Fleece, the Cope of the Virgin Mary.

Queen Elizabeth I, c1575 by Nicolas Hilliard. The costume richly embroidered in blackwork, goldwork and pearls and gems.

Men's suit, 1750s, by Mattheus Verheyden. Gold brocade vest and cuffs, richly embroidered.

precious stones. By the early 17th century the technology for producing metal thread had advanced, resulting in fine threads that could be passed through the fabric.

With this, embroidery techniques and designs changed, adding surface stitches and needlelace to the couching techniques. Fine gold and silver threads were often combined with blackwork and silk embroidery. The gold threads were stitched in coiling stem patterns to link a collection of flowers, birds and insects.

Wealthy households could boast their own embroiderer, or had the wealth to commission professional workrooms to make the piece required.

Smaller items decorated with gold embroidery such as sweetbags, pockets and purses, bookbindings and caskets could be made by the domestic embroiderer.

The decoration of dress at English and Continental courts made lavish use of metal and silk thread embroidery from the late 17th to mid 18th centuries. Couched gold embroidery was back in vogue. The designs created were dramatic with the gleam of gold set against a dark, strong coloured fabric.

Mens' suits were lavishly decorated, the waistcoat fronts at times entirely covered. The embroidered patterns, often imitating the designs of woven silks, were large in scale. The wide skirts fashionable at the time were an exceptional canvas to display wealth and social status.

Embroidery designs grew more naturalistic, with large floral motifs worked in coloured silk and gold embroidery. Towards the end of the 18th century the style of embroidery became much more delicate. Tantalising neoclassical borders were stitched in coloured silks and metal threads, with the extensive use of tiny spangles worked over a trellis or striped fabric.

Military and ceremonial gold embroidery

Throughout the world, goldwork has been used to decorate military uniforms, civil and ceremonial regalia for centuries, often guided by strict protocol. In England and Europe, the ceremonial trappings of horses were also adorned with gold embroidery.

Goldwork for regimental and ceremonial dress uniforms was meticulously couched with the use of card padding, which provided a sharp, crisp outline. Often ornaments were stitched as separate pieces known as 'cut clean-outs'. These backed motifs were edged with pearl purl or milliary wire and attached to the garment through this edging. This method is still being used today in workrooms, such as Hand and Lock in London.

19th and 20th centuries

By the early 19th century, goldwork embroidery had all but disappeared from fashion and had only a limited use in haute couture.

The tradition for ecclesiastical vestments had continued to flourish on the continent. By the mid 1800s it experienced a revival in England, helped along by the 'Gothic revival' so enthusiastically embraced by the Arts and Crafts movement. Architects, such as Augustus Pugin, believed in designing the building as well as everything within it. Influenced or designed by contemporary artists, such as William Morris, Walter Crane and Edward Burne-Jones, the embroidered textiles produced often featured naturalistic motifs filled with richly coloured silks, using gold threads for highlights and outlines.

From the 1950s, gold embroidery was embraced by a growing number of domestic embroiderers. With designs becoming increasingly abstract, embroiderers experimented with colour and texture.

Orphrey for Chasuble English circa 1880s
Cream satin with applied burgundy velvet, tan and green silk with metal thread and maroon silk edging. From the collection of the Embroiderers Guild of America.

Gold embroidery today

Today, gold embroidery is still an important element of military, religious and ceremonial textiles. The design for military pieces is constrained by tradition, but goldwork for religious and ceremonial purposes, as well as domestic embroidery, is often combined with other techniques and materials to create exciting contemporary pieces.

Whereas early examples of goldwork used expensive pure metals, now there are affordable substitutes available and this has contributed significantly to the interest in goldwork today. Art embroidery and an increased interest in fashionable goldwork accessories has seen the technique embraced by embroiderers around the globe. No longer the privilege of the church or the wealthy, it is fabulous that such a time-consuming, but stunning form of embroidery can still attract interest, allowing it to develop and grow in new directions.

First published in France in 1884 in 'The Encyclopaedia of Needlework', Thérèse De Dillmont writes in her introduction to gold embroidery:

"Up to the present time, dating from the end of the eighteenth century, gold embroidery has been almost exclusively confined to those who made it a profession; amateurs have seldom attempted what, it was commonly supposed, required an apprenticeship of nine years to attain any proficiency in.

But now, when it is the fashion to decorate every kind of fancy article, whether of leather, plush, or velvet, with monograms and ingenious devices of all descriptions, the art of gold embroidery has revived and is being taken up and practised with success, even by those to whom needlework is nothing more than an agreeable recreation."

Sampler, 1920–1940. Embroidered by Miss Elizabeth Lewis while studying at the Royal School of Needlework. From the collection of the Embroiderers Guild of Victoria.

Before you begin

Equipment

To achieve a good result in metal thread embroidery it is a good idea to add a few extra tools to your usual sewing kit.

Making a rolled felt bobbin

Cut a rectangular piece of felt approximately 15cm × 20cm wide (6" × 8").

Fold each long edge to the centre. Holding the folded sides in place, fold one short end to the centre.

Begin to roll the felt tightly from the folded short end.

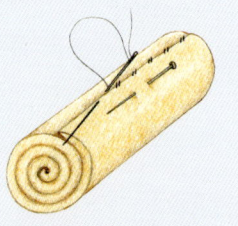

Secure the opposite end of the rolled felt with a pin and stitch the end securely in place.

Awl or stiletto

This is a pointed tool used for making holes in the fabric. By pushing the point of the awl through the fabric the threads are eased apart and a hole is prepared without breaking the fabric threads.

Beeswax

The thread used for couching the metal threads and sewing on beads and purls should always be passed over a piece of beeswax. The wax smoothes the fibres and stiffens the thread, making it stronger and preventing it from knotting while you stitch.

Buy the best beeswax you can find. Lesser quality wax can be crumbly and leave small flakes and marks on the embroidered work.

Bobbin

A bobbin is a reel or spool around which threads can be wound to prevent tangling. Wooden bobbins, also known as Japanese Koma, can be purchased from goldwork suppliers.

A felt bobbin is a handy tool when handling metal threads as it keeps the thread smooth and tidy. It can be pinned to the fabric while you work, preventing it from falling on the floor. Felt bobbins can be made by covering a card cylinder in felt, or just rolling a length of felt tightly.

Wrapping the thread around the bobbin will create extra twist in the thread and make it kink. To avoid this, rotate the bobbin to wind on the metal thread.

Chalk and charcoal (pounce)

These are both used in powder form called pounce, for transferring, using the prick and pounce method described on page 18.

Tailors chalk and chalk pencils are used for drawing patterns and designs onto fabric, but are not often used for goldwork embroidery.

Chalk and charcoal should only be used where the lines will be covered by stitches.

Clamps

It is important to have both hands free to manipulate the metal threads when working metal thread embroidery. Small clamps can be used to secure the hoop or frame to the table.

Couching threads

The metal threads are couched in place using a waxed matching machine sewing thread. Gütermann no. 488 is often recommended for couching gold threads, as the shade of this thread blends very well with the gold. Use very light grey or white when couching silver threads and an ochre colour for copper threads.

Frames and hoops

It is important to keep the fabric taut when working metal thread embroidery to avoid puckering. Ideally the fabric should be stretched onto a square or rectangular frame, but embroidery hoops can be used for smaller projects.

Embroidery hoops are useful for working smaller pieces, or slips, that will be applied to the main embroidery later.

It is useful to use a hoop with a floor or seat stand or to fix the hoop to the table with clamps or weights. It is advisable to use a good quality hoop, with solid brackets and a screw that can be tightened with a screwdriver. The inner ring should be bound with cotton tape to prevent the fabric from slipping while you stitch.

The slate frame is used for larger pieces of embroidery and gives the best result, as it is easily adjustable and holds the fabric at an even tension across the grain.

Slate frames are made from four bars, a roller bar with cotton tape at the top and bottom, and a stretcher bar on each side.

The upper and lower edge of the backing fabric is stitched to the tape on the roller bars and the sides of the fabric are laced to the side bars.

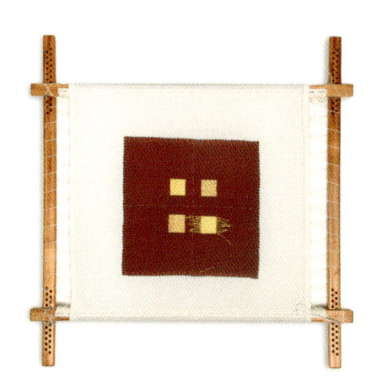

Stretcher frames can be bought from most art suppliers. Made from lengths of wood, they are available ready-made in several sizes, or can be made to specific measurements. The backing fabric and main fabric is stretched onto the frame and held in place with thumbtacks.

The stretcher frame holds the fabrics square and taut in the same way as the slate frame. The disadvantage of this frame is that the thumbtacks have to be removed and replaced to adjust the tension of the fabrics while you work.

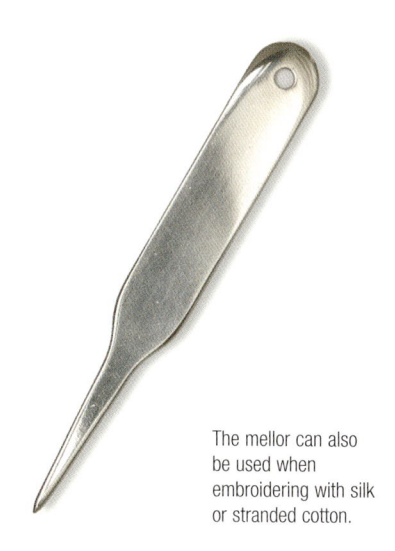

The mellor can also be used when embroidering with silk or stranded cotton.

Mellor

A mellor is a traditional and very useful goldworking tool used for arranging the metal threads. One end is tapered to a blunt tip and is used when turning the threads and for preparing holes in the fabric, in a similar way to an awl. The other end is flat and slightly rounded, much like a spatula. This end is used for pushing rows of laid threads close together.

Needles

A variety of needles are required for different purposes. The most useful needles to have is a selection of crewel needles and a large chenille needle.

Crewel or embroidery needles have an elongated eye making them easier to thread. A no.10 is good for couching laid threads in place and for attaching the larger purls. A no.12 needle is needed for the finer purls. Larger size crewel needles are useful when thicker embroidery threads are used.

Chenille needles have a very large eye and a sharp point. No. 18 or 20 are essential for taking the metal thread tails to the back of the work.

Fine metal threads and cords can be threaded directly into the needle. A sling is made from the chenille needle to take thicker threads through the fabric.

The following types of needles are also useful

Beading needles are very fine and will pass easily through even the finest purl and tiny beads.

Betweens are short needles with a round eye. They are not usually used for goldwork embroidery but can be used instead of crewel needles for couching the metal threads.

Curved needles can be helpful when securing the metal thread tails on the back of the work. Goldwork can be very dense and heavy. It can be difficult to sew into the stitches on the back using a straight needle. The curved needle allows you to stitch around the thread tail without distorting the fabric.

Milliner's or straw needles are rarely used for goldwork. However, a no. 1 needle can be useful if stitching with passing thread and a no.10 for couching or beading through very thick layers of padding.

Sharps are fine needles with a round eye. They can be used for couching, plain sewing and for applying embroidered slips to the main design.

Pliers

It can prove handy to keep a pair of small flat nose pliers in your metal thread workbox. They are useful for pulling the needle through thick layers of padding.

Pounce pad

This tool is made in the same way as the rolled felt bobbin. It is used to apply the pounce when transferring designs, using the prick and pounce transfer method.

Pricking tool

This tool is used for making tiny holes in the traced pattern for the prick and pounce transfer method. Special pricker handles that will hold a no.10 crewel needle are available. Pushing the eye end of a needle into a cork or rubber ball makes it an ideal pricking tool.

Scissors

Craft scissors are useful for cutting templates as well as card and felt padding.

Embroidery scissors are small pointed sharp scissors used for cutting embroidery and couching threads. Avoid using these scissors for metal threads or any other materials, as the fine blades are easily damaged.

Metal thread scissors or small short bladed pointy scissors, such as Fiskars 4" embroidery scissors, are essential for cutting metal threads and purls cleanly. Special metal thread scissors that have serrated blades are also available.

Sewing threads

Light coloured cotton sewing threads are most suitable for tacking and basting. Darker colours may leave marks on light coloured fabrics. Cotton threads break easily and are therefore less likely to damage the fabric or embroidery when removed, than if polyester thread is used.

A stronger thread, such as crochet cotton or no.8 perlé cotton is useful for lacing the fabric to the slate frame and for making the sling.

Sling

This is a tool used to sink the metal thread tails to the back of the work. You will need a no.20 chenille needle and a strong thread, such as no. 8 perlé cotton.

Thimble

Metal thread embroidery can be very hard on your fingers, particularly when pushing the needle through layers of padding and securing the tails.

A thimble is worn on the middle finger and is used to push the needle through the fabric.

When you work with one hand above and one below the frame you may find it useful to wear a thimble on the middle finger of each hand.

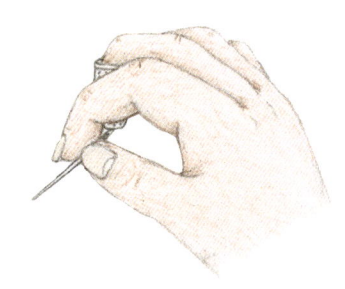

Thumbtacks

These are used to secure the fabric when stretching it onto a stretcher frame.

How to prepare a sling

Cut a 15cm (6") length of strong thread.

Pass the thread over a block of beeswax several times for added strength. Thread the tails into the eye of the needle in opposite directions to create a loop.

Tweezers

Pointed tweezers are used to manipulate the metal threads. They are used to shape the threads when turning corners and sharp points. Tweezers are also used when arranging pearl purls and for picking up and placing small lengths of cut purl. Use the tweezers carefully to avoid damaging the metal.

Velvet covered board

The velvet board is a helpful tool when cutting purls, as the pile in the velvet helps keep the purls steady and prevents them from 'jumping'. The tip of the scissors sinks into the pile around the purl, making cutting more precise.

Weights

Weights can be used to hold the frame or hoop steady on the table in a similar way to clamps. Using weights instead of clamps allows you to easily turn the frame when needed.

A padded and covered brick makes a perfect weight and can double up as a pincushion while you work.

Fabrics

With the exception of stretchy, sheer and very lightweight fabrics, most fabrics can be used for goldwork embroidery as long as they are stabilised with a backing fabric. When choosing your fabric, consider it as part of the overall design, not just as a blank canvas for the embroidery.

Backing fabric

The main fabric is nearly always backed with another fabric to provide extra strength and stability and prevent puckering. The weight of the backing fabric depends on the weight of the main fabric, the amount of goldwork it needs to support and the use of the finished piece.

Calico, fine linen and cotton are all suitable as backing fabrics as they are quite firm. It is important to always launder the backing fabric before use to remove any chemicals and allow for shrinkage. When placing the main fabric over the backing fabric, the grain of the two must be aligned.

Main fabric

To begin, choose a fabric that is closely woven and without any heavy texture as this may distort the evenness of the stitching. As you become more skilled you can choose more open weave and textured fabrics.

If fabric is unsuitable or very difficult to embroider onto directly, such as velvet, the goldwork can be worked on calico or linen and appliquéd onto the fabric.

Gold embroidery is quite heavy and the stitching dense so the fabric will in most cases require a backing fabric for added strength and stability.

Cottons, linens and wools are available in a multitude of weights and textures. Most are firmly woven, making them very suitable for gold embroidery, though they are not traditionally used.

Furnishing fabrics such as damask and jacquard, have patterns woven into the fabric and are not suitable choices for small projects. Stunning results can be achieved when these fabrics are used on a larger scale, such as church vestments, though it does require a certain degree of design skill to achieve a good balance between the embroidery and the fabric.

Man-made fabrics can also be used successfully, but are not as pleasant to handle as natural fibres.

Silk fabric is the most common choice for gold embroidery as the sheen of the fabric creates a wonderful background for the metallic threads. The extensive range of weights, textures and colours gives the embroiderer a wide variety to choose from.

Velvet is a beautiful fabric with a raised pile that does present the embroiderer with a challenge. Embroidery stitches easily disappear into the pile and the fibres in the pile 'creep' up between the rows of couching. For the best result, the embroidery should be worked on a separate piece of fabric and applied to the velvet. Alternatively, material such as felt can be stitched in place onto the velvet and the embroidery worked over the felt. When working with velvet, be aware that the direction of the pile will affect the appearance of the fabric.

Making a velvet covered board

Cut a piece of medium cardboard 10cm × 15cm wide (4" × 6"). Place it onto the wrong side of a piece of velvet.

Cut the velvet 2.5cm (2") larger around all sides for the seam allowance.

Lace or glue the seam allowance over the card along one side at a time, making sure the velvet is taut over the card.

Weights

In the work rooms at the Society of Ecclesiastical Arts and Craft in Copenhagen a collection of antique irons are used as weights.

Materials

Backing fabric
If the backing fabric is not laundered before use, it will often stretch during stitching, causing the finished embroidery to pucker.

Acid free card and paper
Thin card is used for padding under laid fillings and guimped embroidery to achieve smooth slightly raised surfaces with strong, clean outlines.

Heavier firm card is used for mounting the finished piece of embroidery.

Acid free tissue paper is useful to have at hand in which to wrap your metal threads, in order to preserve the quality.

Cotton cord or string
Cotton cord in various thicknesses is used as padding under laidwork and strong lines. It is important that the cord used is firm, smooth and tightly twisted. It can be coloured to match the colour of the threads used.

Felt
This non-fraying material is ideal as padding under laidwork and kid leather to enhance the play of light over the metallic surfaces.

The felt, in a colour to complement the threads, can be placed in a single or several layers to create a soft domed shape.

Kid leather
This is fine soft leather with a metallic coating, available in gold, silver and pewter. Kid leather is ideal to use as a contrast in texture among couched threads, but can be somewhat overpowering if used in large unbroken areas. Kid leather is most often stitched over felt or cord padding to create dimension and improve the play of light.

Soft cotton thread
Thin soft threads, such as floche are used as a smooth padding under narrow areas, such as stems. The threads are waxed and bundled together to achieve the required thickness. The bundle is couched in place and the ends easily tapered by trimming the number of the threads in the bundle.

It is advisable to use cotton matching the colour of the metallic threads.

Tissue paper
This fine semi-transparent paper is used for transferring designs by tacking, as it tears easily.

Tracing paper
This is a transparent paper used for transferring designs onto fabric. When transferring using the prick and pounce method, the tracing paper must be good quality to achieve a good result.

Baking paper can be used as an alternative to tracing paper for other transfer methods.

Metal threads

Most metal threads contain very little or no precious metals, so the colour description refers only to the colour of the thread.

The most precious gold threads readily available contain just 2% gold. These threads are also known as Admiralty or Government gold, the name referring to the quality of the thread, by metal content, used for the British Services' uniforms.

A less expensive range of threads is gilt threads which contain about ½% gold on silver plated copper. It has a similar appearance to Admiralty gold, but will tarnish faster.

Metal threads can be divided into two main groups; couching threads and purl threads.

Couching threads

This group includes braids and cords, imitation Japanese, passing threads, rococo, twists, plate and pearl purl. The textures and sizes of this group of threads vary greatly. The thickness is indicated by a number, the higher the number the finer the thread.

These types of threads are all couched in place on the fabric with a much finer thread, such as sewing thread, stranded cotton or fine silk.

Braid and cord

These are traditionally used to create strong lines and are most often seen on larger pieces such as military regalia, church vestments and banners.

Braids are flat decorative threads or bands made from finer threads that have been plaited to create various widths and patterns. Metallic braids are hard to come by, but lurex threads are available, however they do have a more 'glitzy' appearance.

Russia braid is a very traditionaly braid. It is made from fine metal threads, plaited around two parallel cotton cores in a fishbone pattern.

Cords are round threads made from a number of finer threads, twisted together in various patterns.

Heavy cords are made from groups of twisted threads, twisted again into a cord. The size of the cord is determined by how many groups of threads are twisted together.

Broad plate

This thread is made from a fine wire that has been passed through rollers several times to create a thin flat thread. No. 6 broad plate is readily available, but other sizes are also made, however they are more difficult to come by.

Plate can be couched in place in straight lines or bent back and forth over string or felt padding to cover a shape. The thread can be difficult to work with and once it has been bent it is marked and cannot be re-stitched.

Imitation Japanese thread

Commonly known as 'imitation Jap', 'Jap gold' or 'Jap thread'.

Japanese gold threads were originally made by placing gold leaf onto rice paper. The paper was then cut into narrow strips and wrapped around a core of orange silk fibres.

The imitation and substitute threads commonly used today are made from metallisied polyester strips wrapped around a core of yellow silk, cotton or synthetic threads. They are available in various sizes measured by the thickness of the core; the higher the number the finer the thread.

Couching thread 371 is a very fine couching thread available in a multitude of colours. It is used in the same manner as other couching threads, but its fineness makes it suitable for fine detail.

Imitation Japanese threads are numbered T69 to T72. These threads are traditionally couched in place in pairs and is the most common thread used to fill solid shapes. They are softer in colour and are easier to handle than substitute threads. Imitation Japanese thread is also available in silver and copper.

Substitute Japanese gold threads have a brilliant appearance and are available in four sizes K1 to K4.

no. 2 pearl purl

no. 2 smooth purl

no. 6 smooth purl

no. 8 smooth purl

no. 8 rough purl

no. 3 check purl

no. 6 check purl

371 couching thread

T69 imitation Japanese thread

3ply twist

no. 5 rough purl

no. 8 check purl

T70 imitation Japanese thread

3 ply twist

no. 6 pearl purl

no. 8 smooth purl

Milliary wire

This very textured, rigid wire thread is made from a firm core wire with a finer coiled wire wrapped tightly to it. The wire is used primarily for strong, textured outlines, but can also be used to add interest among rows of solid couching.

Passing thread

This is a smooth, less shiny but very durable thread. Passing thread is made from a core that is twisted in one direction and wrapped with a gold thread in the opposite direction. This produces a strong thread that does not twist.

It is one of the only threads which can be worked through the fabric, and was used extensively by Elizabethan embroiderers to work raised stem bands and chain stitch outlines. If working with passing thread in the needle, use very short lengths and a needle with a large round eye, such as a no.1 milliner's, to accommodate the thread.

Passing thread is traditionally used for underside couching in opus anglicanum and techniques that require a constant coiling or twisting of the laid thread.

Pearl purl

This is made from hard wire, coiled tightly to create a firm hollow spring that looks like a row of beads. It is commonly used to define outlines and fine lines. When pulled slightly the thread becomes rigid and very easy to handle and shape. It is couched in place in a manner which hides the stitches in the grooves between the coils. When pulled open the thread becomes an open spiral ideal for adding texture.

Pearl purl is available in a number of sizes, the higher the number the finer the thread.

Rococo

Rococo and check (also crinkle) threads are shiny threads with an undulating finish. The core of the thread is wrapped with a second thread to create a wavy texture before it is wrapped with a narrow strip of gold foil. Rococo threads have an open wavy texture, while check threads have a tighter crimped appearance. Rococo and check are traditionally couched singularly along smoother threads to add a change in texture.

The threads are available in three sizes; fine, medium and large.

Twists

These metal threads are made from three or more fine threads twisted together. They are available in a number of thicknesses often referred to as ply; the higher the number the thicker the thread.

Most twists are couched in place so the direction of the couching stitches follows that of the twist, allowing the stitches to sink through the thread and become invisible.

Very fine twist, such as Elizabethan twist and metallic threads sold for hand and machine embroidery, can be threaded into the needle and sewn through the fabric. It is advisable to use short lengths and a needle with a round eye large enough to accommodate the thread.

Grecian twist is made in a similar way to twist. It is a heavier 4-ply twist made from two rough and two smooth threads to create a distinct stripy pattern.

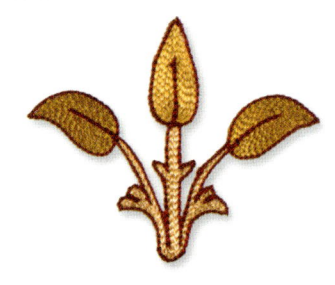

Purl and bullion threads

These are made by spinning fine wire tightly around a needle to create flexible hollow tubes. Textured threads are made in a similar way by using a triangular or faceted needle.

Purls and bullions are available in various thicknesses; the higher the number the finer the thread. The hollow tubes are cut into short lengths and sewn in place like beads, giving them an appearance similar to bullion knots.

With the exception of pearl purl, all bullions and purls are very soft and springy and should be handled with care as they are very easily damaged.

Bullion threads

These are made from very fine wire with a large diameter; up to 5mm (3/16") making them very stretchy and soft. They are available in three textures. Bright check bullion has a sparkly faceted appearance. Bright bullion is shiny and smooth and wire bullion is smooth with a matte appearance.

Purl threads

These are very similar to bullion threads but tend to be a little firmer. They have a smaller diameter; up to 2mm (1/16") and are available in three different textures.

Bright check purl is a textured thread with a faceted surface. It is most commonly cut into very short lengths known as 'chips', which are stitched in place close together to cover a shape.

Smooth purl is a round coil with a very shiny reflection. **Rough purl** is also round, but the coil is made from a much duller wire.

Both smooth and rough purl are available in up to seven sizes; the larger the number the finer the purl. Traditionally available in gold, silver and copper, some sizes are now also available in colours such as blues, greens and mauves.

Other metallic threads

Metal coloured knitting yarns and ribbons are available in many colours and weights. These threads can be successfully incorporated into metal thread embroidery.

Lurex was originally the trademark of the manufacturer, but is now the generic term used for metal covered plastic thread. A wide range of threads is available. The appearance of these threads can be a bit 'glitzy' and at times difficult to tie in with other metal threads.

Metallic machine and hand embroidery threads are available in numerous weights and finishes, from thick metallic perlé to fine blending filaments. All these threads can be used successfully in metal thread embroidery.

Embroidery threads

Coloured silks and cottons are often used in combination with goldwork. They can be used to add shading to the metal or used for surface embroidery to create sprays of colour among the metal thread embroidery.

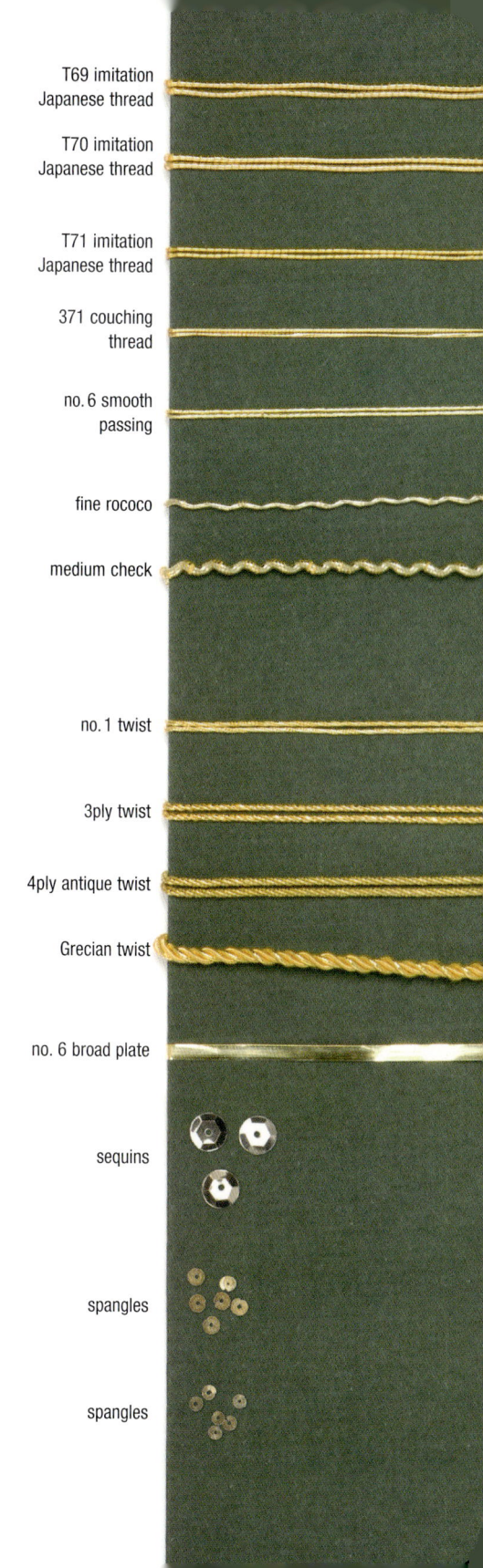

T69 imitation Japanese thread

T70 imitation Japanese thread

T71 imitation Japanese thread

371 couching thread

no. 6 smooth passing

fine rococo

medium check

no. 1 twist

3ply twist

4ply antique twist

Grecian twist

no. 6 broad plate

sequins

spangles

spangles

Embellishment

Beads

Any kind of bead can be incorporated into metal thread embroidery. Beads come in many shapes and sizes and can be made from a large variety of materials, such as glass, porcelain, metal, wood and semiprecious stones.

Beetle wings

Incorporating the hard iridescent coverings of beetle wings into embroidery originated in India. A tiny hole is punched through each end of the piece so it can be stitched onto the fabric.

Sequins

These are punched out shapes with a hole in the centre. Flat or cupped, they are available in a number of sizes and a multitude of colours. Where the term paillette refers to a round shape, sequins are available in many different shapes. Sequins are traditionally used for bead embroidery but also combine well with metal thread embroidery.

Spangle

These are usually much smaller than sequins and are made from metal rings that are hammered flat, making them less uniform than sequins.

Pearls

Pearls have a long history of being incorporated into gold embroidery. They are available in various sizes in a range of soft pastel colours. Both round pearls and the irregular shaped freshwater pearls are usually pierced and sewn in place like beads.

Rhinestones and semi-precious stones

Rhinestones are made from glass or plastic. They have a flat back and a facetted, domed front and are available in many different sizes and shapes, in a vast variety of colours.

To bring out the colour, most rhinestones are backed with metal; some with a backing directly on the stone and others are held in place on the backing with tiny claws. The stones are sewn in place through small holes at the edge. Semi-precious stones used in embroidery are usually made into beads.

Detail, small mat. Early 20th century, India. Fine white cotton embroidered with a border pattern of stylised flowers in silver plate, silver pearl, sequins and beetle wings. From the collection of Embroiderers Guild of South Australia.

Preparing for embroidery

Transfer methods

There are several methods and tools to choose from to help you transfer embroidery designs onto fabric. The method you choose will depend on your choice of fabric, the size and intricacy of the design, the use of the finished embroidery and your personal preference.

Designs can be transferred before or after the fabric is placed taut into a hoop or onto a frame. The advantage of transferring onto a taut fabric is that it won't slip while the design is being transferred. This method also minimises any distortion of the design that could occur when the fabric is stretched after the design is transferred. Some transfer methods require a firm surface behind the fabric. Place blocks, boards or books that fit inside the hoop or frame behind the fabric.

> **Using carbon paper**
> Try not to slide your hand across the paper while you are tracing, as this can cause light smudging.

Carbon tracing

This method is suitable for transferring onto fabrics with a smooth surface. The transferred lines can easily rub off as you work, so it is a good idea to cover areas not being worked with a cloth.

This is a simple method for transferring fine details but the design lines, though faint, are permanent and should be covered by embroidery. Carbon paper is available in a range of colours; choose a colour that will show on the fabric but blends with the overall tone of the embroidery.

To use this method after the fabric is framed up, create a firm surface behind the fabric.

1 Using a fine pen or pencil, trace the design onto tracing paper. Position the tracing over the fabric and pin in place at the upper corners.
2 Slide the carbon paper, with the coloured side facing the fabric, under the tracing. Using a ballpoint pen or sharp pencil, retrace the design lines.
3 Carefully lift one corner of the tracing to make sure all lines have been transferred before removing the tracing.

Direct tracing

This method of transferring is only suitable for fine and light coloured fabrics. By placing the embroidery design and fabric over a light source the embroidery design appears clearly through the fabric.

You can easily transfer fine details using this method. Cover areas not being worked with a cloth as the pencil lines may smudge or rub off as you work.

This method is not suitable after the fabric is placed in the hoop or frame.

1 Use a fine black pen to trace your design onto tracing paper.
2 Tape the tracing onto a light box or over a window.
3 Position the fabric over the tracing and tape in place or hold firmly in place with weights.
4 Use a very sharp, hard pencil (HB or H) or a fine acid free permanent pen to trace the design onto the fabric.

Indirect tracing

This method is only suitable for light coloured fabrics with a smooth surface. To use this method after the fabric is framed up, create a firm surface behind the fabric.

The transfer lines can be a little pale and can easily become paler while stitching. To avoid this, cover sections of the design with a cloth, as for direct tracing, until you are ready to stitch.

1 Use a fine pen to trace the design onto tracing paper or baking paper. Turn the tracing over and retrace the design on the other side with a sharp HB pencil or mechanical pencil.
2 Position the tracing, right side facing up, over the fabric and pin in place. Use a ballpoint pen to retrace the design lines, using a firm even pressure.

The pencil lines on the back will work as a carbon and transfer onto the fabric.

Prick and pounce

~ In Scandinavia the pounce is replaced by a permanent ink. The ink is applied over the pricked design using a rolled felt pad in a similar manner to the pounce. To make sure the ink is pushed through the tiny holes in the pricked tracing, an eraser is used to rub along the design lines in small firm circular movements. The pricked tracing is removed, leaving the design clearly marked on the fabric by tiny dots, eliminating the need to paint along the dotted lines.

~ In France the pounce mixture is made by blending ⅓ of powderised pine resin with ⅔ of charcoal or chalk pounce. Once the pounce mix has been rubbed through the holes in the pricked design the tracing is carefully lifted away. A piece of tissue paper is gently placed over the transferred design. A warm iron is then used over the tissue paper. The heat from the iron melts the resin, fixing the pounce to the fabric and leaving the design marked clearly by small dots.

Prick and pounce

This is the traditional method used to transfer designs for goldwork embroidery and is the method most commonly used in professional workrooms as the pricked design can be used several times.

Prick and pounce is quite labour intensive compared to other methods of transferring, but it is very accurate and ideal where padding is required because the transfer lines are exactly the same for each piece.

When choosing this method, the transfer lines are permanent so it is important only to transfer lines that will be covered by embroidery. Be aware that pounce is not suitable for heavily textured fabrics or velvet.

1 Using a sharp pencil, trace the design onto tracing paper.
2 Place the tracing over layers of craft felt, upholstery felt or a cork mat.
3 Using a pricking tool in a straight upright movement, prick holes along the design lines at 2mm (¹⁄₁₆") intervals.

4 Hold the pricked tracing up to the light to make sure all design lines have been pricked.
5 Use a very fine grade sandpaper or emery paper to lightly sand the wrong side of the pricked design, to remove the rough paper around the tiny holes.

6 Place the fabric on a firm surface and secure it with thumbtacks, tape or weights around all edges to hold it firmly in place. Position the pricked design over the fabric and pin in place.
7 Lightly dip the pounce pad into the pounce. Rub the pad firmly over the design in a circular movement, rubbing the pounce through the holes in the pricked design.

8 Carefully lift away the tracing. Fine lines of pounce dots will make the design visible on the fabric, but are very easily rubbed away. Gently blow away any excess powder that has collected on the surface. The pricked tracing can be wiped clean with a tissue and used again.
9 Choose a watercolour appropriate for the colour of your fabric. Dark grey, white, pale blue or yellow are the most suitable. Use a fine paintbrush (size 1) to carefully paint very fine lines along the dotted lines to permanently mark the design. Leave to dry.

9a Where design lines will not be covered by embroidery, mark the lines by tacking using a pale colour cotton sewing thread.

10 Remove the remaining pounce by shaking the fabric well.

Tacking

This transfer method is mostly used for textured fabrics and velvet, where other methods are not suitable. It is also used where the design lines will not be covered by embroidery.

The tacking is worked in a medium sized, spaced, back stitch. If the tacking is worked in running stitch, as is most common, the stitches will easily distort or break when the tissue paper is removed.

1 Frame up the material and backing fabric before transferring the design to prevent the fabrics from moving.

2 Using a fine black pen, trace the design onto tissue paper. Position the tracing over the fabric and secure around the edges, making sure the tracing is held firmly in place.

3 Using a light coloured cotton sewing thread, tack along the design lines using medium sized, spaced back stitches.

Make sure you secure the tails of the tacking threads firmly.

4 When all the lines are covered, carefully tear away the tissue paper. The tissue paper can be lightly moistened, using a damp cloth to make it tear more easily, but care should be taken not to dampen the fabric if it has a tendency to watermark.

Cotton sewing thread

It is best to use cotton sewing thread for tacking. It breaks easier than polyester thread and there is less risk of damaging the fabric and embroidery when the tacking is removed.

Tacking without tissue paper

Instead of using tissue paper, a mirror image of the design can be transferred onto the wrong side of the backing fabric. Once the fabrics are layered in the frame, the design lines are tacked, making them visible on the right side of the fabric. This method eliminates removing the tissue paper.

Preparing the fabrics

The fabric piece should be a generous size for your embroidery design. Allow approximately 10cm (4") from the edges of the embroidery design to the edges of the fabric.

If the fabric piece has been folded, check that the crease is not dusty or damaged because such marks can be difficult to remove and will spoil your finished piece.

It is a good idea to have a small spare piece of fabric mounted in a hoop so you can practise stitches and experiment with effects and textures before using them on your embroidery.

Once you have chosen your fabric, press it with a steam iron and leave it laying flat, or roll it onto a cardboard roll ready for use.

When embroidering with metal threads the main fabric will always need to be stabilised with a backing fabric. Launder the backing fabric to allow for any shrinkage before use and press while it is still damp. Roll the fabric onto a roll ready for use in the same way as the main fabric.

Framing up

It is essential to use a hoop or frame for goldwork embroidery to keep the fabrics taut throughout the stitching and to leave both hands free for arranging the threads.

Embroidery hoop

An embroidery hoop or ring frame can be used for smaller pieces of goldwork embroidery. To give the hoop a better grip on the fabrics the inner ring should be bound with cotton tape.

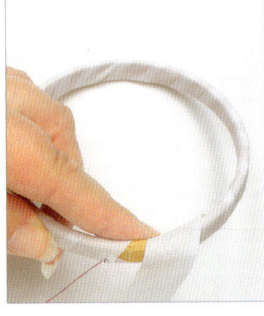

Wrap the binding around the hoop, ensuring there are no creases and the layers of binding overlap. Secure the end with small stitches.

Cut the fabrics at least 10cm (4") larger than the diameter of the hoop. Neaten the raw edges of the fabrics with a machine zigzag or overlock stitch to prevent fraying.

1 Centre the main fabric over the backing fabric, making sure the straight grain of the fabrics is aligned.
2 Keep the layered fabrics flat. Using a light coloured cotton sewing thread, tack from the centre along the grain, dividing the fabrics into quarters.
3 Place the layered fabrics over the inner ring of the hoop. Slide the outer ring into place over the fabrics. Pull the fabrics firmly on the straight grain to a taut even tension.

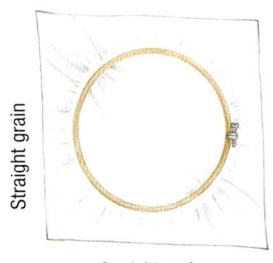

4 Tighten the screw of the hoop.

The tacking can be removed gradually as the embroidery is being worked. Leave the fabrics in the hoop until the embroidery is complete.

Stretcher frame

The backing fabric and main fabric are cut to the same measurements, allowing enough fabric to cover the sides of the frame.

Neaten the raw edges of each fabric with a machine zigzag or overlock stitch.

1 Place the backing fabric with the right side facing down. Centre the frame over the fabric, ensuring the straight grain is aligned with the sides of the frame.
2 Pull the fabric over one side of the frame and pin in place with a thumbtack at the centre of one side.

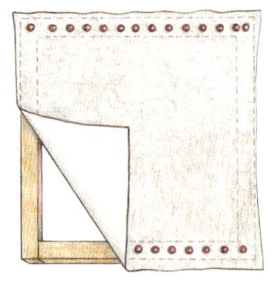

3 Working from the centres outwards, pin the remaining two sides of the fabric. Place the thumbtacks at regular intervals, pulling the fabric taut as you work.
4 Repeat for the remaining two sides.
5 Centre the main fabric over the backing fabric, making sure the straight grain of the fabrics is aligned.
6 Pin the main fabric in place in the same manner as the backing fabric, placing the thumbtacks between the previous.

Using an embroidery hoop

~ Avoid tightening the layered fabrics by pulling at the corners as this will stretch them and distort the grain, causing puckering.

~ The fabrics should be left in the hoop until the embroidery is complete. If you remove layered fabrics from a hoop and place them back later, the fabrics may shift, which will cause puckering. As the hoop will mark the fabric, it is important that the size of the hoop is large enough to encompass the complete design.

Tacking layered fabrics

Fabrics should always be tacked together or to stretcher bars, from the centre to the sides, to prevent the materials from 'walking'.

Slate frame

Cut the backing fabric to fit the frame. Allow the upper and lower edge to overlap the cotton tape on the frame and add a 1cm (⅜") wide double hem at each side. Cut the main fabric 10cm–15cm (4"–6") larger than the embroidery design.

Preparing the backing fabric

1 Neaten the upper and lower edge of the backing fabric with a machine zigzag or overlock stitch.
2 Fold a double hem over a fine string along each side of the backing fabric and stitch in place, leaving a tail of string extending at each corner.
3 Remove the stretcher bars from the frame. Mark the centre of the tape on the upper and lower bar and on the upper and lower edge of the backing fabric.
4 Place the upper edge of the backing fabric over the tape on one roller bar, aligning the centre marks. Working from the centre to the sides, overcast stitch the backing fabric to the tape.

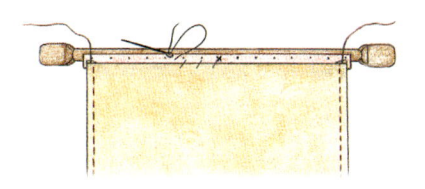

Repeat to attach the fabric to the second bar.

5 Re-assemble the stretcher frame and position the pegs to hold in place. Tie the string tails to the side bars above the rollers.

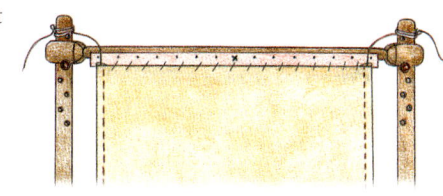

6 Use a strong cotton thread, such as perlé cotton, from the ball to allow a continues length of thread. Lace each side of the backing fabric to the stretcher bars, stitching around the enclosed string. Knot the thread tails around the corners of the frame. This enables you to adjust the tension of the lacing as required.

7 Relax the backing fabric by adjusting the position of the pegs.

Positioning the main fabric

8 Centre the main fabric over the backing fabric, ensuring the straight grain of the fabrics is aligned.

Use light coloured cotton sewing thread to tack the fabrics together along the centres. Leaving a long tail, begin each row of tacking at the centre and work to one side at a time.

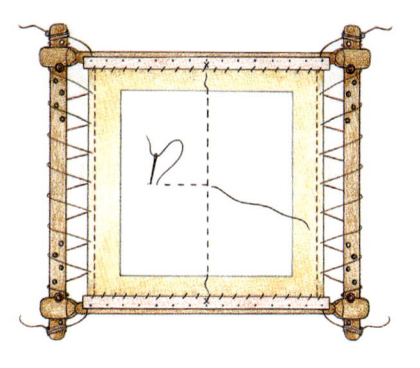

Using a stretcher frame

~ The main fabric can be cut to fit inside the stretcher frame and mounted on top of the backing fabric in the same manner as when using a slate frame.

~ The disadvantage of using a stretcher frame is that to retighten the fabrics while the work is in progress, the thumbtacks will have to be removed and replaced.

9 For large pieces, tack the fabrics together in a grid to prevent puckering. Begin each row at the centre and place the rows at 2.5cm (1") intervals.

10 Stitch the sides of the main fabric to the backing fabric with long and short overcast stitch. Repeat for the upper and lower edge.

Tightening the frame

11 Reposition the pegs and tighten the lacing so the fabrics are drum tight.

Remove the rows of tacking across the fabric as the embroidery progresses.

Finishing work

Once you have completed your embroidery the piece needs to be 'finished'. Cleaning and pressing your work is just as important a part of the process as the actual stitching.

Cleaning

In the case of most other embroidery this would often involve washing or dry cleaning. However, most metal threads are unsuitable for these forms of cleaning, as the cleaning will cause the threads to tarnish much faster. It is therefore very important that you cover your work at most times. If you are embroidering on a very large piece, cover the sections that you are not working on to prevent them from becoming soiled. It is important to keep your hands very clean while you work, as oil from your skin will cause tarnishing. Also resist the temptation to apply hand lotion before you commence stitching.

Pressing

Embroidery should always be pressed from the wrong side to avoid flattening the stitches. This is particularly important with padded and textured work. Place the embroidery with the right side facing down on a well padded surface, such as a towel folded into several layers. Press the piece using the setting appropriate for the fabric.

When pressing goldwork, only press the fabric surrounding the embroidery, avoiding the stitched areas as the steam from the iron may hasten the tarnishing of the threads.

Embroidery worked in silk will benefit from being pressed or steamed to enhance the shine and brightness of the threads. Hold a steam iron just above the right side of the embroidery and leave the piece laying flat until it is completely dry.

Lacing embroidery

Before being placed into a frame the embroidery needs to be laced over cardboard to hold the surface smooth. Cut a piece of acid free cardboard at least 1cm (⅜") larger on all sides than the opening required in the mount. Cut a piece of thin wadding to the same size.

1 Place the wadding over the card.

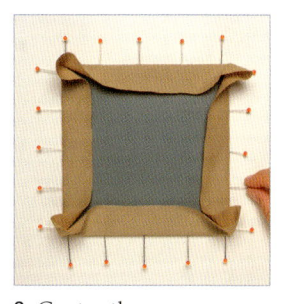

2 Centre the embroidered fabric over the wadding. Pin in place, pushing pins into the ends of the card around all sides. Turn to the wrong side and fold the excess fabric to the back.

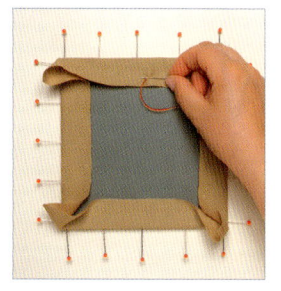

3 Secure a long doubled length of strong thread in the middle of the over-lapping fabric on one side.

4 Make a small horizontal stitch through the over-lapping fabric on the opposite side.

5 Pull the thread firmly. Work a small stitch on the first side. Pull firmly. Make sure that the front of the work is smooth.

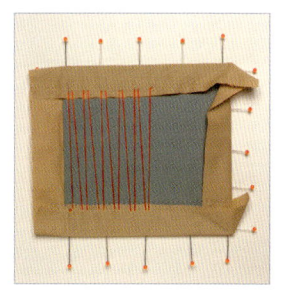

6 Continue stitching from side to side in this manner until reaching one edge. Tighten the lacing and secure the thread.

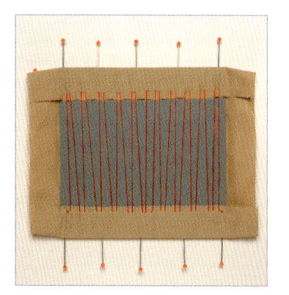

7 Repeat for the remaining half. Tighten the lacing as you work and ensure the edges and front of the work is smooth.

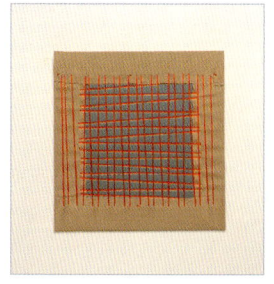

8 Lace the remaining two sides in the same manner. Remove the pins.

Caring for old embroidery

~ If you are lucky enough to own a piece of old embroidery, there are a few tips that can help you preserve your piece in the best condition possible. The aim when conserving a textile is to stabilise it and store it in the most suitable manner. It is advisable to seek help from a trained textile conservator if the item needs cleaning, as the task of stabilising the condition of old textiles is quite specialised.

~ Avoid pressing and ironing, as this will hasten deterioration. Roll flat objects onto card tubes covered in acid free tissue, interleaving the item as you roll. Clothing should be stored in a large flat box lined with acid free tissue, as sharp creases will damage the fabric. Any folds should be supported with acid free tissue. Store your pieces in a dry, well-ventilated place, away from natural light.

Starting and finishing techniques

The methods for starting and finishing metal threads differ from the methods most commonly used for other embroidery. Appliqué and padding are important elements for achieving a good finish.

APPLIQUÉ

This is a stitching technique in which fabric shapes, or pieces of embroidery, are cut out and stitched in place on the main fabric. The embroidered and cut out shape is often referred to as a 'slip'.

Appliqué is a useful method when embroidering large pieces, such as vestments or banners. The goldwork slip is worked on a small frame, before being cut out and applied to the main fabric. The fabric on which the goldwork is worked, should be backed for stability and strength. To avoid puckering it is very important that the grain of the fabric for the appliqué piece is aligned with that of the main fabric.

Outlines

Decorative outlines become a distinct part of the overall design. It is important to consider the most suitable finish, weight, colour and texture for the outline, so that it will complement and not overpower the overall design.

Method one ~ concealed edge

The embroidered piece can be cut out and applied to the main fabric before the raw egdes are neatened by decorative cords or blanket stitch.

1 Complete the metal thread embroidery of the appliqué shape, working on closely woven, backed fabric, eg double layers of calico.

2 Using fine sharp scissors, carefully cut out the prepared shape, leaving a 3mm (⅛") seam allowance. Position the piece on the main fabric.

3 Tack or pin in place, taking care not to damage or distort the metal thread embroidery, ensuring the grain of the fabrics is aligned.

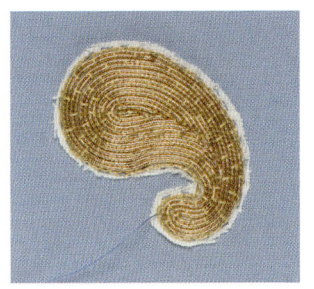

4 Using a matching thread, stitch the piece in place with small stitches along the edge of the embroidery.

5 Conceal the seam allowance with twisted cord, braid or laid metal threads.

6 Alternatively, stitch the appliqué piece in place by working close blanket stitch over the seam allowance.

Method two ~ neatened edge

The edges of the appliqué piece can be neatened with a close blanket stitch or machine zigzag to prevent fraying. The neatened edge can be incorporated as a design outline or covered with threads, cords or braids for a more decorative finish. Work the slip on a backed, firm fabric.

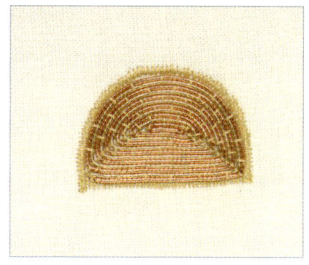

Securing appliqué

To hold larger pieces securely in place, they may require small stitches to be worked through all layers along some design lines within the shape.

1 Outline the shape with a close row of stitching by hand or machine. Fill the shape with metal thread embroidery inside the stitched outline.

2 Using fine sharp scissors, carefully cut out the prepared shape close to the neatened edge, trimming any fuzzy threads.

3 Position the piece on the main fabric and tack or pin in place, taking care not to damage or distort the metal thread embroidery.

4 Using a matching thread, stitch the piece in place with small stitches. Bring the needle to the front at the edge of the shape and to the back through the edging. The stitches will sink into the zigzag edge.

5 Outline the appliqué shape with couched threads covering the previous stitching.

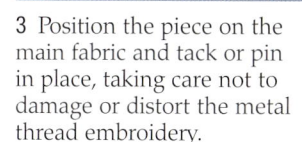

Method three ~ turned edge

The appliqué piece is cut with a small seam allowance that is turned under and the piece is stitched in place by hand.

1 Complete the metal thread embroidery of the appliqué shape, working on closely woven, backed fabric, eg double layers of calico.

2 Back of work. Turn the piece over and trim the backing fabric as close to the back of the embroidery as possible.

METHOD THREE ~ TURNED EDGE - CONTINUED

3 Work running stiches along the centre of the seam allowance along all curved edges.

4 Cut out the embroidered piece leaving a 6mm (¼") seam allowance.

5 Back of work. Gently pull up the running stitches to gather the seam allowance over the back of the work.

6 Back of work. Tack the seam allowance in place.

7 Position the prepared piece on the main fabric. Pin or tack in place through the folded edge, taking care not to distort the embroidery.

8 Stitch the appliqué piece in place with ladder stitch along all edges.

9 The turned edge can be finished with cord, threads or braid for a decorative outline if desired.

Christ the Victorious

Detail of embroidered slip, appliquéd onto a chasuble. The face is embroidered in fine silk and the robes in or nué. Embroidery by the Society for Ecclesiastical Art and Craft from design by Hans Georg Skovgaard, circa 1950s.

APPLYING PADDING

Adding padding under areas of metal thread embroidery enhances the play of light on the threads. Card, felt and soft cotton are the most commonly used types of padding, but carpet felt and fibre-fill can also be used. Always complete all the padded areas within a design before you begin the metal thread embroidery.

Tacking card in place

Do not stitch through the card as the needle holes will damage the surface and may show through the design.

CARD PADDING

Card padding gives a smooth area with sharp edges. It can be used to create highlights within a design filled with solid couching or used as padding under narrow isolated shapes. The card padding should not be any wider than 1.5cm (⅝") to prevent the laid threads from slipping.

The card can be covered with a layer of felt or lightweight fusible wadding for a softer surface without losing the sharp edges. Layers of card can be glued together to vary the height of the padded area.

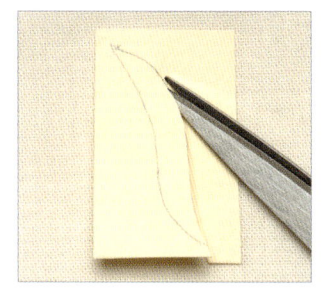

1 Transfer the shape onto the card. Cut out just inside the marked design line to allow the gold thread to lie over the card without enlarging the design.

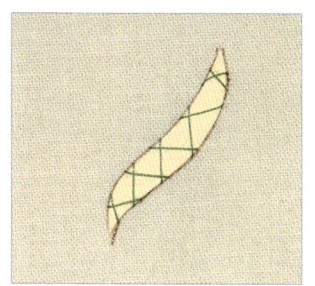

2 Position the card shape onto the fabric and hold in place with tacking stitches across the card. The design line should be visible around the edge of the card. The tacking is removed as the metal threads are laid.

3 The card can also be held in place by using double-sided acid free tape.

CORD PADDING

Cord padding gives a strong undulated line. It is useful for creating borders and defining design details.

The cord should be closely twisted with a smooth hard surface. The thickness should be in proportion to the design area.

Use matching waxed machine sewing thread to wrap the ends of the cord and stitching it in place.

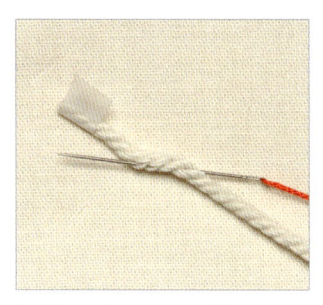

1 Wrap the ends of the cord with tape to prevent it from unravelling. Knot the end of the thread. Insert the needle along the length of the cord, emerging 15mm (⅝") from the end.

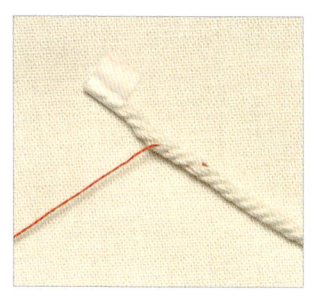

2 Pull the thread firmly to sink the knot into the cord.

CORD PADDING – CONTINUED

Fine cord

The tails of very fine cord can be sunk to the back and secured in the same way as the metal thread. There is no need to wrap the ends.

3 Wrap the thread firmly around the cord three or four times. Take the needle through the cord.

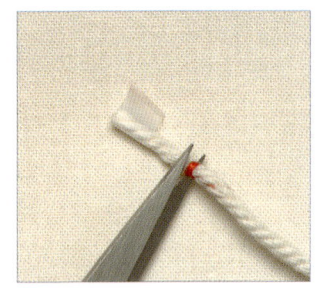

4 Stitch through the cord a few times to secure the wrapping. Trim the end of the cord close to the wrapping.

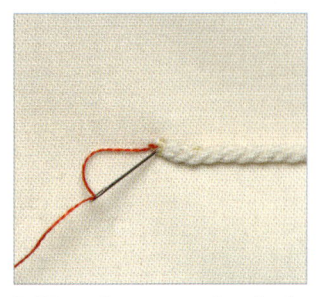

5 Place the wrapped end of the cord on the fabric. Bring the thread to the front at the end of the cord and stitch the end firmly in place, stitching across the end into the wrapping.

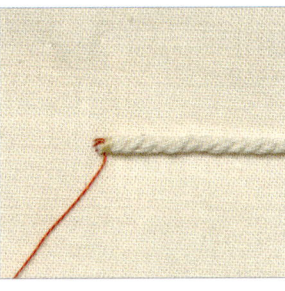

6 Rotate the cord to maintain the twist and hold it taut. Bring the thread to the front at the edge of the cord.

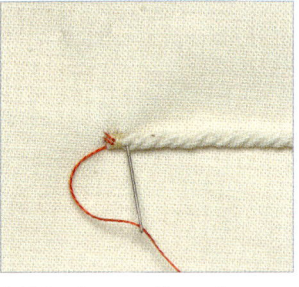

7 Take the needle to the back through the edge of the cord, so the stitch follows the direction of the twist.

8 Pull the stitch to sink it into the twist of the cord. Bring the needle to the front on the opposite side. Work a stitch following the direction of the twist in the same manner.

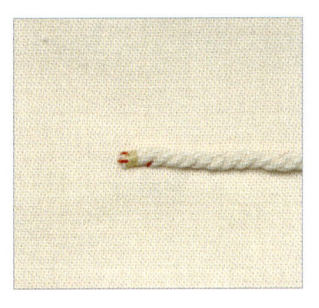

9 Continue to stitch the cord in place in this manner, alternating the stitches from side to side.

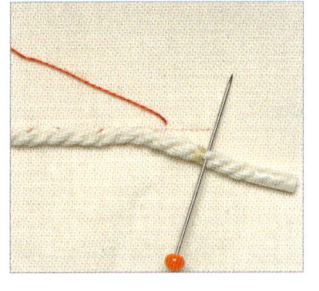

10 When you near the opposite end, measure the cord to the exact length and mark with a pin. Wrap the end as before.

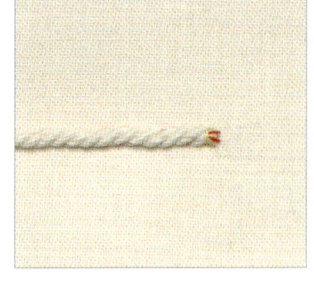

11 Trim close to the wrapping. Stitch the remainder of the cord in place, finishing with a couple of stitches across the end into the wrapping.

CORD INTERSECTION

Where sections of cord padding meet, such as on a cross, the cord ends should be cut and butted closly together.

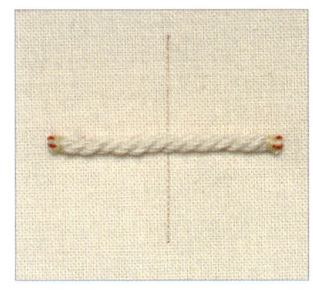

1 Stitch the cord padding in place in one direction as described on page 28. Prepare a second length of cord.

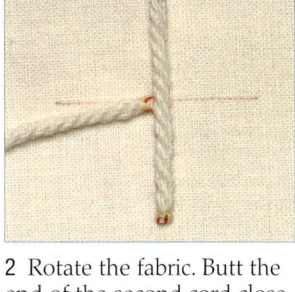

2 Rotate the fabric. Butt the end of the second cord close to the first piece and stitch the wrapped end in place, bringing the needle to the front at an angle under the attached cord.

Butting cords

If the lengths of cord are not butted together closely enough, the laid metal threads will fall into the gap at the intersection.

Twist tension

Keep the twist in the cord tight by rotating the cord regularly between your fingers. Hold the cord straight and taut while you stitch it in place, taking care not to stretch it.

3 Stitch the second length of cord in place.

4 Prepare and stitch the remaining piece of cord in place in the same manner as the second piece.

FELT PADDING

Felt padding gives a smooth round shape. It can be used in a single layer or several pieces can be layered to create a dome. The felt pieces are graduated in size with the largest piece placed on top. Three layers of felt are enough to create a soft dome in most cases, but the design and the area determine the number of layers required. Use felt and sewing thread to match the colour of the threads or leather you are using.

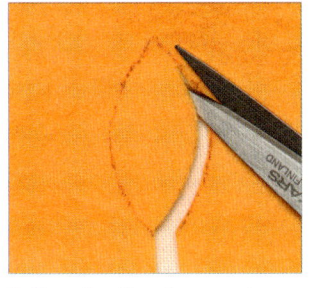

1 Transfer the shape onto the felt and cut out just inside the design line. This allows the gold thread to lie over the felt without enlarging the design.

2 Cut a second piece the same shape, but slightly smaller, and a third piece smaller again.

3 Position the smallest piece on the fabric at the centre of the shape.

FELT PADDING – CONTINUED

4 Bring the thread to the front at the edge of the felt. Take the needle to the back through the felt, placing a small stitch at a right angle across the edge.

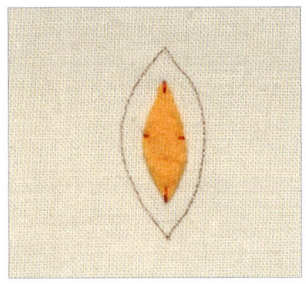

5 Work a small stitch over the edge of the felt in this manner at each quarter point to hold the piece in place.

6 Work small stitches over the edge of the felt around the entire shape at 4mm ($3/16$") intervals.

7 Centre the second piece over the first and hold in place with a small stitch at the quarter points.

8 Work small stitches around the shape in the same manner as before.

9 Position the largest piece over the previous pieces and hold in place at the quarter points. Stitch around the edge of the piece at 2mm ($1/16$") intervals. The design line should be visible around the edge of the felt padding.

REVERSE FELT PADDING

Applying the largest piece of felt padding first and finishing with the smallest piece will result in a more graduated style of padding. When using this method each layer is usually covered with a different technique.

1 Reverse felt padding. The felt pieces are stitched in place in the reverse order, resulting in a less rounded padding.

SOFT COTTON PADDING

This type of padding is mainly used under very narrow, tapered shapes. Usually cut purls are used to cover this type of padding. The soft cotton thread used for the padding is waxed and stitched in place using a matching doubled waxed sewing thread. We used contrasting thread for photographic purposes.

1 Pass the cotton thread several times over a block of beeswax until it is stiff and easy to control.

2 Fold the thread in half several times until you have a bundle thick enough to cover the widest section of the shape.

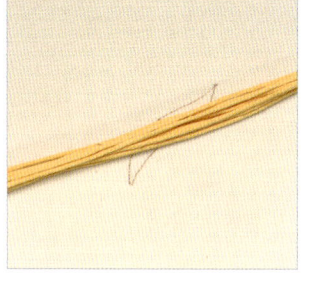

3 Cut the folded ends and pull the threads straight. Place the thread bundle along the length of the shape, making sure the threads are not twisted.

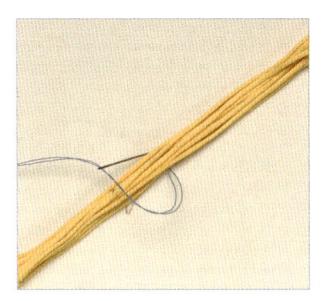

4 Bring the thread to the front just inside the marked line, at the widest section. Take the needle to the back just inside the marked line on the opposite side of the cotton padding.

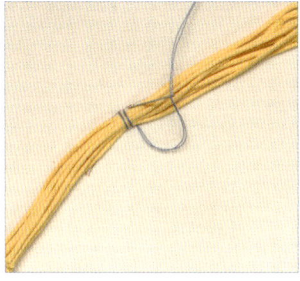

5 Begin to work stitches over the padding at 2mm ($1/16$") intervals.

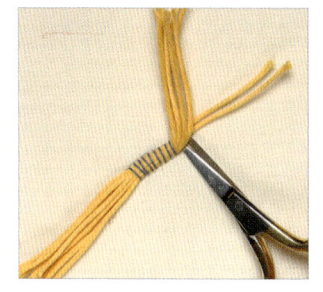

6 As the shape begins to narrow, lift the cotton threads and trim one or two threads from underneath.

SOFT COTTON PADDING – CONTINUED

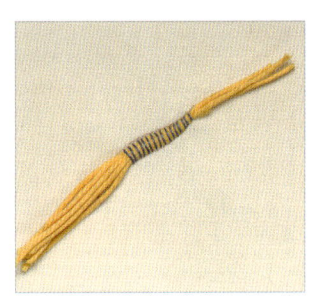

7 Continue to oversew and gradually trim the cotton threads towards the tip of the shape.

8 At the tip, trim the underlying threads just back from the design line. Trim the upper threads on the design line.

9 Bring the sewing thread to the front at the tip of the shape and work a stitch into the padding.

Soft cotton padding

The threads are gradually cut from underneath. The upper threads hold the cut tails in place, creating a smooth surface for the embroidery.

10 Work the last stitch across the padding to hold the ends in place.

11 Complete the remainder of the padding in a similar manner.

SECURING THREADS

Securing couching thread

Metal threads are couched in place using a fine waxed silk or sewing thread. Usually a matching thread is used for the couching, however contrasting thread may be used to create various effects.

1 Starting. Cut the sewing thread 30cm (12") long or the distance from your thumb to your elbow.

2 Run the thread over a piece of good quality beeswax for added strength.

3 Thread a no. 10 crewel needle and tie a knot in the end of the thread. Bring the thread to the front on the marked line, a short distance from the starting point where it will be covered by the laid thread.

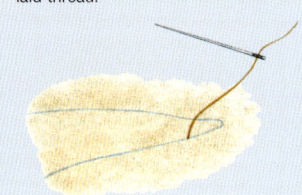

4 Work two or three back stitches to secure the thread. You are now ready to begin your couching.

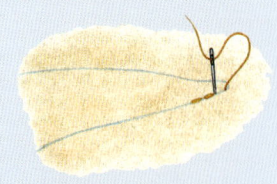

5 Finishing. Work several back and split stitches into the backing fabric and stitches on the back of the work.

SINKING METAL THREADS

The tails of the metal thread are taken to the back of the work, one at a time, and secured after the couching is complete.

Method one ~ large needle

This method can be used for fine metal threads such as fine twists, passing thread and fine imitation Japanese thread.

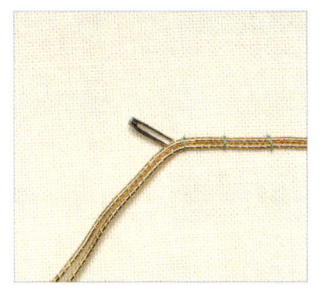

1 Insert a no. 18 chenille needle at the end of the stitched line. Push the needle through until just the eye is above the fabric.

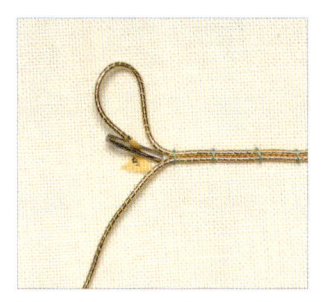

2 Insert the tip of a metal thread tail into the eye of the needle.

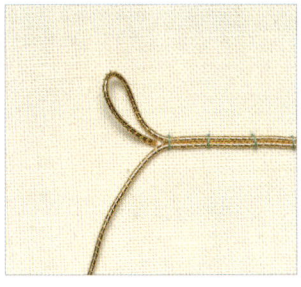

3 With one hand below the frame, begin to pull the needle through. Gently rotate it from side to side between your fingers if necessary, to ease the thread through.

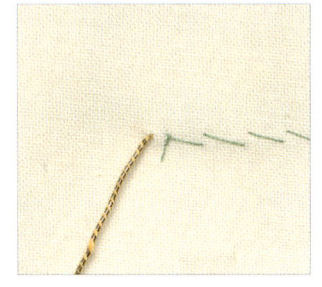

4 Back of work. Turn the work over and pull the thread tail to the back.

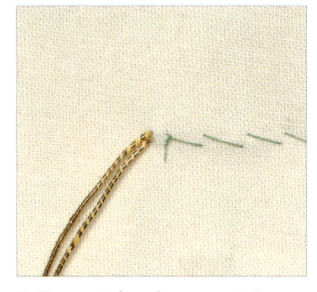

5 Repeat for the remaining metal thread tail, taking it through the fabric just next to the first.

Storing your threads

Wrap your threads in acid free tissue paper when you are not using them. This will ensure the quality of your threads will last longer.

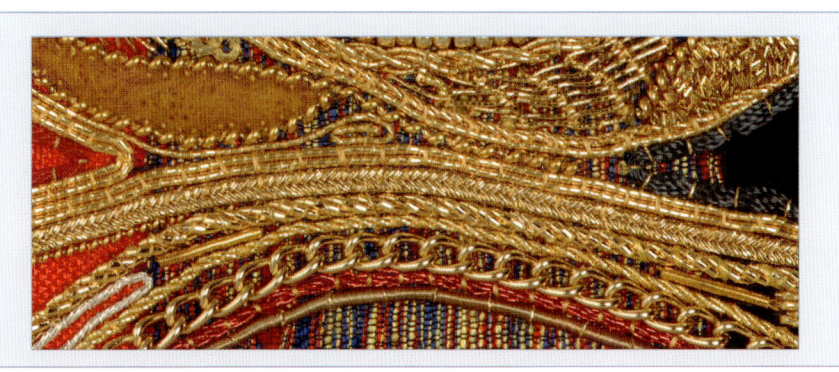

Detail of panel on page 93.

Method two ~ sling

This method is particularly useful for heavier threads, twists and cords, but can be used for all threads.

Make a sling by threading a length of strong waxed thread, such as no. 5 perlé cotton, into a no. 18 chenille needle, see page 10.

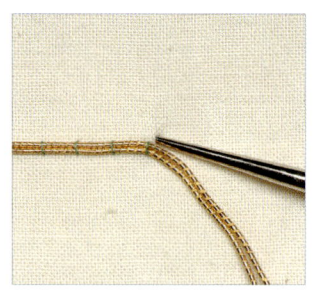

1 Using an awl or mellor, prepare a hole in the fabric where the thread tail is to be taken to the back. This step can be omitted when sinking finer metal threads.

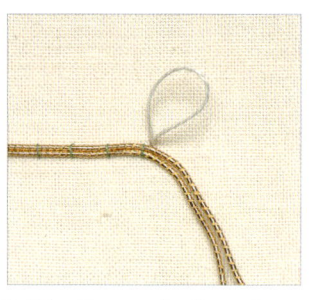

2 Take the needle through the prepared hole, leaving the thread loop on the front.

3 Place the tip of the gold thread tail into the loop.

4 With one hand below the frame, pull the needle to tighten the loop and lock the tail against the fabric.

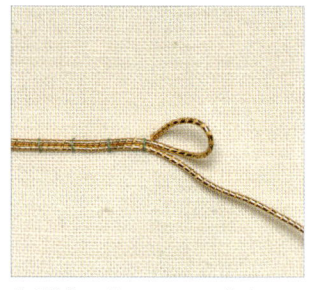

5 With a firm tug, pull the loop through the fabric, taking the metal thread with it.

6 Release the loop and gently pull the metal thread tail to the back.

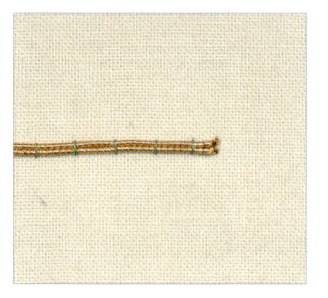

7 Repeat for any remaining metal thread tails.

Detail from laidwork on page 75. The metal thread tails ready to be sunk to the back and secured.

SECURING METAL THREADS

The metal thread tails are secured on the back of the work using a waxed sewing thread.

Method one ~ fine and/or single threads

1 Back of work. Fold the metal thread tail back under the work.

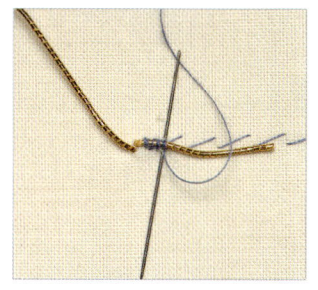

2 Using the sewing thread, work several overcast stitches over the thread tail and into the back of the work to secure.

3 Trim the metal thread close to the overcast stitches. Secure the sewing thread by working several back stitches into the back of the work.

Method two ~ heavy and/or groups of threads

Where many metal thread tails are taken to the back close together, or the metal thread is thick, it may be necessary to reduce the bulk of the thread(s) on the back. To do this, the foil around the thread core is carefully removed before each thread is folded back and secured.

1 Trim the metal tail to 1.5cm (5/8").

2 Gently unravel the metal foil and trim 5mm (3/16") from the fabric.

3 Fold the thread core under the work.

4 Using the sewing thread, stitch the thread core securely in place into the back of the work.

5 Secure the sewing thread with several back stitches worked into the back of the work. Trim the thread core close to the overcast stitches.

Securing tails

It can be helpful to use a fine curved needle when securing the metal thread tails, as this makes it easier to stitch into the stitches on the back of the taut fabric.

Goldwork stitches and techniques

BASIC COUCHING

This is an embroidery method in which a thread, or a pair of threads, are laid on the fabric and stitched in place by another thread passed through the fabric at regular intervals. The couching stitches are worked from top to bottom over horizontally laid thread or from right to left over vertically laid threads.

Gold threads are usually couched in place using matching gold coloured sewing thread. White or light grey sewing thread is most commonly used for silver threads. Beautiful and subtle effects can be achieved by using other colours.

We used contrasting couching threads throughout for photographic purposes.

Pair of threads cross section

The stitch should fit snugly around the laid threads, holding them firmly together.

COUCHING A PAIR OF THREADS

Metal threads are most often couched in place in pairs. Wind the thread onto two separate spools or bobbins to prevent them from getting tangled. The couching stitches are worked at a right angle across the laid threads.

1 Leaving 2.5cm (1") tails, centre a pair of gold threads along the marked line. Secure the couching thread and bring it to the front above the threads.

2 Take the needle to the back at a slight angle under the laid threads on the opposite side.

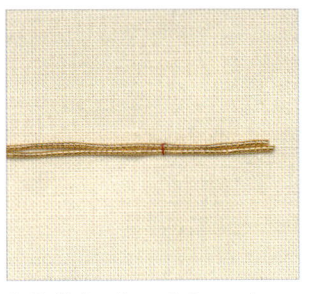

3 Pull the thread through, keeping the laid threads straight and firm. The couching stitch should be at a right angle to the laid threads.

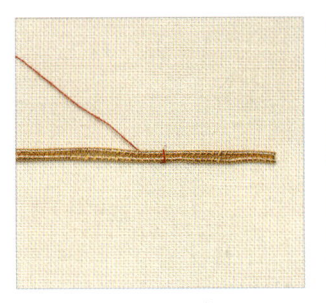

4 Angling the needle slightly, bring the thread to the front above the laid threads, 5mm (3/16") from the first stitch.

5 Repeat step 2 While holding the laid threads straight and taut with one hand, pull the couching stitch taut with your other hand below the frame.

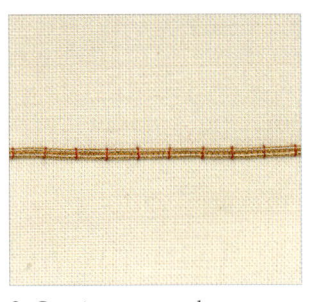

6 Continue to work couching stitches at 5mm (3/16") intervals, keeping an even tension on the laid threads and the couching thread.

COUCHING DOUBLED METAL THREAD

The metal thread can be cut to double the required length and folded in half. The folded end is couched in place and only the tails at the opposite end will need to be taken to the back.

1 Fold the metal thread in half, using tweezers to carefully pinch the fold closed.

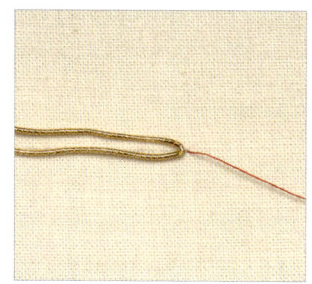

2 Place the fold on the end of the line to be covered. Secure the couching thread and bring it to the front on the design line just outside the fold.

Couched threads

When laid side by side the two threads stabilise one another. The couching stitches are worked at a right angle across the laid threads.

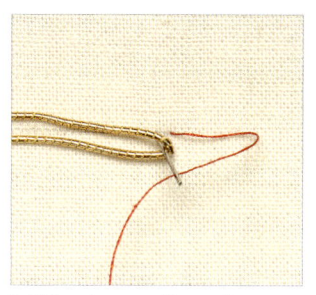

3 Take the needle to the back inside the fold, placing the stitch at a right angle over the folded end.

4 Bring the thread to the front above the laid threads, just back from the folded end. Take the needle to the back at a slight angle under the laid threads on the opposite side.

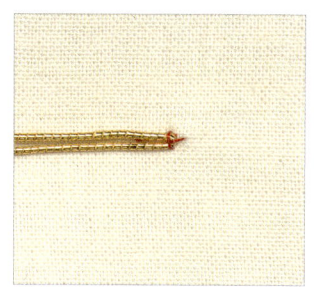

5 Holding the doubled thread straight and taut with one hand, pull the couching thread through with your other hand below the frame.

6 Bring the thread to the front above the laid threads, 5mm (3/16") from the first stitch.

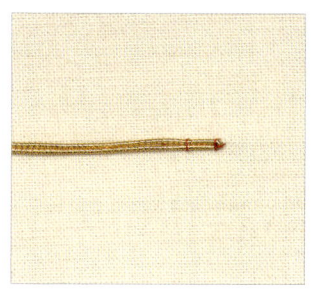

7 Take the needle to the back on a slight angle on the opposite side of the laid threads. Hold the threads firmly and pull the stitch taut.

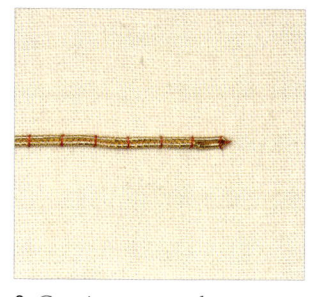

8 Continue to work couching stitches at 5mm (3/16") intervals, keeping even tension on the laid threads and the couching thread.

37

COUCHING A SINGLE THREAD

When couching a single thread along a marked line, care has to be taken when placing the couching stitches. The metal thread has a tendency to roll and can be difficult to couch in place accurately. The couching stitch should be as wide as the diameter of the metal thread to hold it firmly in place.

1 Leaving a 2.5cm (1") tail, place the metal thread along the marked line. Secure the couching thread and bring it to the front just above the laid thread.

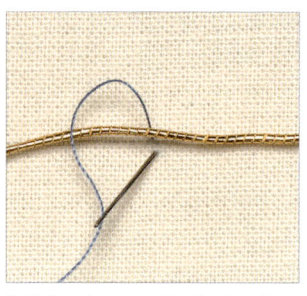

2 Take the needle the back at a right angle through the fabric below the laid thread.

3 Hold the laid thread straight and taut while pulling the couching thread through with your other hand below the frame.

4 Bring the thread to the front above the laid thread, 5mm (3/16") from the first stitch. Take the needle to the back at the opposite side.

5 Continue to couch in this manner at 5mm (3/16") intervals, keeping an even, firm tension on the gold thread.

Single thread cross section

The couching stitch is as wide as the diameter of the thread to hold it firmly in place and prevent it from rolling.

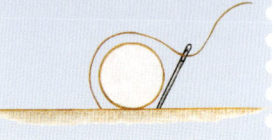

COUCHING ROCOCO AND CRINKLE THREADS

The wave in these threads makes them ideal for adding texture when couched among smooth threads. Unlike other metal threads, these are usually couched in place singly, as the texture in the thread makes it difficult to pair them neatly. Couch the thread in place following the instructions for single thread above, adjusting the couching stitches to the texture of the thread.

OUTLINING AN EMBROIDERED SHAPE

A single laid gold thread is often used to outline an embroidered shape.

1 Leaving a 2.5cm (1") tail, lay the metal thread along the edge of the embroidered shape.

2 Secure the couching thread and bring it to the front outside the laid thread.

3 Take the needle to the back on the opposite side of the laid thread at a slight angle under the embroidered shape.

4 Hold the metal thread firmly with one hand while pulling the couching stitch taut with the other hand below the frame. The stitch pulls the gold thread snugly against the edge of the embroidery.

5 Bring the thread to the front outside the laid thread 5mm (3/16") from the first stitch. Take the needle to the back at a slight angle under the embroidered shape.

6 Repeat step 4.

7 Continue to couch the gold thread at regular intervals around the embroidered shape, keeping an even tension on both threads.

8 Sink and secure the thread tails one at a time, following the instructions on pages 33–35.

CORNERS

It is important to have the correct placement of the couching stitches when turning a corner or a sharp point, in order to maintain good definition of the shape.

ACUTE CORNER

To achieve an accurate point it can be helpful to tack a centre line through the corner point.

1 Couch the pair of gold threads in place along the marked line following the steps for basic couching on page 36 Stop just before reaching the corner.

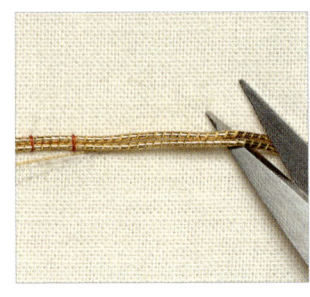

2 Cut the gold threads, leaving 2.5cm (1") tails.

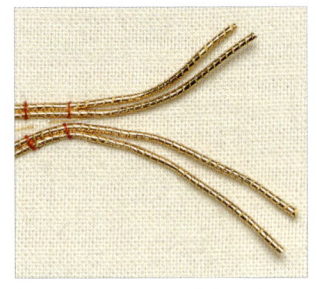

3 Leaving 2.5cm (1") tails, restart the pair of threads along the adjacent side. Couch the threads in place along the adjacent side, placing the first couching stitch just after the corner point.

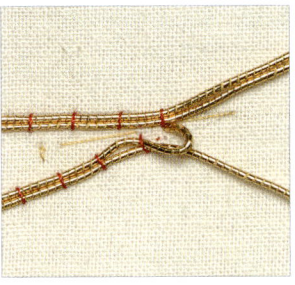

4 Following the instructions on page 33 or 34, sink the innermost thread on the centre line of the point and secure on the back.

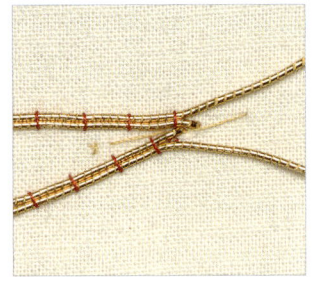

5 Sink the second inner thread on the centre line just above the first thread in the same manner.

6 Sink the two outer threads, one after the other, in the same manner.

Detail of rank badge on page 57.

RIGHT-ANGLED CORNER

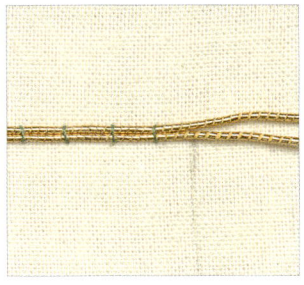

1 Couch the pair of gold threads in place along the marked line following the steps for basic couching on page 36.

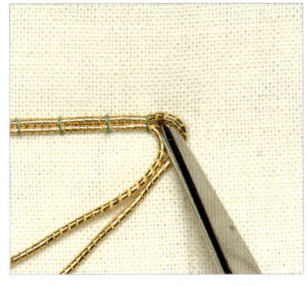

2 Place the tip of a mellor or awl at the corner. Manipulate the outer thread around the mellor to kink the thread.

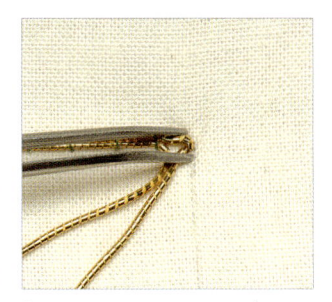

3 Use tweezers to gently pinch the fold to shape the point.

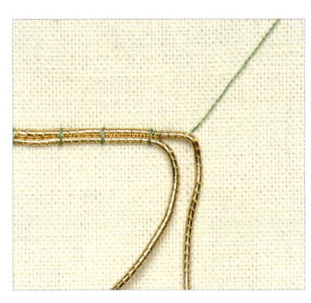

4 Bring the thread to the front at the corner point on the outside of the outer thread.

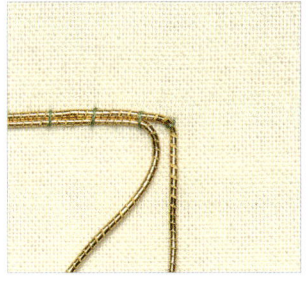

5 Take the needle to the back on the inside of the outer thread. Pull the thread through, forming a diagonal couching stitch.

6 Manipulate the inner laid thread in a similar manner to fit snugly into the corner. Bring the thread to the front on the inside of the inner laid thread.

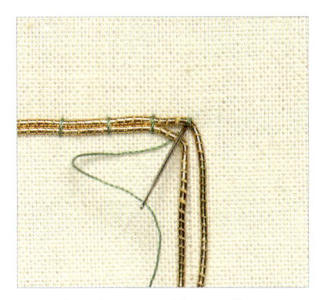

7 Take the needle to the back between the gold threads, angling it slightly under the outer thread to pull the threads together.

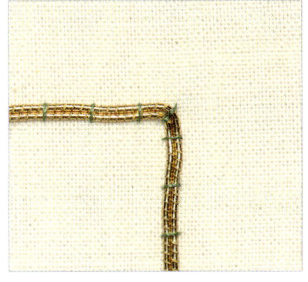

8 Couch along the adjacent side at regular intervals, bringing the needle to the front on the outside and to the back on the inside of the laid threads.

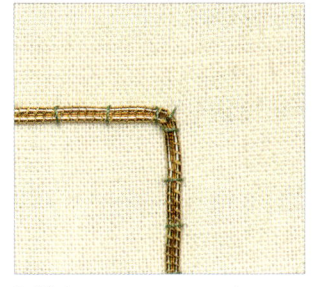

9 If the corner occurs just after a couching stitch, the diagonal stitch over the inner thread can be omitted.

SHARP CORNER

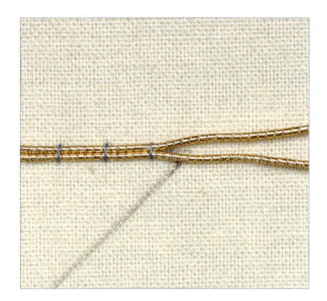

1 Couch the pair of gold threads in place along the marked line following the steps for basic couching on page 36 Stop just before reaching the corner.

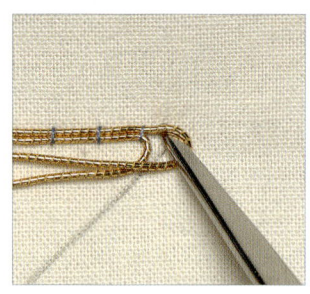

2 Place the tip of a mellor or awl at the corner point. Manipulate the outer thread around the tip.

3 Use tweezers to gently shape the folded thread at the point.

4 Bring the thread to the front at the point on the outside of the outer thread.

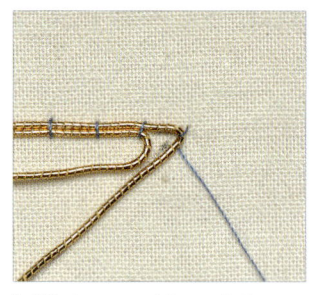

5 Work a couching stitch over the outer thread. Bring the thread to the front a short distance from the point outside the thread on the adjacent side.

6 Work a couching stitch diagonally across both sides of the outer thread.

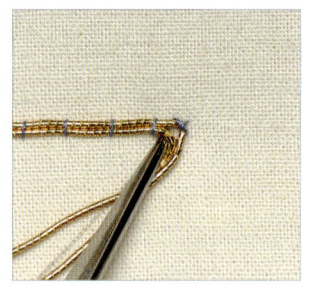

7 Use a mellor and tweezers to manipulate the inner thread into the point as closely as possible.

8 Bring the thread to the front inside the inner thread. Take the needle to the back between the two laid threads, angling it under the outer thread.

9 Keeping a firm, even tension on the laid threads, couch along the adjacent side at regular intervals.

COUCHING TWISTED THREADS

Twisted threads, also referred to as 'twists', are fabulous for borders, outlines and defining designs. They are pliable and easy to manipulate. Wrap a small piece of tape around the end of the twist while working to prevent it from unravelling.

With the exception of very fine twists, most are couched in place so the stitches sink into the grooves and become invisible.

Stitch direction

The twist should lie so the stitches can be angled forward in the direction of the grooves in the twist.

Method one ~ fine twist

Fine and medium threads are very easy to work with. The tails of these threads are taken to the back and secured.

1 Leave a 2.5cm (1") tail and place the twist along the line to be covered. Hold the tail in place with a couple of tacking stitches.

2 Secure the couching thread and bring it to the front above the first groove in the twist.

3 Gently unwind the twist by rotating the thread between your fingers. Take the needle to the back on the other side, following the direction of the twist.

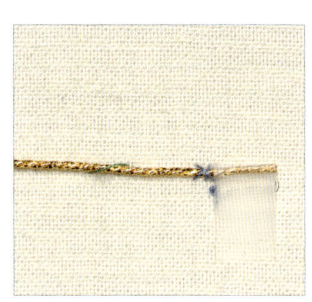

4 Rotate the thread in the opposite direction to re-tighten the twist, while pulling the stitch taut with your other hand below the frame.

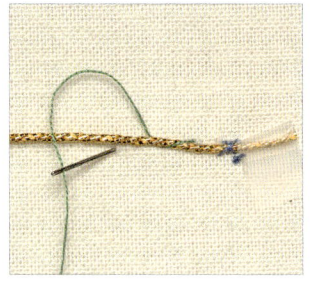

5 Bring the thread to the front above a groove in the twist, a short distance from the first stitch. Unwind the twist slightly and place a second stitch following the direction of the groove.

6 Re-tighten the twist while pulling the stitch taut.

METHOD ONE ~ FINE TWIST – CONTINUED

7 Continue to couch the twist in place, positioning the stitches at regular intervals and sinking them into the grooves.

8 Gently remove the tape and tacking stitches. Take the tails to the back using a sling, following the instructions on page 34.

9 Twist outline. When outlining an embroidered shape, bring the needle to the front on the outside and to the back on the inside of the twist, following the direction of the grooves.

Method two ~ heavy twist

It can be difficult to sink the tails of thick twisted cords to the back of the work neatly. The tails of these threads are wrapped and secured on the front. Use a matching machine sewing thread, invisible nylon thread or fine metal hand embroidery thread to wrap the ends. We used contrasting machine sewing thread for photographic purposes.

1 Knot the end of the sewing thread. Insert the needle along the length of the twisted cord, emerging 1.5cm (⅝") from the end.

2 Pull the thread to sink the knot into the cord. Wrap the thread firmly around the cord three or four times.

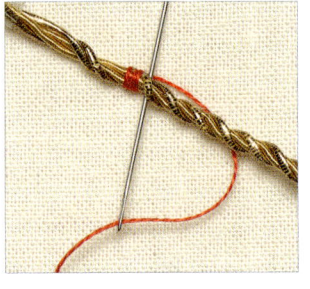

3 Take the needle back through the cord three or four times and pull tight to secure the wrapping.

4 Trim the wrapping thread. Trim the end of the cord close to the wrapping.

44

METHOD TWO ~ HEAVY TWIST – CONTINUED

5 Place the cord on the line to be covered. The cord should lie so the stitches are angled forward in the direction of the grooves. Bring the couching thread to the front above the wrapped end.

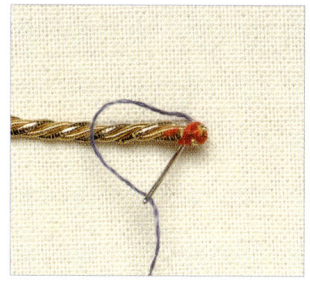

6 Take the needle to the back on the opposite side of the wrapped end.

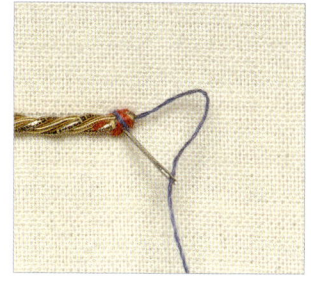

7 Pull the stitch taut with one hand below the frame. Bring the thread to the front at the end of the cord and take the needle to the back over the first stitch, through the wrapping.

8 Pull the stitch through with one hand below the frame, securing the wrapping and holding down the end. Bring the thread to the front next to the first groove in the twist.

9 Stitch the cord in place following steps 3–7 for fine twist, see page 43 until nearing the opposite end.

10 Measure the cord to the exact length and mark with a pin. Wrap the end securely in the same manner as before. Trim close to the wrapping.

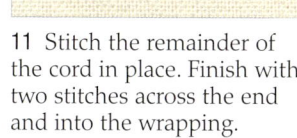

11 Stitch the remainder of the cord in place. Finish with two stitches across the end and into the wrapping.

Detail of bookbinding on page 4.

EMBELLISHED COUCHING

The laid thread(s) can be couched in place with beads, cut purls, ribbon or other materials for added interest. In some cases the gold threads need to be couched in place before the embellishment is added to ensure they are held firmly in position.

Copper and gold imitation Japanese thread couched in place with delica beads.

Gold imitation Japanese thread couched in place with seed beads.

Gold imitation Japanese thread, couched in place with no. 6 smooth and rough purl.

Double laid copper imitation Japanese thread embellished with fine gold couching thread, couched in a zigzag pattern.

Couching with beads

Delica beads are the perfect size for couching a double width of T69 imitation Japanese thread.

Framed panel, 1966, 45cm × 55cm wide (17¾" × 21⅝"). Worked in a rich variety of stitch techniques in coloured threads, gold and silver threads with some kid appliqué. Design and embroidery by Mrs E.M. John, Doncaster School of Art, U.K. From the collection of the Embroiderers Guild of Victoria.

LAID WORK

This term is used when threads are placed closely side by side to fill a shape. The gold threads are laid across the shape in rows or following the contours and spiralling towards the centre. The reflection of light will vary depending on the chosen method. The colour and pattern of the couching stitches also affects the overall appearance of a design. The most common method of couching gold thread to fill a shape is in a brick pattern where each row of couching is worked by placing the stitches halfway between those of the previous row. The stitches will line up in alternate rows. Imitation Japanese threads, passing threads and twists are all suitable for laid work. Lay the threads in horizontal rows working upwards, or vertical rows from left to right. We used contrasting threads for photographic purposes.

Couching laid work

Couching by following the outline of a shape and working towards the centre gives the metal threads a good change of direction and play of light, adding life and dimension to the shape. This method wastes little thread as very few tails are taken to the back. However, this method is not suitable for narrow shapes, because too many tight turns will distort the overall design.

Couching across or along a shape creates a very smooth surface with an even play of light. For shapes with narrow ends, lengths of gold thread are laid along the full length and shorter pieces are used to fill the gaps.

The following points should be considered before you begin to fill a shape.

1 Decide on the most suitable way to fill the shape with the best possible continuous line or lines, to avoid creating awkward holes or gaps.
2 Consider the direction of the couching of each shape in relation to the overall design. For example, filling all shapes within a design from the outside to the centre is likely to give a very 'busy' result, where clarity of the overall design is lost.
3 Determine the most suitable placement of the couching stitches to achieve a flowing pattern.
4 Consider starting and finishing points that will not disrupt the design and the flow of the gold thread.

'Justicia' mid 20th Century 30.5cm × 23cm wide (12" × 9 1/16")
Face worked in Japanese gold thread. The direction of the laid threads is skilfully used to create dimension and shape with the use of coloured couching thread for shading.

Embroidery by Mrs Edna Wark from design by Con. Bolton. From the collection of Embroiderers Guild of Victoria.

FILLING SHAPES

Filling a shape with laid work by following the contours is an effective method for creating dimension within the shape. When using this method, the laid work is most often worked from the perimeter towards the centre of the area.

ANGULAR SHAPES

When filling angular shapes the couching stitches will form dominant lines at the corners, so it is important that they are placed accurately. To achieve this, mark the centre lines at each point to ensure sharp, crisp lines.

To begin, position the laid threads so the outer thread is aligned with the marked line. Bring the couching thread to the front on the marked line outside the outer thread.

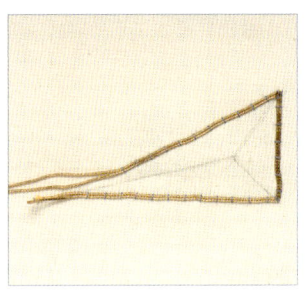

> **Laid work**
>
> Interesting play of light is achieved when a shape is filled from the outer edges towards the centre, adding to the appearance of the design.

1 Keeping a firm tension on the laid threads, couch them in place along the outline. Follow the steps on pages 40–42 for working the corners.

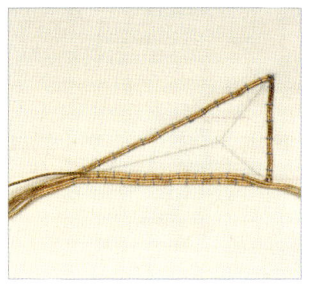

2 Begin the second round, placing the couching stitches halfway between those of the first round to form a brick pattern.

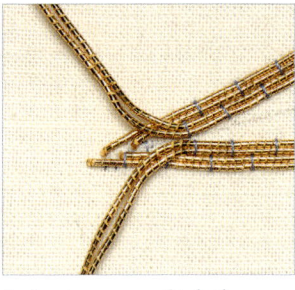

3 Acute corner. Sink the threads in the first row following steps 4–6 for acute corners on page 40. Cut and restart both threads in the same manner as the first row. Couch along the adjacent side.

4 Sink and secure the four tails from the second round on the marked line, alternating from side to side.

5 Continue to fill the shape. Take the four thread tails to the back on the marked centre line after each round and secure.

6 Right angled corners. Using tweezers, manipulate the outer thread to fit snugly into the corner. Bring the needle to the front inside the outer thread.

48

ANGULAR SHAPES – CONTINUED

7 Take the needle to the back, angling it slightly towards the previous thread to pull the gold thread into the corner.

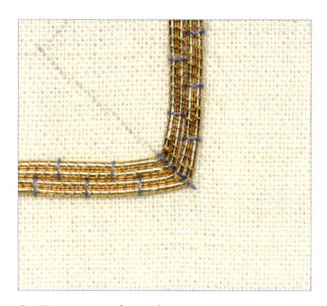

8 Repeat for the inner thread. Continue to couch along the adjacent side in a brick pattern.

9 Work towards the centre of the shape, placing the corner stitches carefully along the diagonal of the corner.

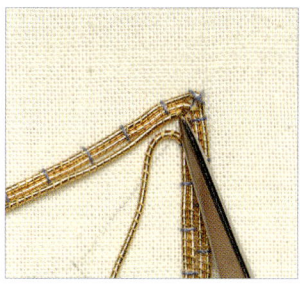

10 Sharp corners. Manipulate the outer thread as far as possible into the corner using a mellor and pinching the fold with tweezers.

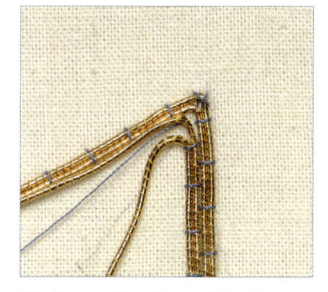

11 Bring the thread to the front on the inside of the outer thread, halfway across the corner.

12 Couch in place, pulling the thread into the corner. Repeat for the inner thread.

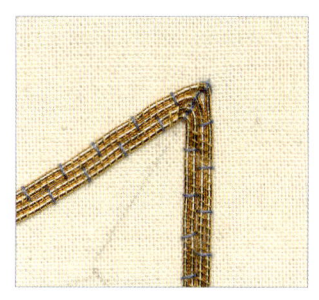

13 Continue to couch along the adjacent side, placing the stitches in a brick pattern.

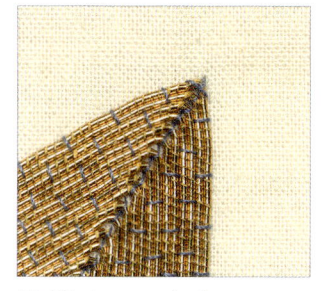

14 Work towards the centre of the shape, placing the corner stitches carefully on the marked line.

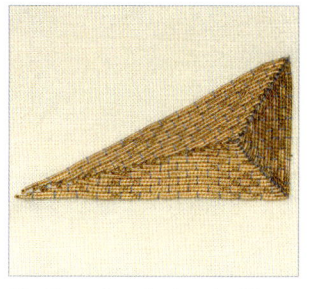

15 Completed triangle. The couching stitches form distinct lines at the corners.

CIRCLE FROM CENTRE

Couching a circle from the centre can be necessary if an exact centre needs to be pinpointed. However, couching from the outside is the most accurate method to achieve a perfect circle.

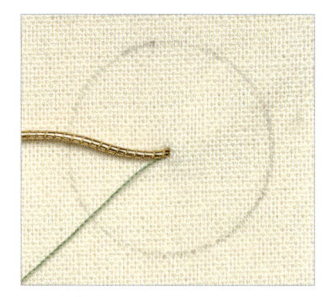

1 Sink the tail of one thread to the back at the centre. Bring the couching thread to the front next to the gold thread.

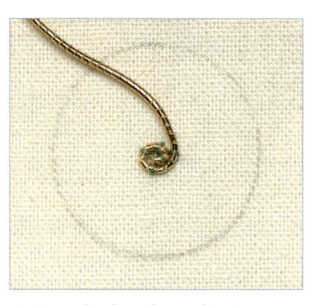

2 Couch the thread into a tight coil, stitching from the outside towards the centre. Keep the thread tail out of the way on the back of the work.

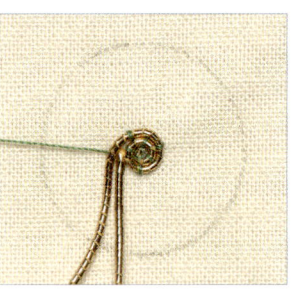

3 When the circle reaches 3mm–4mm (1/8"–3/16") add a second thread inside the first. Sink the tail to the back of the work.

4 Bring the couching thread to the front outside the laid threads. Couch the pair in place, pulling the laid threads close towards the previous round.

5 Stagger the couching stitches to form a brick pattern. The distance between the stitches will increase as the circle grows and extra stitches will need to be added.

6 On the final round finish the inner thread leaving a 2.5cm (1") tail. Continue to couch over the outer thread only.

7 Finish the outer thread on the opposite side to the inner thread.

8 Sink the two outer tails. Secure the four thread tails on the back of the work one at a time.

CIRCLE FROM OUTLINE

The best way to achieve a perfect circle is to work from the outside towards the centre.

1 Leave a 2.5cm (1") tail of one thread. Begin couching at the base of the circle, bringing the couching thread to the front on the marked line and to the back inside the laid thread.

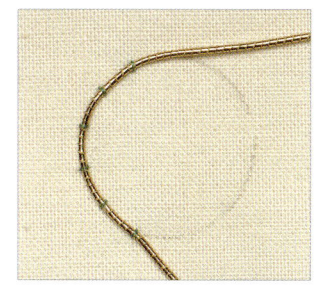

2 Couch halfway around the circle, placing the stitches at 5mm ($3/16$") intervals.

3 Leaving a tail, place a second gold thread along the inside of the first thread.

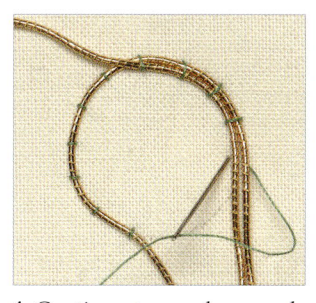

4 Continue to couch around the circle over both threads, bringing the couching thread to the front on the marked line outside the laid threads.

5 Adjust the spacing of the couching stitches when nearing the starting point. Place the pair of threads inside of the previous round.

6 Bring the needle to the front inside the laid threads and to the back on a slight angle under the previous round. Couch in a brick pattern.

7 Continue to couch in this manner. Decrease the number of stitches, as the circle becomes smaller to avoid solid stitching.

8 Cut the outer thread near the centre and complete the final tight turns with just one thread.

9 Taking care to fill the centre and keeping a smooth outline, sink the four tails to the back, one at a time, and secure.

LAID WORK ~ TURNING ROWS

Where a shape is filled with parallel rows of thread laid across the area, the threads will need to be turned or finished off at the edges.

Method one ~ turned threads

In this method, the two laid threads are both turned at the end of each row. This wastes little gold thread, because not many tails need to be sunk to the back. This method is most suitable for shapes that will be outlined with other threads, as it produces a slightly 'stepped' outline.

> **Sinking thread tails**
>
> When filling larger shapes, pause to sink and secure the thread tails after every 8–10 rows.

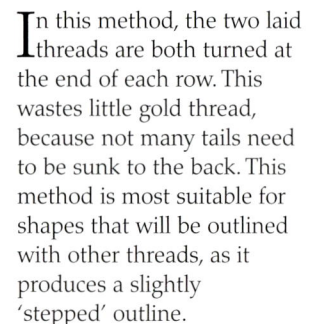

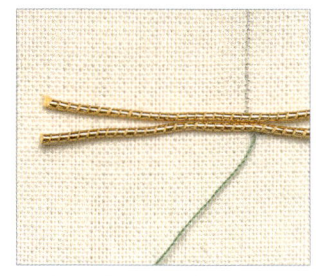

1 Place the pair of gold threads along the marked line, leaving 2.5cm (1") tails. Bring the couching thread to the front on the marked line.

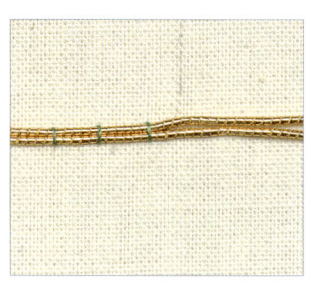

2 Couch the threads in place following the instructions for basic couching. Finish just before the edge of the shape.

3 Turning. Turn the outer thread back on itself, aligning the fold with the design line. Use a mellor and tweezers to shape the fold.

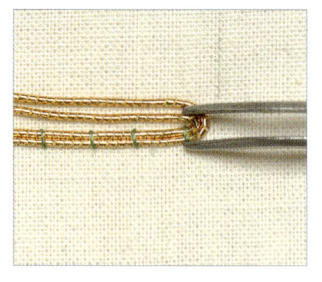

4 Turn the inner thread in the same way to fit snugly inside the outer thread. Use tweezers to gently pinch the fold closed.

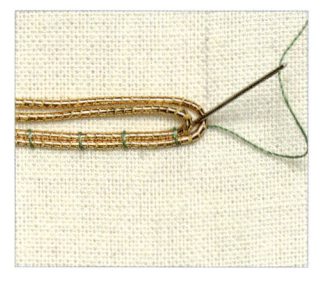

5 Bring the couching thread to the front on the marked line outside the outer thread. Take the needle to the back between the two threads.

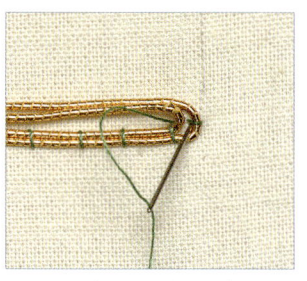

6 Bring the couching thread to the front on the inside of the inner thread. Take the needle to the back between the threads, angling it under the outer thread.

7 Bring the thread to the front above the threads, over the last stitch on the previous row. Take the needle to the back at a slight angle under the previous row.

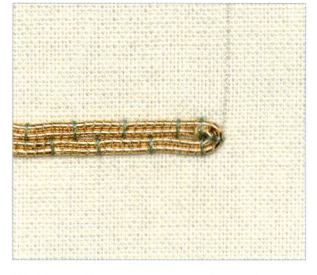

8 Keeping an even tension on the threads, couch the turned threads in place, positioning the stitches halfway between those of the previous row.

METHOD ONE ~ TURNED THREADS – CONTINUED

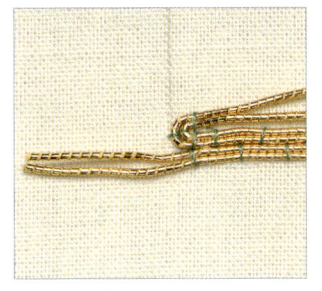

9 Place the last stitch just above the first stitch at the opposite side. Turn the threads one at a time following steps 3–7.

10 Couch the laid threads, placing the couching stitches directly above those of the first row and halfway between those of the previous row.

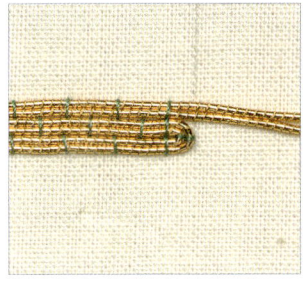

11 Work the last stitch directly above the outermost stitch of the previous row.

12 Continue to fill the shape, placing the couching stitches in a brick pattern. Sink the tails one at a time and secure.

Tension

~ To keep the tension on the couching thread, work a small back stitch at regular intervals to anchor the thread. Place the back stitch where it will be covered by the laid threads.

~ The laid threads should be held at an even, firm tension without stretching while being couched.

~ Turn the laid threads regularly and gently between your fingers to tighten the foil around the thread core. This will prevent the foil from becoming loose and revealing the thread core.

Method two ~ turn one, cut one

This is the most commonly used method for turning metal threads. The inner gold thread is turned and the outer is cut at the end of each row. This method uses more gold thread than method one, but produces a neater and smoother outline.

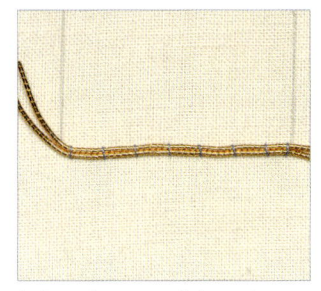

1 Lay the pair of threads along the marked line. Couch in place following the instructions for basic couching. Place the first and last stitch just inside the design line.

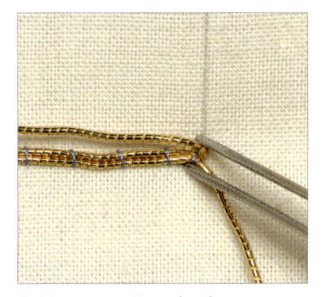

2 Turning. Cut the lower thread, leaving a 2.5cm (1") tail. Turn the upper thread back on itself, aligning the fold with the design line. Use tweezers to gently pinch the fold closed.

53

METHOD TWO ~ TURN ONE, CUT ONE – CONTINUED

Tension

You may find it helpful to rotate your work for each row as you stitch, to maintain a constant stitch direction and tension.

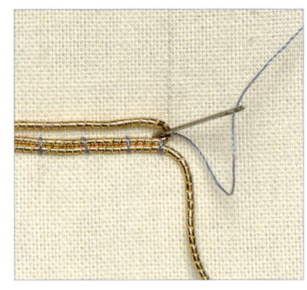

3 Bring the couching thread to the front on the design line outside the fold and place a stitch at a right angle over the fold.

4 Leaving a 2.5cm (1") tail, rejoin the cut thread alongside the turned thread. Bring the needle to the front above the pair of threads.

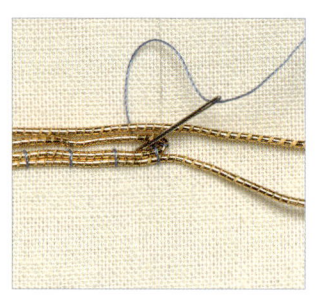

5 Take the needle to the back on a slight angle under the previous row, pulling the rows close together.

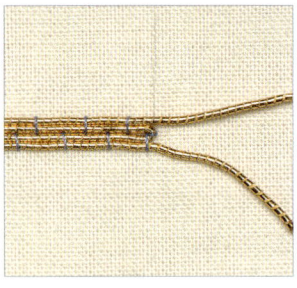

6 Keeping a firm tension on the laid threads, couch them along the previous row. Place the stitches halfway between those of the first row, bringing the needle to the front above the laid threads and to the back under the first row.

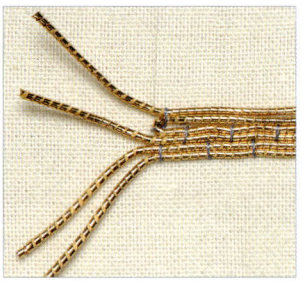

7 At the end of the row, cut the thread that was turned last, leaving a 2.5cm (1") tail. Turn the upper thread back on itself in the same manner as before. Rejoin the cut thread.

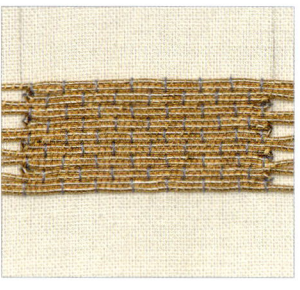

8 Continue to couch in a brick pattern to fill the shape, cutting the lower and turning the upper thread at each side.

Achieving close rows

Taking the needle to the back at a slight angle under the previous row will help pull the rows close together.

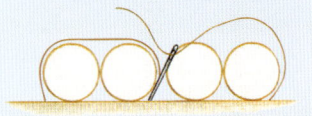

9 For every 8–10 rows sink the tails on the marked line, one at a time following the steps on pages 33 or 34.

10 Back of work. Trim and secure the thread tails one by one.

54

Method three ~ cut threads

In this method both gold threads are cut at the end of each row. This results in a very accurate outline making it suitable for very small shapes, where turned threads would distort the edge of the design. Using this method involves sinking many gold thread tails and therefore has more wastage.

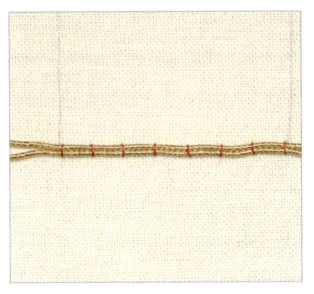

1 Lay the pair of threads along the marked line and couch in place following steps 3–7 for basic couching. Finish just before the edge of the shape.

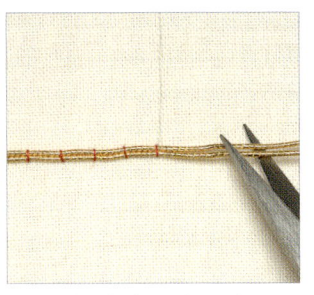

2 Cut both threads at the end of the row, leaving 2.5cm (1") tails.

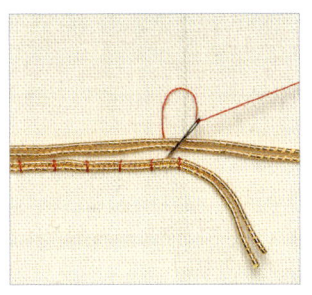

3 Place a new pair of gold threads alongside the first row. Bring the couching thread to the front above the laid threads, halfway between the last two stitches of the previous row. Take the needle to the back at a slight angle under the previous row.

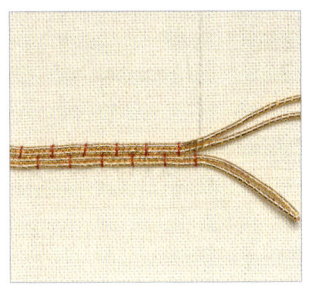

4 Couch the new pair of threads in place, bringing the thread to the front above the laid threads and placing the stitches halfway between those of the first row.

5 Work all subsequent rows in a brick pattern, cutting both laid threads at the end of each row.

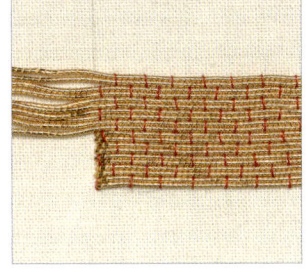

6 Sink and secure the tails, one at a time, at regular intervals following the instructions on page 33 or 34.

LAID WORK ON VELVET

The pile of velvet offers a small challenge for the embroiderer. Many surface embroidery stitches will sink into it and become lost. Cords and braids can be couched in place in the usual way, but if filling a shape with laid work the pile will often show between the laid threads. To avoid this, a single layer of felt is stitched to the velvet before embroidering. Alternatively, the design can be stitched on a separate piece of fabric and appliquéd to the velvet. See pages 24–26 for how to work appliqué.

1 Preparation. Transfer the design onto a piece of felt using a template or the prick and pounce method. Cut out the felt piece along the marked line and position onto the velvet. Tack in place.

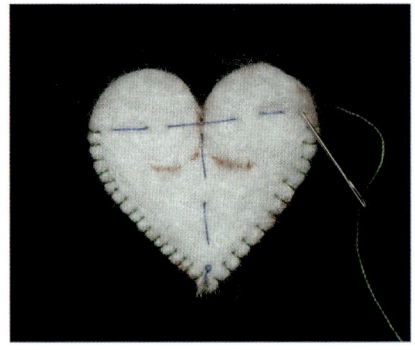

2 Stitch the felt piece in place, bringing the thread to the front at the edge of the felt and to the back through the edge. Place the stitches at a right angle to the felt at 2mm (1/16") intervals.

3 Metal threads. Work the first row, bringing the couching thread to the front through the velvet at the edge of the felt. Take the needle to the back through the felt.

4 Continue to fill the design with metal thread work over the felt, using your chosen technique.

Indian bag

Gold thread embroidery reached great proficiency in India during the height of the Mughal Empire under the patronage of Akbar the Great (1555–1605). The imperial style of metal thread embroidery, called Zardozi embroidery was revived in North India after independence in 1947. However, the threads used now are generally silver or gold coloured copper.

Black velvet bag. Early 20th century, India. From the collection of Embroiderers Guild of Victoria.

LAID WORK PATTERNS

When filling shapes, the positioning and spacing of the couching stitches will influence the appearance of the finished design.

Bricking or brick pattern

This is the most basic and commonly used couching pattern. The coucing stitches are placed halfway between those of the previous row and directly above the stitches in the alternate row (fig 1).

When worked with matching thread, the brick pattern is quite subtle and does not interfere with the overall design.

fig 1

Diamond and geometric patterns

The positioning of the couching stitches can be used to form geometric or scrolling patterns within the design. The patterns should be drawn onto the fabric and the couching stitches worked on the marked lines.

When a matching couching thread is used the result is a subtle pattern of light and shade (fig 2).

More striking patterns can be achieved if darker shades of gold, brown or strongly coloured threads are used (figs 3 and 4).

Small patterns need couching along the design lines only. Larger scale patterns may need extra couching stitches worked in matching sewing or invisible nylon thread between the main stitches. The distance between couching stitches should in most cases not exceed 10mm–12mm (⅜"–½") (fig 5).

fig 2

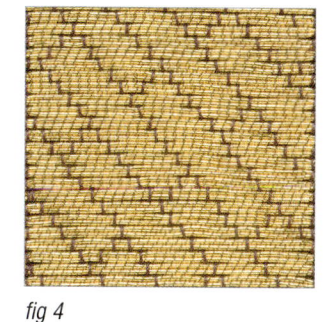

fig 3

fig 4

fig 5

Chinese rank badge (female), late 19th century. Black silk ground with couched metal threads depicting crane among symbols and clouds on a wave base.

From the collection of the Embroiderers Guild of America.

OR NUÉ

Pronounced 'ornway', this colourful and beautiful technique is worked by covering an area with a fine metal thread, or pair of threads, laid in close rows. The metal threads are couched in place using fine coloured silk or cotton to achieve a coloured or shaded pattern. The background, where no colour is needed is couched in self-coloured thread. The couching stitches are worked closely together where intense colour is needed and further apart for softer shading.

Each colour of couching thread is threaded into a separate needle to allow all the couching along each row to be completed at the same time. The design outlines are transferred onto the fabric, but it is advisable also to keep a coloured working drawing as a reference for colour changes and shading within the design.

Couching or nué

Couching with just a single strand of silk or cotton makes this technique fairly slow.

Using two or three strands of thread will cover the laid gold threads more quickly.

However, the thickness of the threads will push the laid rows further apart. This will allow the background fabric to show through between the rows or make it very difficult to keep the rows of laid threads straight.

1 Leaving 2.5cm (1") tails, couch the metal threads along the edge of the design area, using matching thread for the background. When reaching the coloured area, leave the couching thread on the front of the work, ready for the next row.

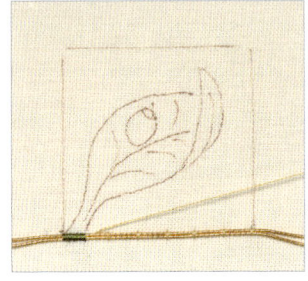

2 Using the coloured thread continue couching across the coloured section, placing the stitches close together.

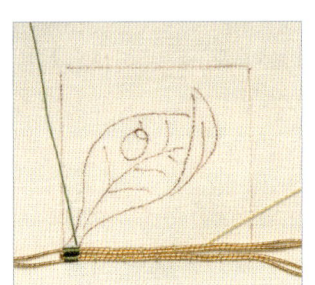

3 Turn the laid threads using your chosen method. Couch the second row, changing between the coloured and background threads. Place the coloured stitches close together and the background stitches in a brick pattern.

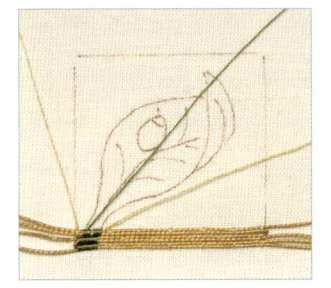

4 Continue in this manner, adding a new thread for each area within the design. Keep the couching threads not in use on the front of the work to prevent them becoming caught in the stitching on the back.

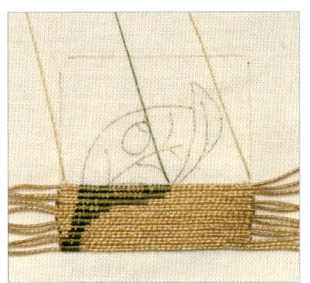

5 Place the coloured couching stitches close together for deep colour. Work the stitches in a brick pattern and further apart for soft shading.

OR NUÉ – CONTINUED

6 Introducing a new length of thread as you reach each area within the design. Keep the threads that are not being used on the front.

7 Continue until the area is completely covered. Sink and secure the metal thread tails at regular intervals.

8 Back of work. The metal thread tails are taken to the back and secured at regular intervals.

Gold lily. 1992, Denmark. Large lily worked in or nué on the back of a chasuble. The gold threads are laid following the flow of the flower petals and shading is achieved using coloured silk for the couching.

Embroidery by Mrs Lilian Christiansen, design by HM Queen Magarethe II.

Courtesy Society for Ecclesiastical Art and Craft, Copenhagen.

OR NUÉ ~ CIRCULAR

When working or nué in a circle the best result is achieved when using a passing thread as the constant 'coiling' of the thread will cause other types of couching thread to twist.

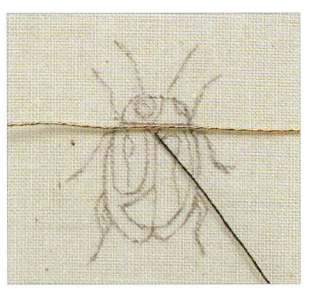

1 Leaving a 2.5cm (1") tail, place the metal thread across the centre of the design. Bring the required colour couching thread to the front at the centre.

2 Work a couching stitch over the metal thread.

3 Place a second stitch over the first ensuring the laid thread is firmly secured.

4 Bend the tail of the laid thread upwards so it is vertical to the fabric. Continue couching in a tight circle around the thread tail.

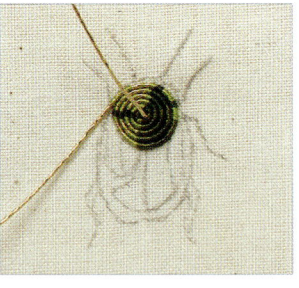

5 Changing colours as required and keeping the thread tail out of the way, continue to couch approximately ten close rounds.

6 Using a sling, insert the tip of the needle at the centre of the circle so the eye shows. Place the tip of the metal thread tail into the sling.

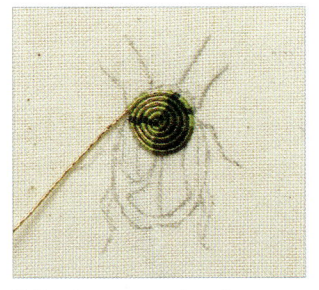

7 Begin to ease the sling loop through, using a short firm tug to get the tip of the thread tail through. Ease the entire thread tail to the back.

8 Back of work. Trim and secure the metal thread tail on the back of the work.

OR NUÉ ~ CIRCULAR – CONTINUED

9 Continue spiralling the metal thread and changing the coloured couching according to the design.

10 Use a self-coloured thread for the background, placing the couching stitches here further apart in a brick pattern.

11 To fill corners around the completed circle, couch the metal thread back and forth using the tweezers to pinch the folds closed.

12 Continue to the tip of the corner. Trim the laid thread, leaving a 2.5mm (1") tail and take it to the back using a sling.

13 Rejoin the metal thread at each remaining corner and complete in the same manner.

'Small Wonders' by Jo Dixey.

61

UNDERSIDE COUCHING

This is a distinct part of opus anglicanum, in which it was used extensively to fill large areas of background. It is different from all other couching as no stitches are visible on the front. The result is more flexible than surface couching, making it suitable to fill large areas on items that have movement. Underside couching also results in a more durable piece, as the couching thread is kept on the back of the fabric and is therefore protected from wear. The stitches are placed in a geometric pattern and the shadows formed allow the patterns to show up extremely well.

Underside couching is usually worked on firm, closely woven linen. The laid threads are placed vertically, following the warp of the fabric. The metal thread used must be firm and pliable, with passing thread the most suitable. A waxed thread of similar thickness to the gold thread is used for the couching. We used contrasting no. 8 perlé cotton for photographic purposes. Use a no. 28 tapestry needle to avoid splitting the fabric threads. Mark the couching pattern on the fabric.

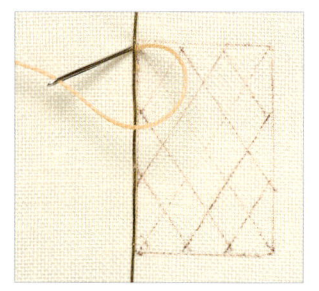

1 Leaving a 2.5cm (1") tail, lay the gold thread along the left hand edge of the design. Bring the couching thread to the front on the marked line. Take the needle over the laid thread and back through the same hole in the fabric.

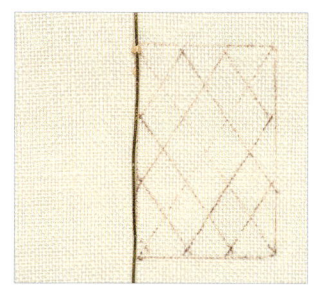

2 Pull the couching thread taut to lock the laid thread against the fabric.

St Stephen, mid 20th century. Australia. Figure worked in coloured silks. Background stitched in underside couching. From the collection of the Embroiderers Guild of Victoria.

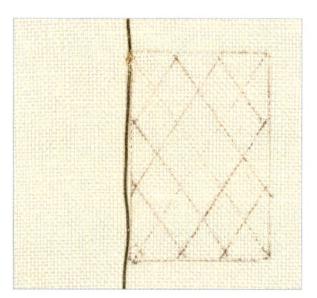

3 Hold the laid thread firmly, but not taut. With your other hand below the frame, pull the couching thread with a short tug, pulling a small loop of gold thread through to the back.

4 Back of work. The metal thread loop on the back will lock the couching thread to the back of the fabric.

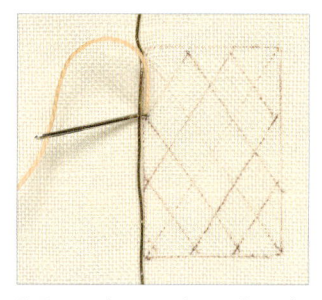

5 Bring the couching thread to the front on the design line at the position for the next stitch. Take the needle over the laid thread and to the back through the same hole in the fabric.

UNDERSIDE COUCHING – CONTINUED

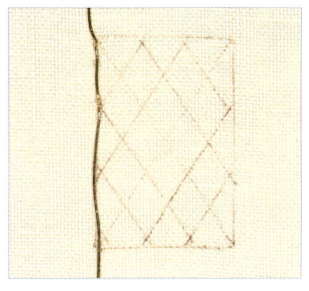

6 Hold the laid thread firmly, but not taut and pull the second stitch through with a short tug in the same manner as before.

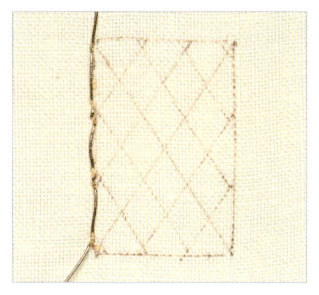

7 Continue to stitch in this manner to the end of the row.

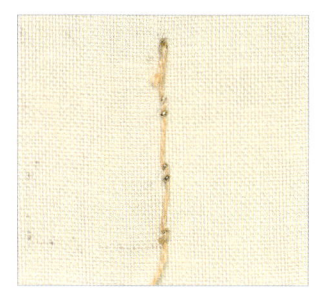

8 Back of work. A series of metal thread loops lock the couching thread in place on the back of the work.

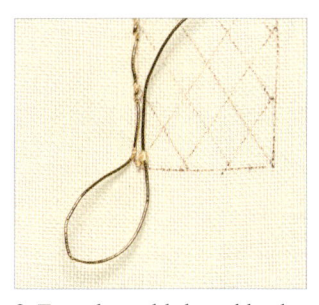

9 Turn the gold thread back on itself, leaving a 5cm (2") loop. Lay the turned thread snug against the first thread. Take the needle over the laid thread and back through the same hole.

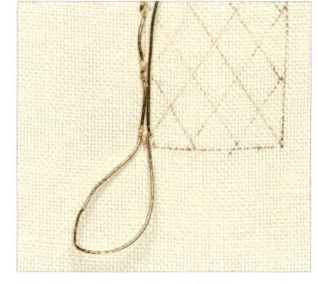

10 Keeping the laid thread taut, pull the stitch to the back with a short tug.

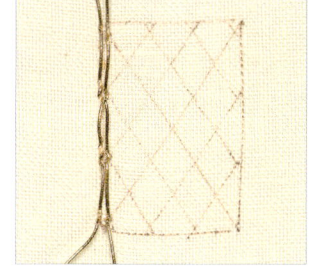

11 Work the second row of underside couching just next to the first row, placing the stitches on the design lines. Ensure the laid threads are pulled close together.

12 Continue in this manner to fill the shape, leaving a 5cm (2") loop at each turn.

13 Cut the loops. Sink and secure the thread tails at regular intervals.

14 Back of work. The series of loops makes the design clearly visible on the wrong side of the work.

COUCHING OVER PADDING

A variety of materials can be used as padding under the laid threads to achieve different textures and enhance the play of light on the threads. The material used for padding should be a similar colour to the thread that will be covering it.

BASKET STITCH FILLING

This is the best known type of cord padding. A highly textured surface is formed with metallic threads couched across parallel lengths of cord in patterns, imitating woven basket ware. Basket stitch filling is quite rigid and therefore best suited to flat items such as book covers, panels and boxes. The couching thread should be of matching colour to the laid thread or a little darker, which will accentuate the pattern. We used contrasting thread for photographic purposes.

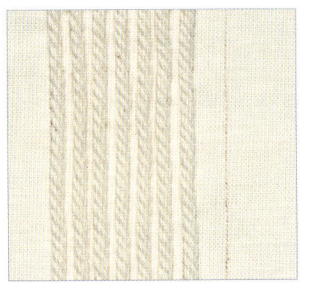

1 Stitch parallel lengths of cord in place at regular intervals across the shape following the instructions on page 27.

2 Leaving 2.5cm (1") tails, lay a pair of gold threads across the cords. Secure the couching thread and couch the laid threads in place at the edge of the shape.

3 Work a double couching stitch close to the first cord. Bring the couching thread to the front halfway between the first and second cords.

4 Work a couching stitch over the laid threads. Pull the stitch taut, pulling the laid threads into the groove between the cords.

5 Work a second couching stitch over the first.

6 Lay the gold threads over the next two cords and couch in place between the third and fourth cords in the same manner.

BASKET STITCH FILLING – CONTINUED

7 Continue to couch double stitches in every second groove between the cords in this manner to the end of the row. Work a double couching stitch outside the last cord in the row.

8 Turn the laid threads and place across the cords. Work a double couching stitch next to the first cord, directly above the previous stitch. Bring the couching thread to the front above the laid threads, halfway across the alternate groove of the previous row.

9 Take the needle to the back next to the previous row, pulling the laid threads into the groove and the rows closely together. Work a second couching stitch over the first.

10 Couch the laid threads in place between the alternate rows of cord, working the couching stitches towards the previous row. Place the last stitch just after the last cord in the row.

11 Continue in this manner to fill the shape.

12 By changing the number of cords over which the laid threads are carried the texture of the basket weave can be varied.

Outlining basket stitch filling

To neaten the shape and prevent the laid threads from falling off the ends of the cord, the design can be outlined with laid threads or cord.

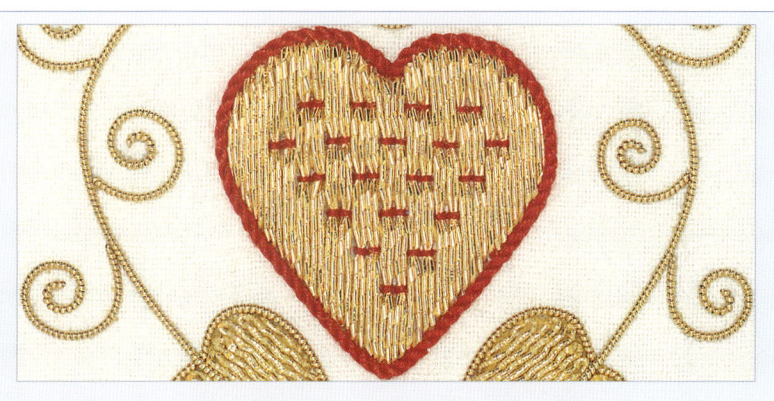

Fil d'or by Tanja Berlin

GUIMPED COUCHING

This technique is traditionally worked over card, vellum or parchment to form isolated, narrow shapes. It works well for petals and leaves.

The thread is laid across the card shape in the direction that is shortest, as it is very difficult to hold the thread in place if positioned along an edge.

Use a fine thread, such as passing thread for the best result.

Close-up bonnet embroidery, 1840s. Guimped embroidery over vellum, spangles, purls and silk embroidery. From the collection of Greve Museum, Denmark.

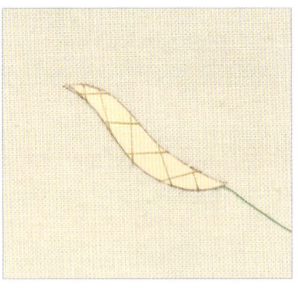

1 Prepare the card padding following the instructions on page 27 Bring the couching thread to the front at the lower edge of the card.

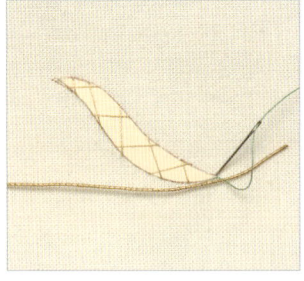

2 Leaving a 2.5cm (1") tail, lay the gold thread across the card. Couch the thread in place at the point.

3 Carry the couching thread across the back of the work and couch the laid thread with a back stitch at the opposite side.

4 Turn the gold thread back on itself, using tweezers to pinch the fold closed.

5 Take the couching thread across the back of the work to the opposite side of the card. Bring it to the front at the edge, above the laid thread.

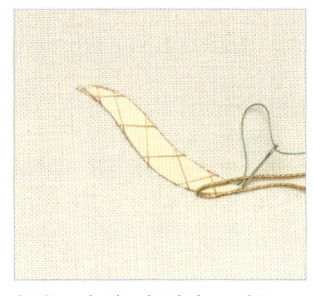

6 Couch the laid thread in place with a back stitch at the edge of the card.

GUIMPED COUCHING – CONTINUED

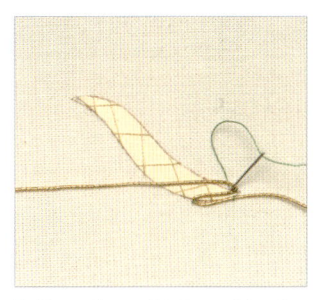

7 Turn the gold thread back on itself. Bring the couching thread to the front above the fold and work a back stitch over the fold.

8 Bring the couching thread to the front at the opposite edge of the card, above the laid thread.

9 Continue to turn the laid thread back and forth across the card, couching it in place at each side.

10 As the work grows, use the flat edge of the mellor to push the laid threads together.

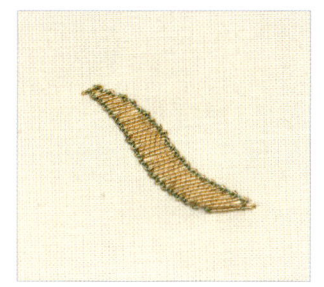

11 Sink each metal thread tail to the back at the edge of the card and secure.

12 Back of work. The couching thread is carried back and forth across the back of the shape.

Hedebo bonnets

From the late 18th century to the early 20th century one could tell by the head costume worn by Danish country woman, which region she was from.

In the Hedebo region near Copenhagen and Roskilde, the farmers were very wealthy, which was evident on their ornately painted and carved furniture, white on white embroidered textiles and beautiful costume of which a heavily gold or silver embroidered bonnet back was an important part. It is known that the bonnets were embroidered and made by professional woman, and that they were an important status symbol. A wealthy farmer's wife could own several. Some woman of the region continued to wear this type of bonnet until the after WW1.

Bonnet, Denmark 1850–55
5-folded bonnet back embroidered with silver threads and spangles.
Courtesy Greve Museum, Denmark.

APPLYING KID LEATHER

Attaching kid leather

To achieve smooth neat edges, always bring the needle to the front through the design line and take to the back through the leather.

Kid leather is usually applied over felt padding. Use a short, fine needle such as a no. 10 crewel or sharp. Leather needles will leave too large a hole or tear the leather. Use matching waxed sewing thread or nylon thread for attaching the kid leather.

We used contrasting thread for photographic purposes.

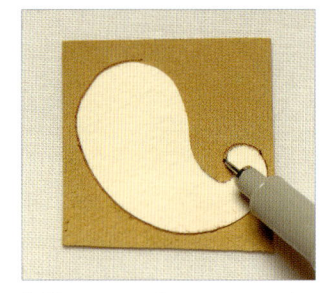

1 Use a template to trace the shape onto the wrong side of the leather. The template should be a mirror image of the design.

2 Using small sharp scissors, cut the piece out along the marked line.

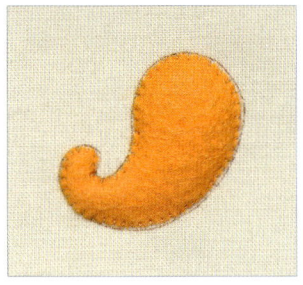

3 Prepare the felt padding following the instructions on page 30.

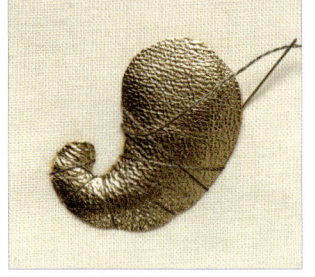

4 Position the leather over the felt padding. Hold it in place with long tacking stitches across the leather. Do not stitch through the leather as the needle holes will show.

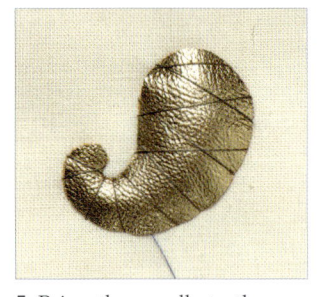

5 Bring the needle to the front at an angle under the edge of the leather.

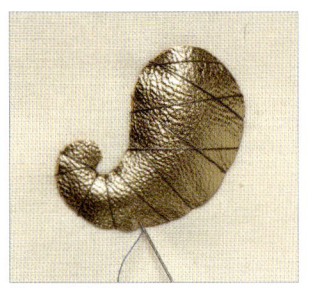

6 Take the needle to the back through the leather, placing a small stitch at a right angle across the edge.

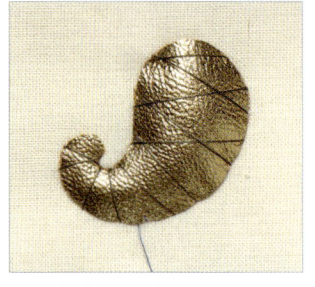

7 Pull the stitch taut, rounding the edge of the leather. Bring the thread to the front at the edge of the leather 2mm ($1/16$") from the first stitch.

8 Continue to stitch around the edge of the shape in this manner, placing the stitches at 2mm ($1/16$") intervals. Carefully remove the tacking stitches.

68

LAID WORK OVER CARD

The couching stitches need to be up against both sides of the card and an even tension must be applied to the laid thread to achieve a smooth shape. The width of the card should be no more than 15mm (⅝").

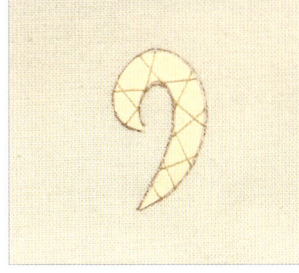

1 Prepare the card padding following the instructions on page 27.

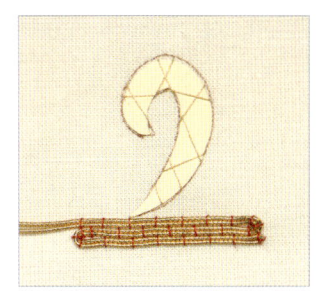

2 Begin couching the laid threads in a brick pattern following the instructions for laid work on pages 52–55 until reaching the edge of the card.

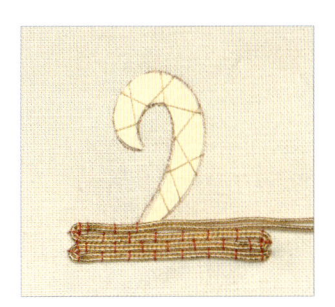

3 Begin couching the next row of thread until reaching the card. Place a stitch on the design line at the edge of the card.

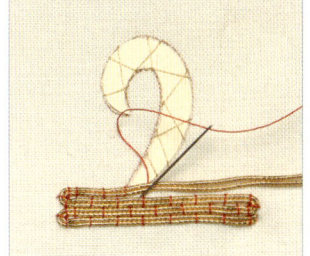

4 Lay the gold threads across the card and place the next couching stitch at the opposite side.

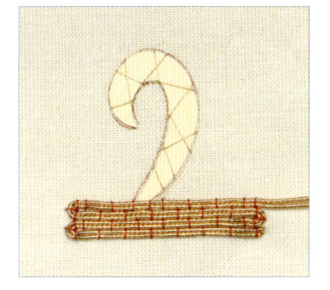

5 Continue couching in a brick pattern to the end of the row.

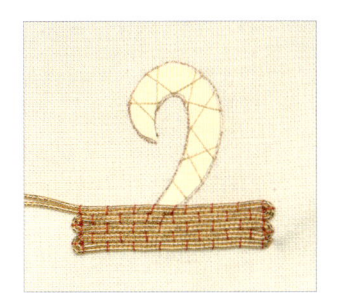

6 Turn the laid threads and couch until reaching the card again. Lay the gold threads across the card, placing a stitch at each side of the card. Continue to the end of the row.

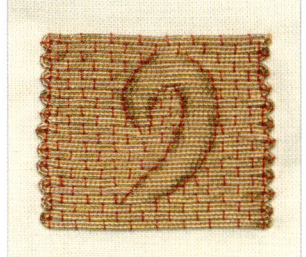

7 Continue to work in this manner, removing the tacking stitches over the card as you work.

Outlining kid leather

The leather shape can be outlined with braid, cord, pearl purl or threads for a decorative finish. Bring the needle to the front on the outside of the outlining thread and to the back at the edge of the leather.

LAID WORK OVER CORD

Cord padding creates strong design lines under laid work.

The couching stitches need to be up against both sides of the cord and an even tension must be applied to the laid threads to achieve a smooth shape.

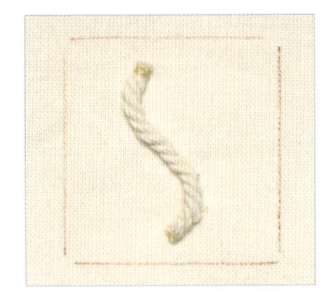

1 Stitch the cord in place following the instructions on page 27.

2 Begin couching the laid threads in place in your chosen pattern, until reaching the cord.

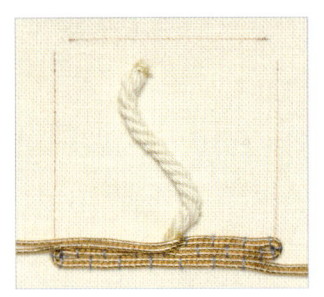

3 Begin to couch the next row of threads as before, placing the last couching stitch at the edge of the cord.

4 Carry the laid threads over the cord. Place a couching stitch close to the edge on the opposite side of the cord. Couch to the end of the row.

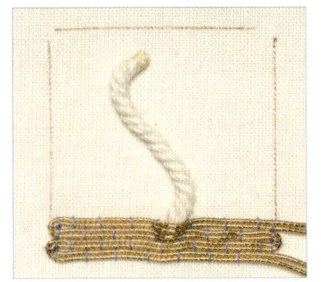

5 Turn the laid threads and couch the next row in a similar manner, placing a stitch on each side of the cord.

6 Continue to couch back and forth in this manner, placing couching stitches on each side of the cord.

Trumpet banner, UK 2004
Banner being completed at Toye Kerning & Spencer, U.K. The ceremonial banner is used in the Trooping of the Colour and other ceremonies. Courtesy Benton & Johnson, U.K.

LAID WORK OVER FELT

Filling a padded shape from the edge

Covering a padded shape from the outline towards the centre is done in the same manner as designs worked directly onto the main fabric. For the first row, bring the needle to the front at the edge of the felt and stitch over the laid threads into the felt to ensure the edge will be covered.

Couching across or along padding

Threads can also be laid and couched along or across a padded shape in the same manner as shapes worked directly onto the main fabric.

Reverse felt padding

For some designs the felt layers can be attached in the reverse order to achieve a crisper defined edge between each layer. Apply the layers of padding beginning with the largest piece and finishing with the smallest.

Padded shape filled with laid work from the outline.

Padded shape covered with laid threads placed and couched along the length.

Use a different goldwork technique over each section of the padding.

Flower brooch

To make a similar brooch, you will need :

15cm × 30cm wide (6" × 12") piece of calico

10cm (4") embroidery hoop

Brooch pin

Small pieces of yellow and white felt

Small piece of gold kid leather

Threads

Selection of gold and silver threads. We used silver rough and smooth purl, imitation Japanese thread and Grecian cord; gold pearl purl and check purl.

How to make the brooch

Fold the fabric in half and place in the hoop. Cut a piece of felt for each layer of padding; one full size, one for petals and one centre and stitch in place in the centre of the doubled piece of fabric, following the instructions on page 91.

Cover each layer of padding using a different type of thread and goldwork technique. We used kid leather, purls and chip work. Outline each area using a heavy cord to outline the design.

Constructing the brooch

Cut out the design leaving a 1cm (⅜") seam allowance. Work running stitch halfway along the seam allowance around the design. Gather up the running stitches, drawing the seam allowance to the back. Secure with a few stitches to the back of the work.

Cut a piece of felt to match the size of the brooch and stitch in place on the back. Stitch the brooch pin securely in place in the centre.

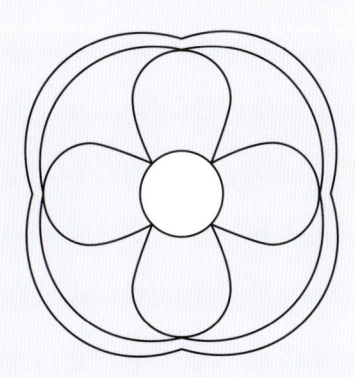

FILLING PATTERNS

Many different techniques can be used to fill shapes, creating interesting patterns and textures within a design.

BURDEN STITCH

This stitch is most often used in crewelwork. When worked with metallic threads or purls, interesting textures can be created.

Method one ~ coloured couching

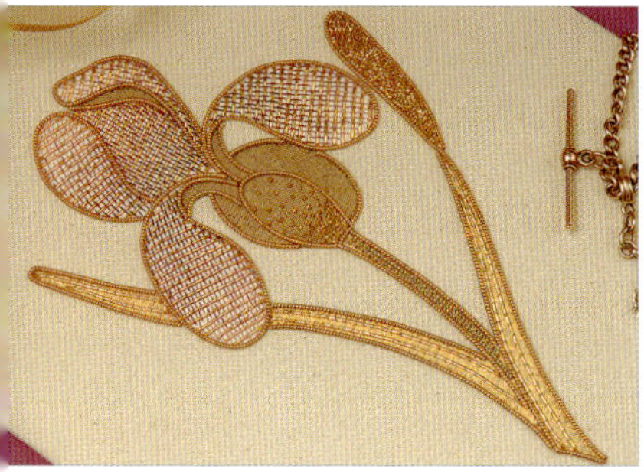

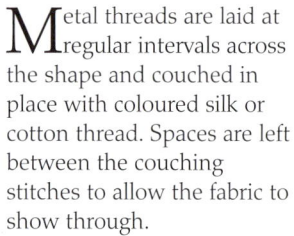

Golden Grace by Tracy A Franklin

Metal threads are laid at regular intervals across the shape and couched in place with coloured silk or cotton thread. Spaces are left between the couching stitches to allow the fabric to show through.

Imitation Japanese threads, passing thread and twists are all suitable as laid thread. Use waxed stranded silk or cotton for the couching.

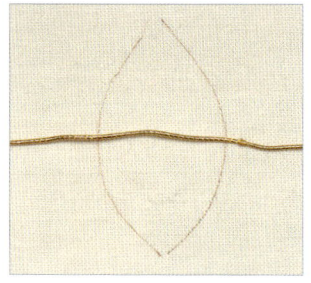

1 Leave a 2.5cm (1") tail. Place the metal thread across the widest section of the shape. Hold the tail in place with a few tacking stitches outside the design line.

2 Bring the couching thread to the front at the edge of the shape next to the laid thread.

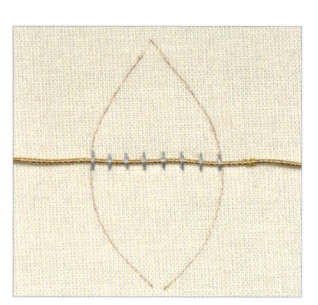

3 Hold the metal thread straight and firm across the shape. Work wide couching stitches over the laid thread at 4mm ($3/16$") intervals.

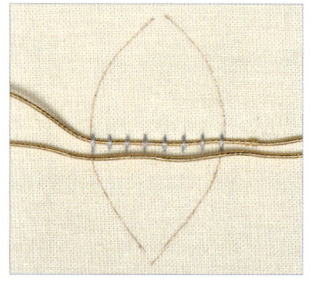

4 At the opposite side, turn the metal thread back on itself, leaving a 5cm (2") loop. Place the metal thread across the shape, along the tips of the couching stitches of the previous row.

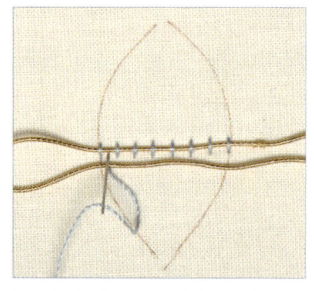

5 Hold the metal thread straight and firm. Bring the couching thread to the front 2mm ($1/16$") from the laid thread, halfway between the couching stitches of the previous row. Take the needle to the back under the previous laid thread.

72

METHOD ONE ~ COLOURED COUCHING – CONTINUED

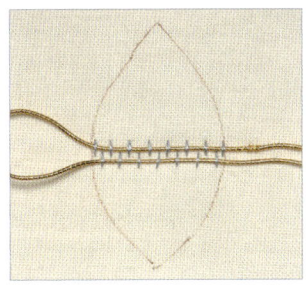

6 Continue to couch the turned thread, placing each stitch halfway between those of the previous row in a brick pattern.

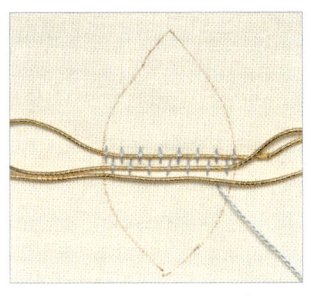

7 Repeat step 4 Bring the thread to the front 2mm (1/16") from the turned thread, halfway between the previous couching stitches.

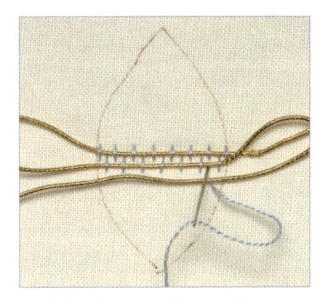

8 Take the needle to the back under the previous laid thread, aligning the stitch with the couching stitch of the first row.

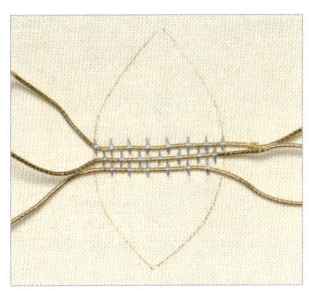

9 Continue to couch along the row, placing the stitches directly below those of the first row.

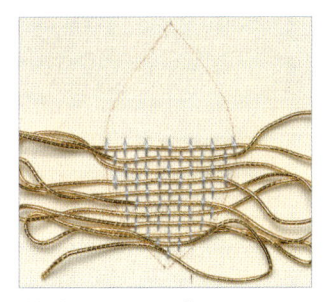

10 Continue in this way to fill one half of the shape.

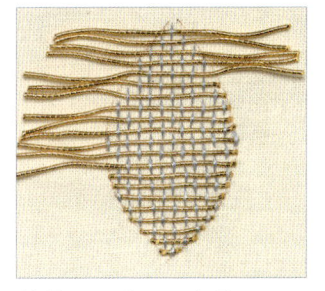

11 Rotate the work. Restart the metal thread and fill the remaining part of the shape in the same manner. Cut the loops at each side. Sink and secure the metal thread tails one at a time.

12 Shading ~ method one. Shading can be added to the burden stitch by gradually changing the colour of the couching thread.

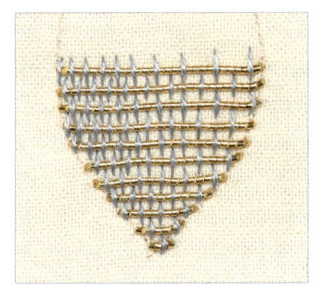

13 Shading – method two. The density of colour can be graded by varying the spacing of the couching stitches.

Burden stitch cross section

Each laid thread is stabilised by the long couching stitches worked over the rows on either side. These create a valley, preventing the laid thread from rolling.

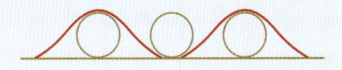

Method two ~ using cut purl

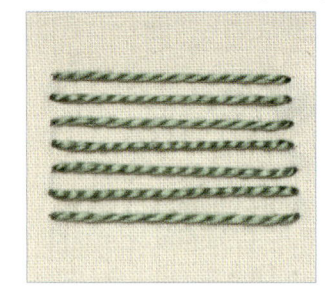

Purls can be spaced and stitched in place over coloured cords, string, perlé threads, ribbons and single or doubled metallic threads. The texture of the pattern is easily changed by the spacing of the purls and the number of laid threads they are stitched across. We used no. 6 smooth purl over no. 3 perlé cotton. Stitch the purls in place using double waxed sewing thread.

1 Couch or stitch parallel rows of thread in place across the shape at regular intervals. Sink and secure the thread tails if required.

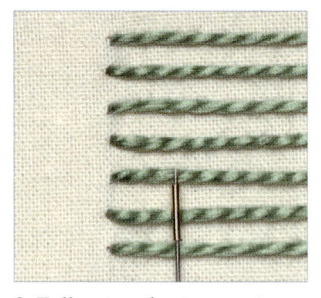

2 Following the instructions on page 91, measure and cut lengths of purl to fit across a laid thread and covering the space on each side.

3 First row. Bring the couching thread to the front above the first laid thread. Slide a length of purl onto the thread.

4 Stitch the purl in place at a right angle over the second laid thread.

5 Bring the thread to the front above the second laid thread, next to the first purl.

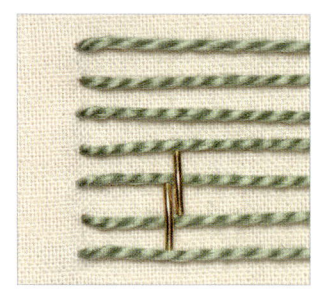

6 Stitch a length of purl in place at a right angle over the third laid thread.

7 Continue to attach purls, alternating over the second and third laid threads to the end of the row.

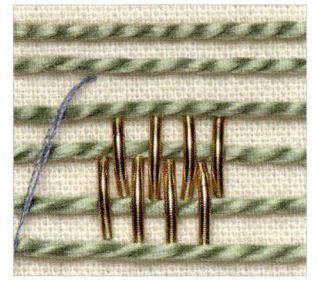

8 Second and subsequent rows. Bring the needle to the front two laid threads above a purl in the first row.

9 Slide a cut purl onto the thread and place it across the fourth laid thread. Take the needle to the back next to the third laid thread, aligning the stitch with the purl in the previous row.

74

METHOD TWO ~ USING CUT PURL – CONTINUED

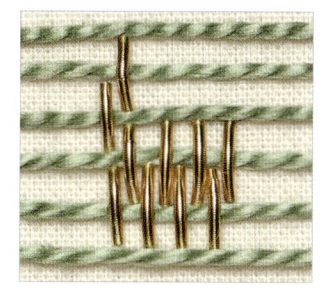

10 Stitch the next purl in place in a similar manner, stepping the position to fit.

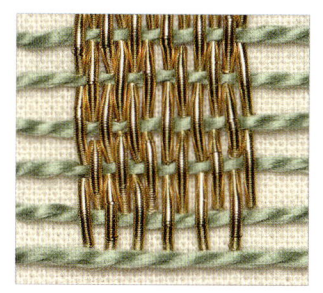

11 Continue to stitch the cut purls in place across the laid threads in a brick pattern to fill the shape.

12 Measure and cut shorter lengths of purl and stitch in place over the outer laid threads to fill the edges.

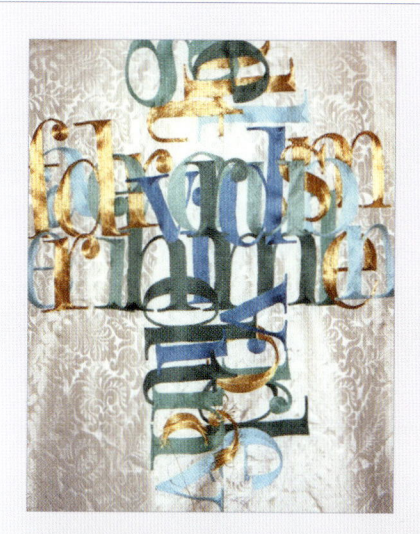

Embroidered letters

Lettering on ecclesiastical textiles, insignia and personal monograms is an important part of embroidered ornamentation. Many different techniques and types of thread can be used to create wonderful effects.

Left: Back of chasuble, 1995 The letters from the first sentence of 'the Lord's prayer' arranged in a cross. Worked in silk and imitation Japanese threads laid, following the outline of the letters. Courtesy Society of Ecclesiastical Arts and Craft, Copenhagen.

Below left: Detail of mini cope, page 97. IHS embroidered in cut purl, embellished with pearls and mirror glass. Collection of the Embroiderers Guild of America.

Below right: Detail of orphrey, page 7. English. IHS worked in purl and bullion over felt padding. Outlined with pearl purl.

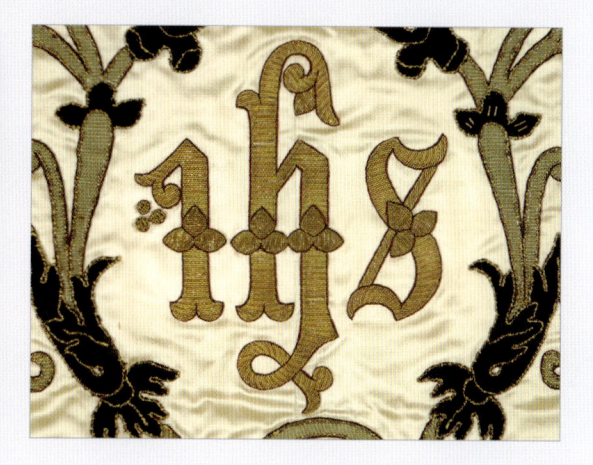

COILED FILLING

This technique creates a highly textured surface. The texture can be easily varied by the size and spacing of the coils.

A firm, pliable metal thread, such as passing thread, is most suitable because the constant twisting will untwist threads such as imitation Japanese thread.

Work in horizontal rows from the top of the shape towards you.

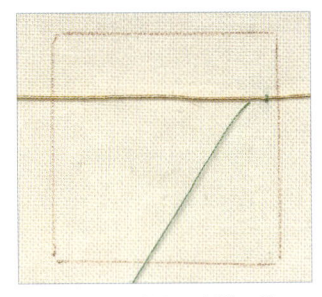

1 Leaving a 2.5cm (1") tail, secure the thread with a couching stitch at the edge of the design. Bring the couching thread to the front at the position for the first coil.

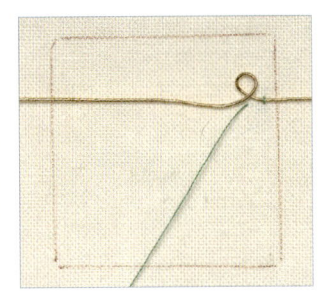

2 Twist the metal thread into a coil, crossing it at the point of the emerging couching thread.

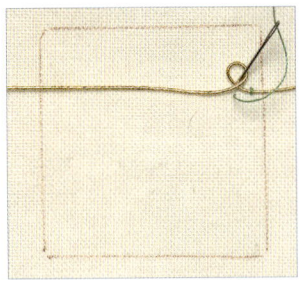

3 Take the needle through the coil and to the back on the opposite side of the crossover point.

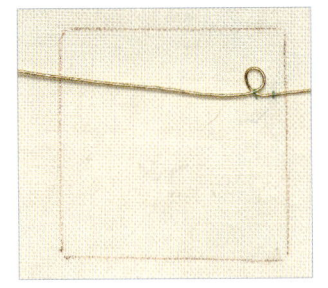

4 With one hand below the frame, begin to pull the thread through. Using the other hand, gently pull the metal thread to adjust the size of the coil. Pull the couching stitch taut.

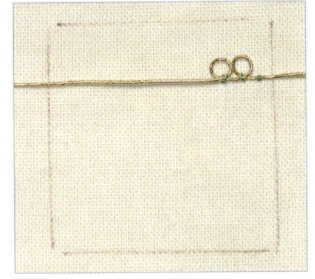

5 Bring the thread to the front at the position of the second coil. Twist the metal thread and couch in place in the same manner.

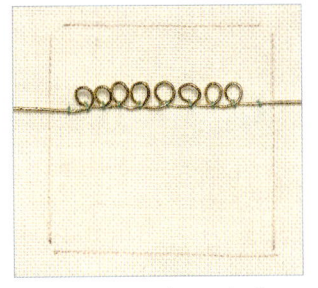

6 Continue to the end of the row. Place a couching stitch at the edge of the design and cut the thread, leaving a 2.5cm (1") tail.

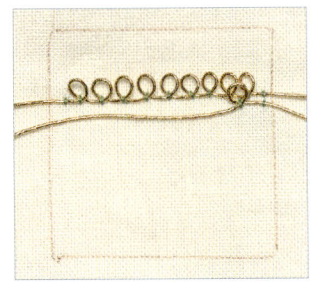

7 Leaving a tail, restart the metal thread. Twist the thread into a coil halfway between and slightly overlapping the coils of the first row. Couch the coil in place as before.

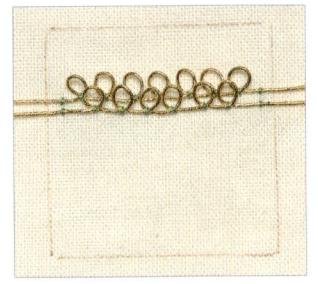

8 Continue to the end of the row, placing the coils between those of the first row. Cut the thread, leaving a 2.5cm (1") tail.

COILED FILLING – CONTINUED

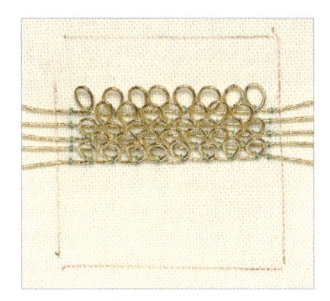

9 Stitch the third and subsequent rows in the same manner, offsetting and overlapping the coils in each row.

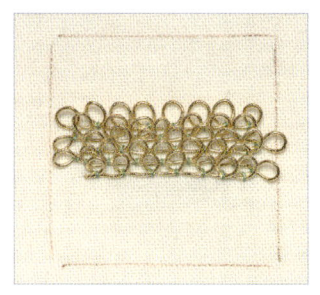

10 To create a more loose and 'fuzzy' outline, coil the metal thread back on itself at the end of each row.

11 To create an interesting design line, work two rows of coiled thread, with the coils facing in opposite directions. A wider line is achieved by working the coiled threads on either side of a laid thread, twist or plate.

Damascening

This couching technique creates a flowing filigree effect. The gold threads are couched in circular, spiralling movements into a swirly pattern.

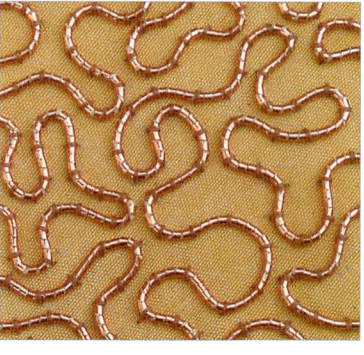

Vermicelli

This is an open meandering couching pattern suitable for filling large background areas.

Golden Dreams by Antonia Lomny

OPEN LAID FILLING

Metal threads can be laid in a grid pattern to fill a shape, allowing the background fabric to show through and become part of the design.

The laid threads are held in place with a couching stitch at the crossover points using a matching waxed sewing thread.

The intersections of the laid threads can be decorated with extra couching stitches worked in silk thread, beads or short lengths of cut purl for added colour and texture.

We used contrasting sewing thread for all couching for photographic purposes. Transfer the design and gridlines onto the fabric.

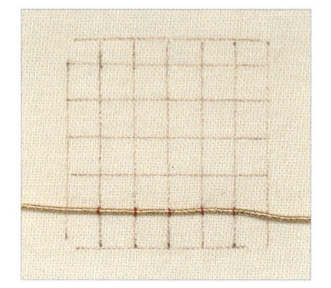

1 Leaving a tail, lay the metal thread along one line of the grid. Keeping the laid thread taut, work a couching stitch at each intersection of the grid.

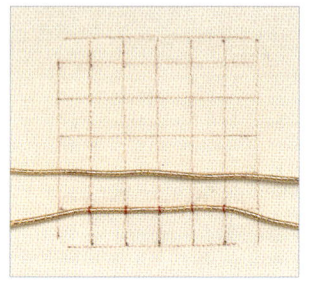

2 Turn the metal thread and lay it along the next parallel line in the grid, leaving a 5cm (2") loop at the edge of the design.

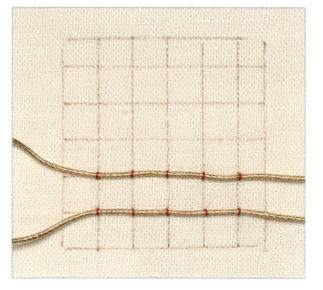

3 Couch the laid thread in place along the grid lines in the same manner as before.

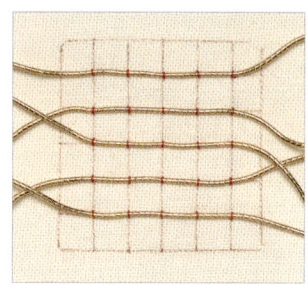

4 Continue in this manner until all the lines are covered in one direction of the grid.

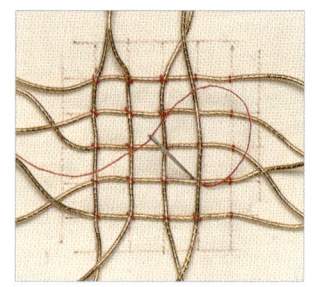

5 Lay and couch the metal thread along the grid lines in the opposite direction in the same manner. Place the couching stitches diagonally over the previous stitches and laid threads.

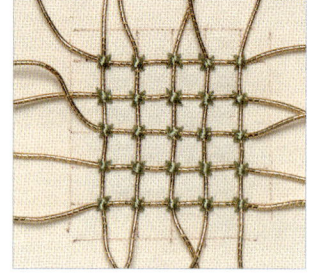

6 The intersections in the laid filling can be embellished with your chosen stitches. We used cross stitch worked in two strands of silk.

7 Cut the metal thread loops in half. Sink and secure the metal thread tails following the instructions on page 33 or 34.

OPEN LAID FILLING OVER SATIN STITCH

Fine metal thread, such as passing thread, forms a very delicate lattice when worked over a satin stitch ground. Fill the shape with satin stitch or other filling stitches such as long and short stitch, chain or stem stitch. Trace the design shape and gridlines onto tissue paper. Making sure the gridlines are at an angle to the underlying stitches, position the tracing over the embroidered shape and tack in place around the edge.

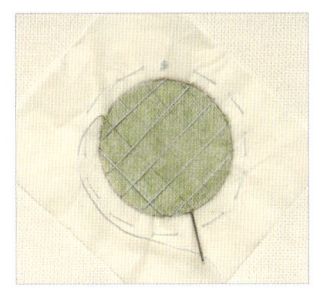

1 Using a contrasting cotton sewing thread, work long tacking stitches across the shape to mark the gridlines.

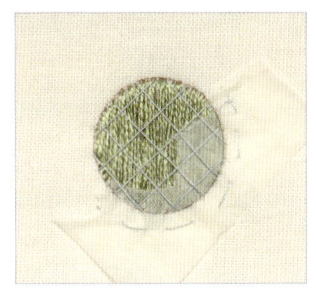

2 Gently tear and remove the tissue paper taking care not to distort the underlying embroidery.

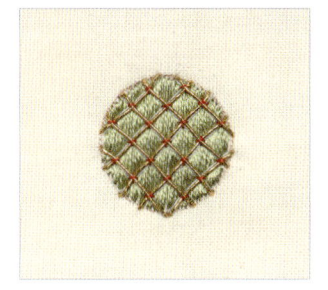

3 Work the laid filling following the instructions on the opposite page. Sink the tails along the edge of the embroidered shape. Carefully remove any tacking stitches still showing.

Open laid filling patterns

Patterns can be built up with several layers of grids, using different threads for added textures (figs 1 and 2).

The open spaces within the grid can be embellished with beads, cut purls, spangles etc. (figs 3 and 4).

See instructions for the laid filling patterns on page 141–143.

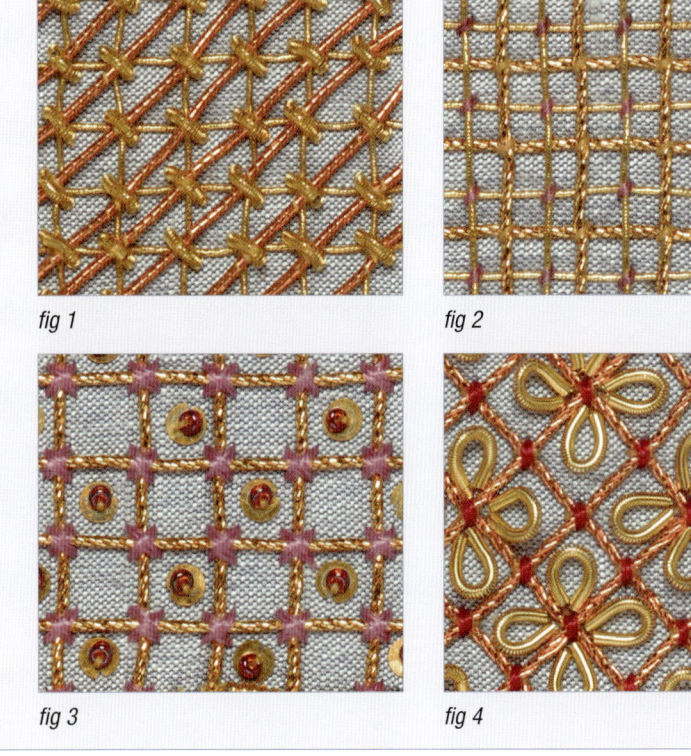

fig 1

fig 2

fig 3

fig 4

79

PEARL PURL

Pearl purl is mainly used to outline shapes, to neaten edges or for strong flowing lines such as stems. It can also be used with other threads and purls for laid work and to form centre veins along leaves and petals.

Use strong short bladed scissors for cutting pearl purl and matching waxed sewing thread for the couching. We used contrasting thread for photographic purposes.

Ra, the sun, heavily padded and embroidered in silk threads and outlined with two rounds of pearl purl.

'The Egyptian Beetle' by Wendy Innes.

COUCHING PEARL PURL

Pearl purl is very springy however, when pulled gently it becomes rigid and easy to manipulate.

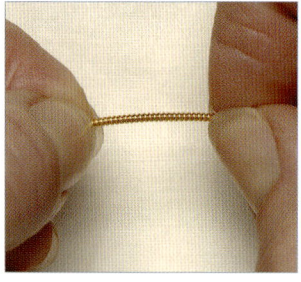

1 Hold each end of a piece of pearl purl and gently pull to stiffen. Take care not to distort the piece by pulling too hard.

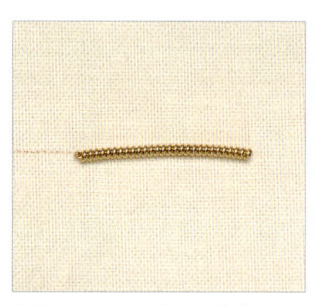

2 Trim one end to a full coil. Position the pearl purl with the full coil facing up on the design line.

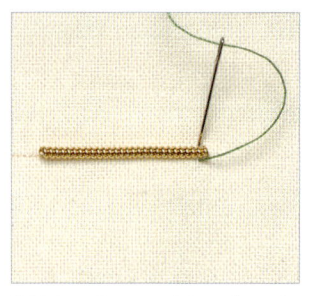

3 Bring the couching thread to the front next to the first groove between two coils. Work a stitch over the purl, following the direction of the groove. Take the needle to the back, angling it under the pearl purl.

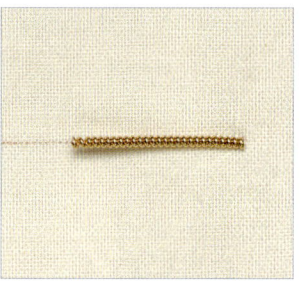

4 With one hand below the frame, pull the thread with a small tug, clicking it into the groove to stitch the first coil in place.

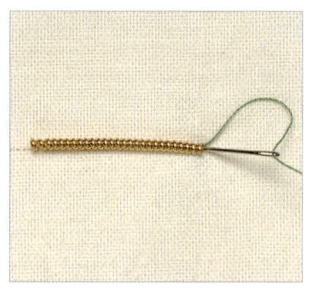

5 Bring the thread to the front at the end of the pearl purl. Work a stitch into the end of the first coil, securing the end.

COUCHING PEARL PURL – CONTINUED

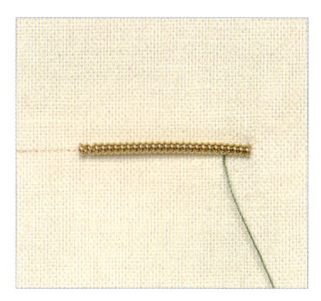

6 Bring the thread to the front at an angle under the pearl purl, two or three grooves from the first stitch.

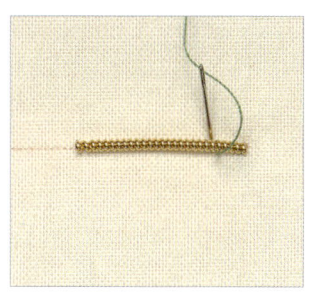

7 Take the needle to the back at the opposite side, angling the stitch to follow the groove.

8 Pull the thread with a small tug, clicking it into the groove as before.

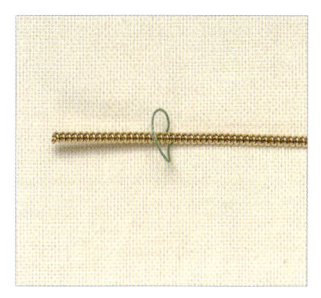

9 Continue to stitch the pearl purl in place in this manner, placing the stitches three to four coils apart.

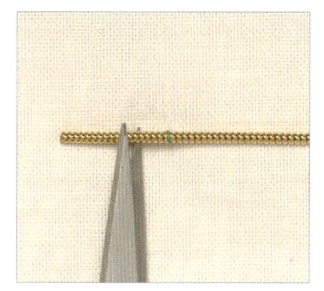

10 As you near the end, measure and trim the end of the pearl purl so a full coil is facing up.

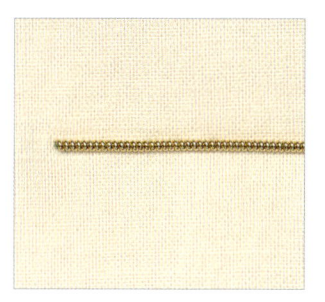

11 Secure the end of the pearl purl with a stitch into the last groove and a second stitch over the end.

Milliary wire

Milliary wire is highly textured and is excellent for adding texture and outlining shapes.

It is couched in place using matching sewing thread, the stitches placed through every 2 to 3 loops in the wire, in a similar manner to overstretched pearl purl.

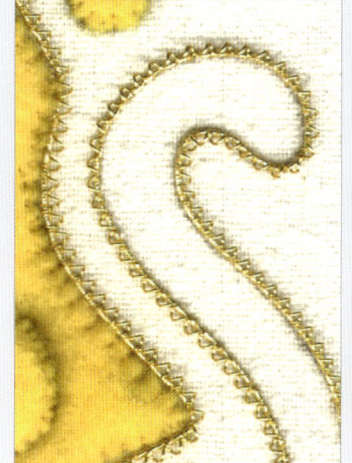

PEARL PURL ~ TURNING CORNERS

When outlining angular shapes such as squares you should start and finish at one corner.

1 Couch the pearl purl in place along one side. Place the point of a mellor or an awl at the corner point. Bend the pearl purl around the point.

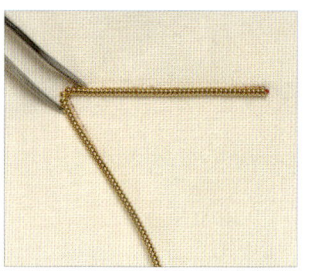

2 Taking care not to stretch the pearl purl, use tweezers to carefully pinch the point to the correct angle.

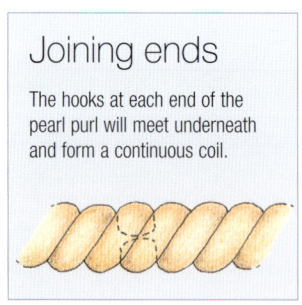

3 Bring the couching thread to the front outside the point. Place a stitch over the pearl purl.

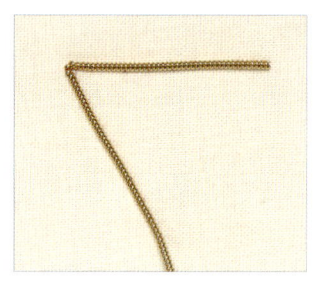

4 Click the stitch between the coils as before. Continue to stitch along the second side.

Joining ends
The hooks at each end of the pearl purl will meet underneath and form a continuous coil.

PEARL PURL ~ JOINING ENDS

When couching circles and other smooth shapes the join should be at the base of the shape.

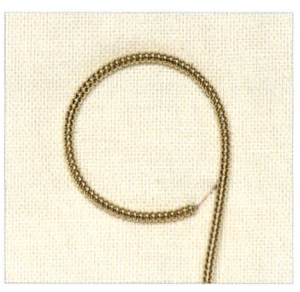

1 Couch the pearl purl in place around the shape.

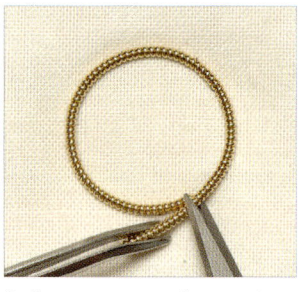

2 Once you near the starting point, use tweezers to manipulate the pearl purl into position to measure the exact length and trim to a full coil.

3 Use the tweezers to manipulate the pearl purl into position, so the ends align and form a continuous coil. Couch in place.

OVERSTRETCHED PEARL PURL

An open textured spiralling thread is created when pearl purl is pulled open. This changes the texture of the thread, allowing the background fabric to show through, giving the line a softer look. Use a matching waxed sewing thread for the couching. We used contrasting thread for photographic purposes.

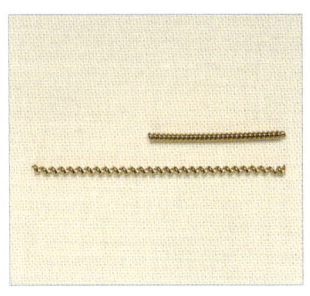

1 Cut a piece of pearl purl to half the required length. Hold each end of the piece firmly and pull to stretch it to twice its original length.

2 Position the piece so the hook at the end sits on the fabric. Bring the couching thread to the front next to the first open groove.

3 Take the needle to the back on the opposite side of the pearl purl, making sure the direction of the stitch follows the groove.

4 Bring the thread to the front at the end of the pearl purl and couch the hook in place.

5 Couch the overstretched pearl purl in place, working a stitch over every second groove.

6 As you near the end, measure and trim the pearl purl, making sure the hook rests on the fabric.

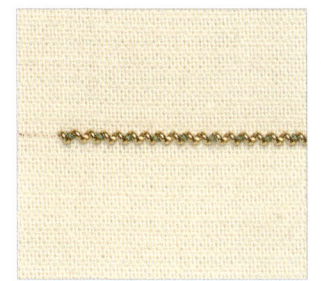

7 Couch to the end of the pearl purl and secure in the same manner as before.

Gold cuff, Slovakia, early 20th Century

In many regions of Slovakia gold thread is wrapped around pieces of leather and applied to lace. The result is raised gold embroidery that can be found on sleeves, scarves, and caps. The goldwork is not washable, so when a garment is soiled or worn the goldwork is lifted and reapplied to a clean surface. Often very old goldwork can be found on new garments, having been recycled. Courtesy the National Czech & Slovak Museum and Library, Iowa.

OVERSTRETCHED PEARL PURL ~ COLOURED

Colour can be added to the overstretched pearl purl in two ways, producing a textured candy-stripe effect. This is achieved either by stitching it in place with a coloured thread over every groove, or by wrapping coloured thread into the pearl purl before couching it in place. Prepare the pearl purl following step 1 for overstretched pearl purl.

Method one ~ coloured couching

Several strands of coloured silk or cotton are stitched across each groove of the overstretched pearl purl. The number of strands needed is determined by the size of the pearl purl. We used three strands of cotton.

1 Place the pearl purl so the hook sits on the fabric. Bring the thread to the front next to the first groove. Take the needle to the back on the opposite side, angling the stitch to follow the groove.

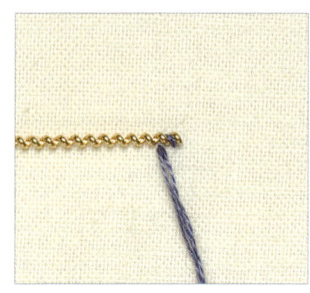

2 Pull the thread through, resting it into the groove. Bring the thread to the front next to the second groove.

3 Work a couching stitch over the second groove in the same manner, taking the needle through the fabric on an angle under the pearl purl.

4 Place a couching stitch over each groove of the overstretched pearl purl in this manner.

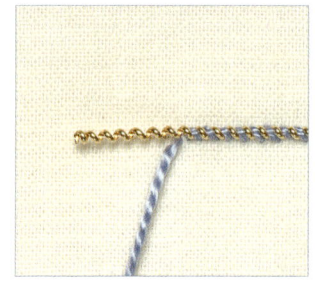

5 Fine perlé thread can also be used for this method. The round thread fills the grooves resulting in a smoother texture.

Robe ornaments, used for decorating ceremonial robes made by Troy Kerning and Spencer.

Method two ~ wrapping

When using this method, the overstretched pearl purl is wrapped with coloured thread(s) before it is couched in place. It is useful where the thickness of the coloured threads makes it difficult to stitch through the fabric, or if thicker perlé threads are used. The number of threads used for the wrapping is determined by the size of the pearl purl.

We used six strands of stranded cotton and a no. 2 pearl purl. The wrapped pearl purl is couched in place using a sewing thread matching the wrapping. We used contrasting thread for photographic purposes. Cut the required number of threads each 10cm (4") longer than the overstretched pearl purl.

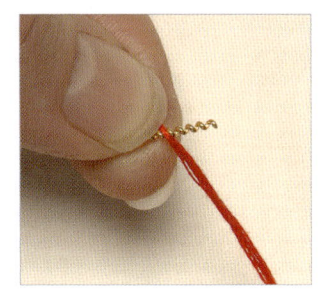

1 Hold one end of the pearl purl. Leave a 5cm (2") tail of the threads extending past the end of the pearl purl. Click the threads into a groove in the pearl purl near the end.

2 Begin to wrap the threads around the pearl purl in an anti-clockwise direction. The threads will slide into the coils. Keep the threads untwisted as you wrap.

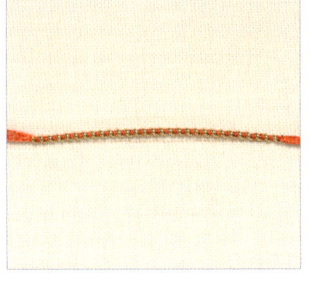

3 When you reach the end, turn the pearl purl around and wrap the threads into the opposite end in the same manner.

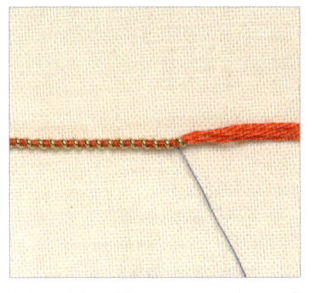

4 Position the wrapped pearl purl resting the end hooks on the fabric. Bring the couching thread to the front next to the first groove.

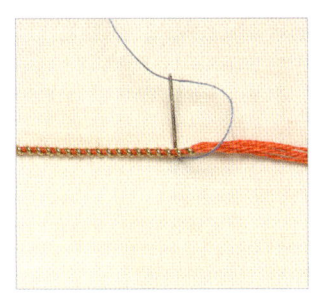

5 Take the needle to the back on the opposite side, angling the stitch to lie along one side of the groove.

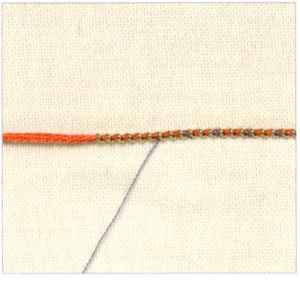

6 Couch the wrapped pearl purl in place by working a stitch over every second or third groove in this manner.

7 Use a large chenille needle to sink the thread tails to the back at each end of the pearl purl.

PLATE

Plate has a very strong shine. Couched across a shape, most often over felt pading, it makes a very smooth and highly reflective surface.

Folding plate

To achieve a precise and sharp fold in the plate, fold it over the pointed end of the mellor and use the flat end to press the fold closed.

FILLING

To fill a shape, plate is couched in a zigzag motion across the shape, often over felt padding to enhance the reflection of light.

1 Turn 2mm (1/16") to the back at one end of the plate, creating a small hook.

2 Secure the couching thread and bring it to the front on the design line at the narrow end of the shape.

3 Lay the plate across the shape with the hook facing towards the fabric. Work a couching stitch over the hook to secure the end.

4 Work a small back stitch inside the design line to anchor the couching stitch. Bring the thread to the front on the design line below the plate, on the opposite side of the shape.

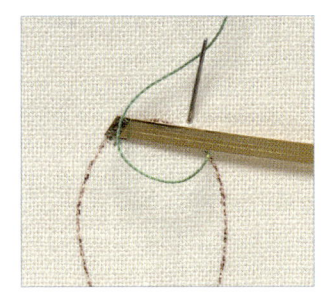

5 Take the needle to the back on the design line above the plate.

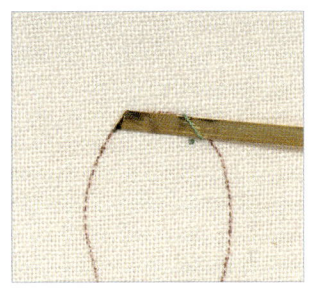

6 Pull the thread through and secure the couching stitch with a small back stitch as before.

86

FILLING – CONTINUED

7 Fold the plate back on itself over the couching stitch, placing it at a slight angle over the first width of plate.

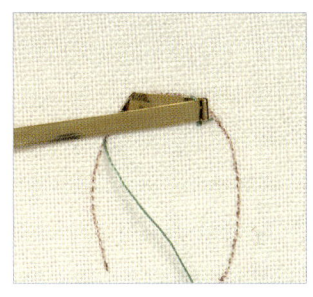

8 Take the thread across the back of the work and bring it to the front below the plate at the opposite side of the shape.

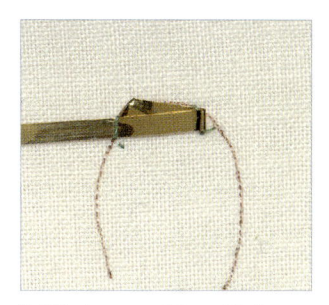

9 Work a couching stitch over the plate and secure with a back stitch in the same manner as before.

10 Continue to fold and couch the plate in this zigzag manner to cover the shape.

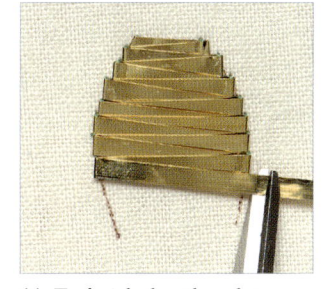

11 To finish, lay the plate across the shape and trim 2mm (1/16") past the outline.

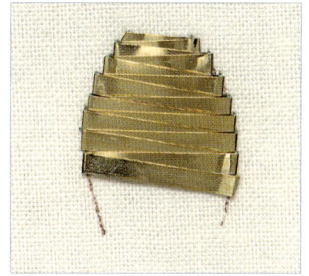

12 Fold the end of the plate to the back and secure with a couching stitch over the 'hook'.

OPEN FILLING

By turning the plate at a wider angle at each side of the shape the background fabric is allowed to show through. This creates a more open filling which still has a very high shine.

This technique is very effective when worked over a ground of padded satin stitch or across a band of laid metallic threads.

COUCHING PLATE WITH CUT PURLS

To create textured straight bands, plate can be couched in place using cut purls. Cut the required number of purls to match the width of the plate following the instructions on page 91.

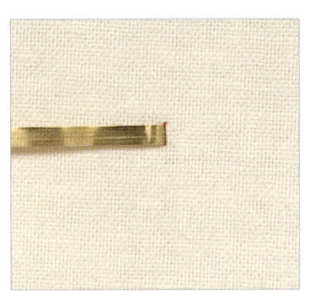

1 Secure the end of the plate following steps 1 and 2 for couching plate.

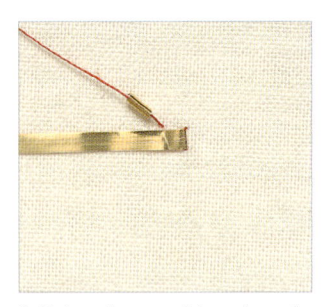

2 Bring the couching thread to the front above the plate. Slide a length of purl onto the thread.

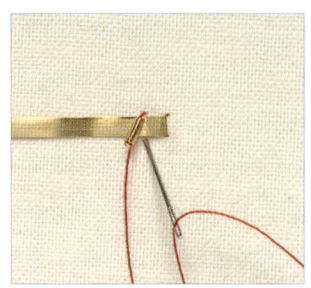

3 Lay the cut purl across the plate. Take the needle to the back on the opposite side of the plate.

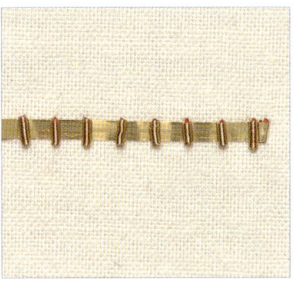

4 Continue to couch the plate in place, positioning the purls at regular intervals.

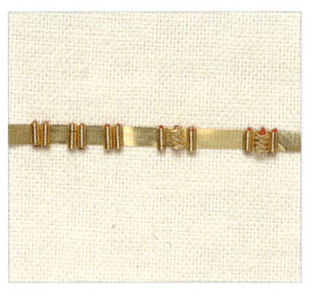

5 Vary the types of cut purl and the intervals at which they are couched to change the textures and patterns.

6 Plate can also be couched in place using short bugle beads, seed or petite beads.

Records from 1517 list that 450 ounces (12.75kg) of gold and 850 pearls were removed from one of Henry VIII's robes.

Portrait of Henry VIII. 1539 –1540 by H. Holbein.

88

PURL

Purl thread, with its flexibility and multitude of sizes and finishes, provide the most magnificent scope for the embroiderer. Whether they are stitched close together over padding, used in combination with sequins or spangles or sewn to the fabric in loops and swirls the beauty of purl thread should not be ignored.

Mixing different types of purl when filling an area is an effective way to achieve a textured finish. Smooth and rough purls are best used in short lengths, usually no longer than 12mm (½"). The cut lengths are stitched in place like beads, often over felt or string padding, with the result being similar to satin stitch.

Short, straight-bladed scissors should be used for cutting the purl cleanly. Cutting on a velvet or felt covered board helps to hold the very springy threads still for accurate cutting. The advantage of using velvet is that the tip of the scissors can be gently pushed into the pile, resulting in more accurate cutting. Cut carefully as purl is easily damaged.

Purls are usually stitched in place using matching doubled waxed sewing thread. We used contrasting thread for photographic purposes throughout.

Detail of green border on page 92.

Detail of banner, 1880s. Purl worked onto leather, over padding and in a rope-like pattern, outlining geormetric shapes and cut out holes.

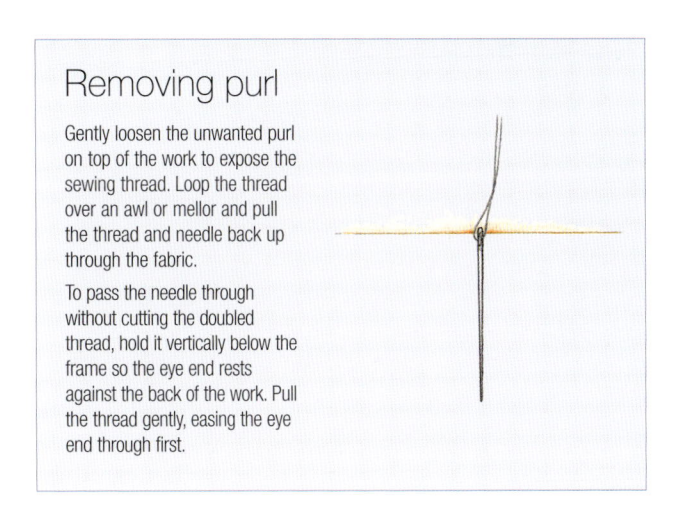

Removing purl

Gently loosen the unwanted purl on top of the work to expose the sewing thread. Loop the thread over an awl or mellor and pull the thread and needle back up through the fabric.

To pass the needle through without cutting the doubled thread, hold it vertically below the frame so the eye end rests against the back of the work. Pull the thread gently, easing the eye end through first.

CHIP WORK

This type of filling is worked using very short lengths of cut purl, called 'chips', stitched in place close together to cover a shape. Check purl is usually used for this technique because the texture of the thread is much more effective than smooth purls. For most goldwork techniques the outlines are worked last, but chip work is stitched in reverse, filling an area already outlined by other stitching.

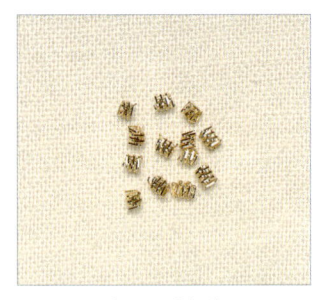

1 Using the padded cutting board, cut the check purl into short lengths, each as long as they are wide, 3mm–5mm (1/8"–3/16").

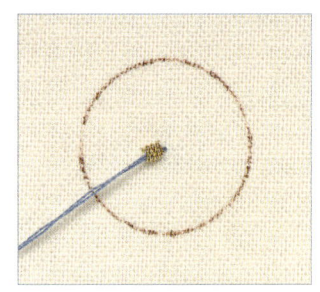

2 Secure the thread and bring it to the front at a central point within the shape. Thread a chip onto the needle and slide it to the base of the thread.

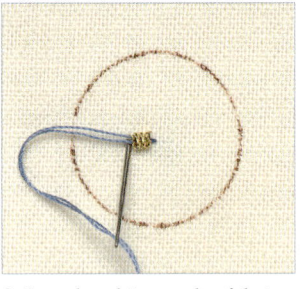

3 Lay the chip on the fabric, making sure the cut ends are facing down. Take the needle to the back at the opposite end of the chip.

4 Bring the thread to the front just next to the first chip.

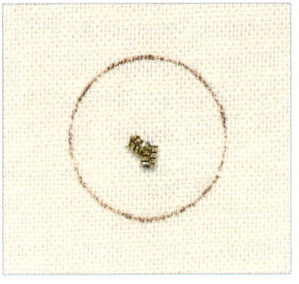

5 Stitch a second chip in place close to the first in the same way as before, but in a different direction.

6 Continue to stitch the chips in place close together and in random directions to fill the shape.

Hint

It is best to fill a shape from a central point towards the sides. Dotting the chips randomly throughout the shape and then filling in the gaps afterwards will create an uneven result.

The check purl chips should lie close together without being crushed, to give the shape a smooth surface with no wire tails sticking up.

CUTTING PURL

The lengths of purl need to be cut very accurately to achieve a good finish. Always set the first cut piece aside and use it as a template for all other pieces. It is advisable to always cut all the pieces needed for a shape before you begin.

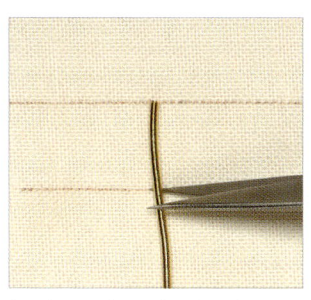

1 Place a length of purl at the correct angle across the shape to be covered. Cut the piece to length.

2 Place the cut purl across the shape to check that the length is correct. Adjust the length if necessary and measure again. Once the correct length is achieved use this piece as a template for all subsequent pieces.

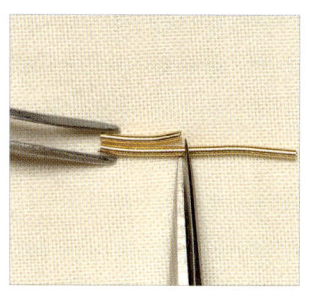

3 Using tweezers, carefully align the ends of the template piece with a full length of purl. Hold in place and carefully cut the second piece to the exact length.

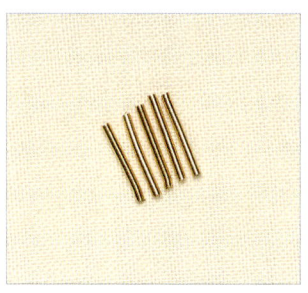

4 Continue to cut as many pieces as required, always using the first piece as a guide.

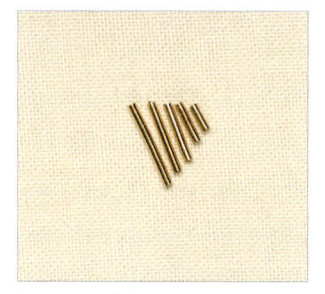

5 Tapered shapes. Measure and cut the longest piece first. Using the first piece as a template cut the subsequent pieces progressively shorter, measuring each against the design as you go.

6 For shapes that taper evenly at both ends, cut two pieces of each length to be used on opposite halves.

Cutting purl

~ to maintain the same length for all cut pieces, always use the first piece of purl as a template when cutting subsequent pieces.

~ it is important to cut the purls at the exact length. If a piece is too long it will buckle or kink, if too short it will not cover the edge of the padding.

~ always discard any damaged pieces of purl, as even the slightest kink or stretch will show as a black mark in the finished work.

~ pieces incorrectly cut or small left-over lengths can be kept aside and will more than likely come in handy at a later stage.

~ if the ends of the purls are not cut cleanly they can easily catch on the thread and unravel.

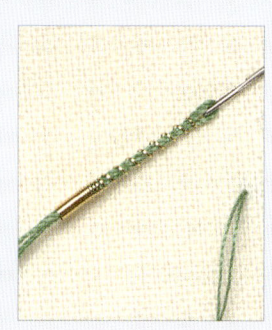

EMBROIDERY STITCHES WITH CUT PURL

Many embroidery stitches can be worked using lengths of cut purl to make textured borders and fillings. Reverse stem stitch or S-ing is a very traditional technique using purls, but chain stitch, fly stitch, herringbone and feather stitch, to name a few, also lend themselves to be worked using cut purl.

Chain stitch

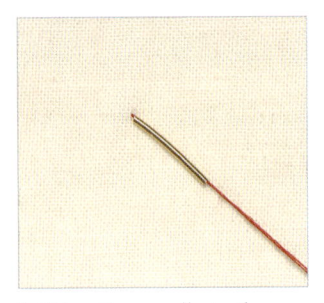

1 Bring the needle to the front and thread on a length of cut purl.

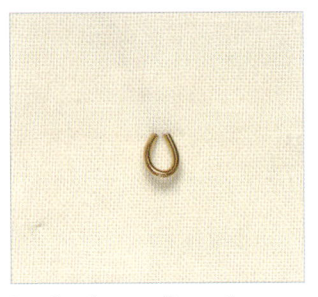

2 Take the needle to the back just next to where it emerged without crushing the purl and gently pull through, leaving a loop on the front.

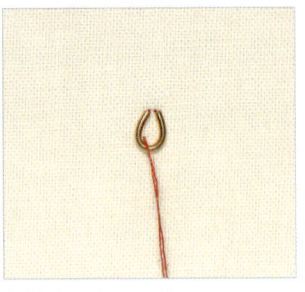

3 Using the mellor or pointed tweezers, lay the loop onto the fabric and bring the thread to the front inside the loop.

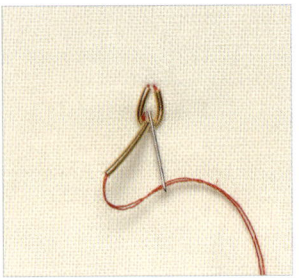

4 Slide a second piece of cut purl onto the thread and take the needle to the back just next to where it emerged.

5 Pull the thread through gently. The second loop holds the first in place.

6 Continue in this manner. To finish, stitch a shorter length of purl in place to anchor the last loop.

Detail of Antependium. 1660, Gent.

Heavily padded ornamentation, worked in laid threads onto dark red velvet.

Detached chain

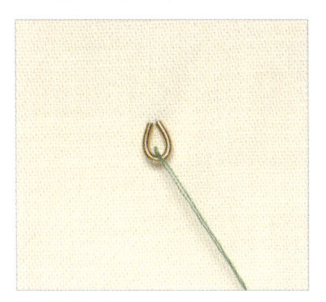

1 Work the first loop following steps 1–3 for working chain stitch.

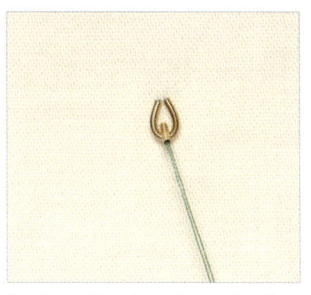

2 Thread a short length of cut purl onto the needle and slide it to the base of the thread, inside the looped purl.

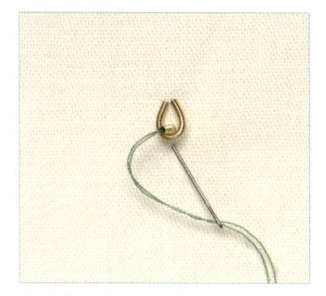

3 Take the needle to the back on the opposite side of the looped purl.

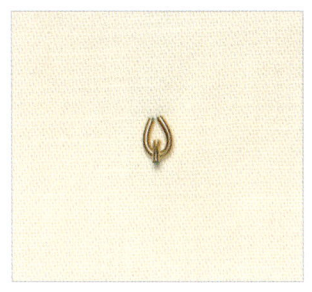

4 Pull the thread through to secure the detached chain.

5 Detached chains worked to form a daisy.

Fly stitch and fly stitch leaf

Thread a length of purl onto the needle for each step of the stitch.

Herringbone and feather stitch

Thread a length of purl onto the needle for each step of the stitch.

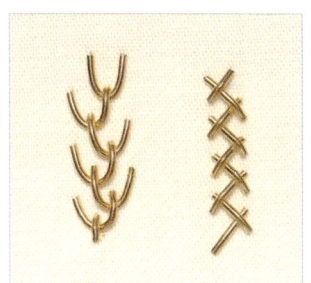

Holy Spirit Shining by Antonia Lomney.
A fabulous variety of threads are used to create this highly textured design on rich coloured fabric.

FILLING ~ CHEQUERED

Planning patterns

Different patterns and borders can be created by placing purls in geometric patterns. Always plan your pattern carefully and ensure the length and width of each group of purls are even.

Short lengths of cut purl can be stitched in place side by side to fill a larger shape with a chequered pattern. Using different types of purl within the pattern can create interesting effects. Measure and cut the purls following the instructions on page 91.

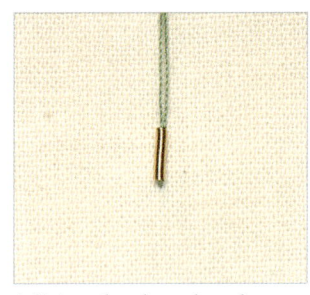

1 Bring the thread to the front. Slide a cut purl to the base of the thread.

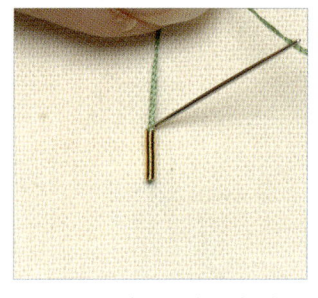

2 Position the purl and take the needle to the back at the opposite end.

3 Bring the thread to the front next to the first purl. Thread on a second purl. Place it snugly alongside the first and stitch it in place.

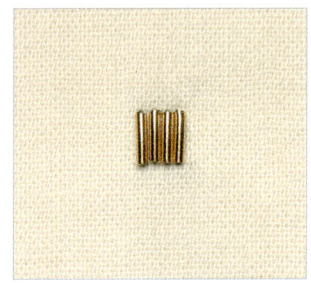

4 Continue in this manner, placing the purls parallel and close together to form a square.

5 To stitch a second square in the opposite direction, bring the thread to the front one purl's length from the previous square. Take the needle to the back under the edge of the previous laid purls.

6 Continue to stitch squares in this manner, alternating the direction of the purls in each square.

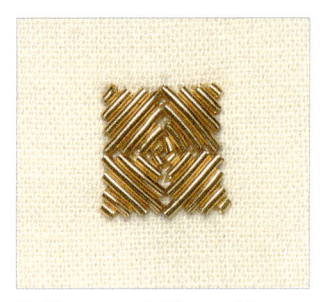

7 Chequered filling with purls placed diagonally across each square. Cut the purls following step 6 for cutting purls, page 91.

Measuring

For accurate stitching, the pattern must be carefully planned and the width of each section must be the same as the set number of parallel purls.

LOOPED PURL

Cut lengths of purl can be worked as loops and couched to lie flat along a line or border. If not couched, the loops can create a scalloped edge, represent petals or stand on the fabric to form a textured area. It is important to consider the use of the embroidered item as long purl loops are easily damaged and therefore not very suitable for items such as garments and cushions.

LOOP ~ BORDER

Longer lengths of cut purl are looped snugly around shorter pieces to form a continuous line. Smooth or rough purl is most commonly used, but check purl is also suitable. Cut all the lengths to size before you begin. We used 4mm and 13mm (3/16" and ½") lengths. Work a few stitches on a sample piece of fabric first to make sure the lengths are correct.

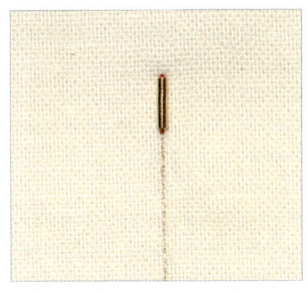

1 Bring the thread to the front at the beginning of the line to be covered. Stitch a short length of purl in place along the marked line.

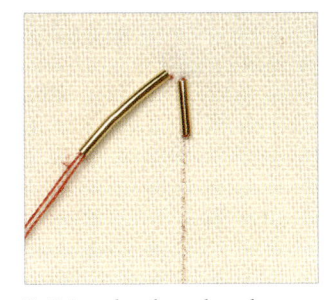

2 Bring the thread to the front next to the end of the short purl. Thread a long purl onto the needle and slide it to the base of the thread.

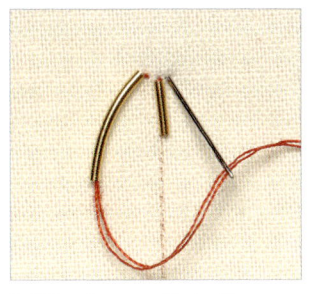

3 Take the needle to the back on the other side of the short purl, without bruising it.

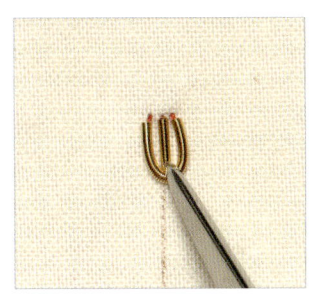

4 Pull the thread through, using a mellor or pointed tweezers to gently manipulate the long purl into a loop around the short piece. The long purl should loop snugly around the short.

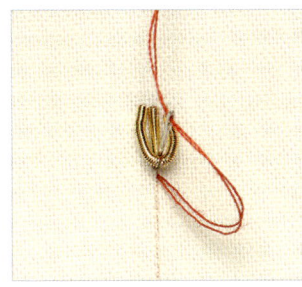

5 Bring the thread to the front on the design line just below the loop. Take the needle to the back inside the loop at the very tip of the short purl.

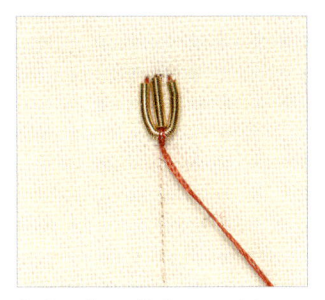

6 Gently pull the couching stitch to hold the loop and re-emerge just below the loop.

LOOP ~ BORDER – CONTINUED

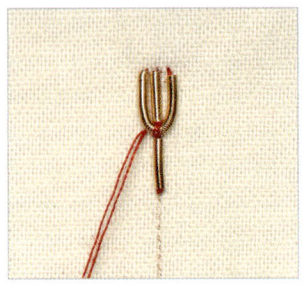

7 Stitch a second short piece in place along the design line. Bring the thread to the front next to the end of the short purl, below the first looped purl.

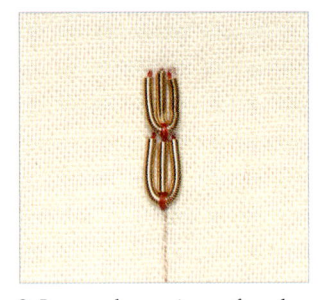

8 Loop a long piece of purl in place around the short piece and couch the loop in place in the same manner as before.

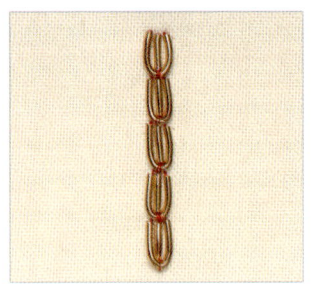

9 Continue to stitch purls in place in this manner to form a border or textured line.

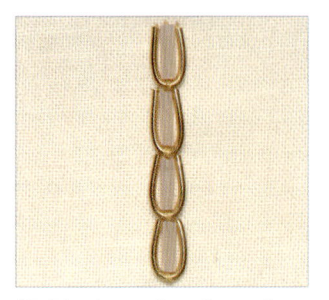

10 The looped purls can be worked around coloured bugle beads instead of short lengths of purl to add colour to the design.

LOOP ~ COUCHED

Longer loops that need to lie flat on the fabric need a small couching stitch to hold them in place. Pull the couching stitches very carefully to just hold the purl loop without distorting the coils in the purl.

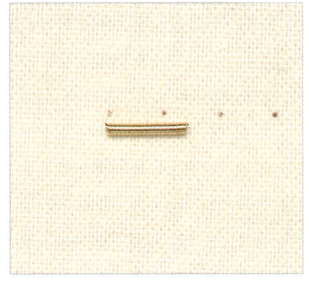

1 Measure and cut the purls to the required lengths. The cut purl should be a little longer than the distance it is to cover.

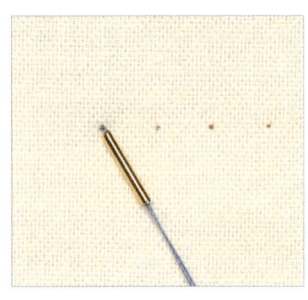

2 Bring the thread to the front. Slide a length of purl to rest on the fabric.

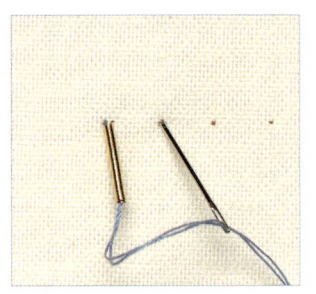

3 Take the needle to the back a short distance from where it emerged.

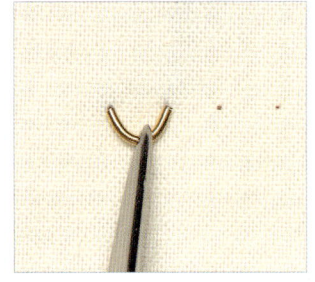

4 Gently pull the thread through, using a mellor or pointed tweezers to manipulate the loop.

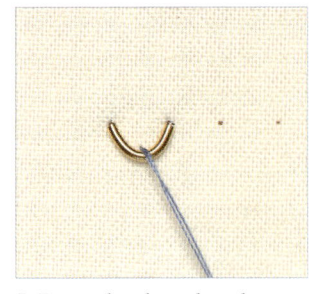

5 Bring the thread to the front just inside the loop.

LOOP ~ COUCHED – CONTINUED

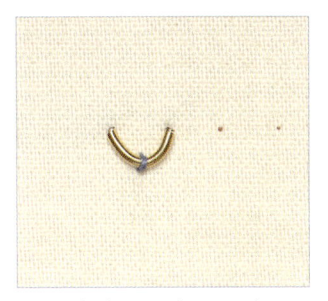

6 Work the stitch over the purl without crushing it to hold the loop in place.

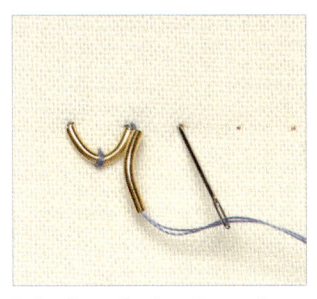

7 Scalloped edge. Bring the thread to the front next to the first purl. Slide a second length onto the fabric.

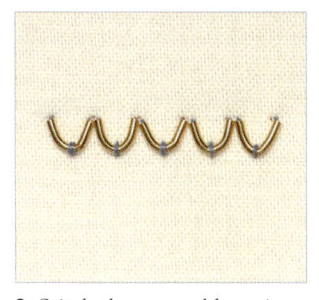

8 Stitch the second loop in place in the same manner as the first. Continue to stitch the loops in a continuous row to create a scalloped edge.

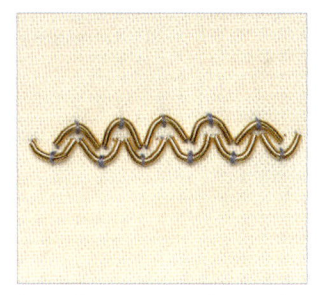

9 Working a second row of couched looped purls opposite the first creates an decorative scalloped line.

Couching purl

The coils in the purl are very fine, so the couching stitches will not sink into the purl and are likely to show.

To avoid the stitches showing, matching or invisible thread can be used.

Miniature cope, German, circa 1798. Semi-circle of blue silk lined with rose taffeta with bobbin lace border. Embroidered with gold thread in a seashell pattern, flowers in silk embroidery and embellished with mirror glass stones, and metal rosettes. Inscribed "Francisca 1798 Von Schatten". Possibly made for Madonna statue or Infant of Prague or adorning saints on holy days.

Collection of Embroiderers Guild of America

LOOP ~ SCALLOPS

Where looped purls are not couched in place they will sit slightly raised above the surface, forming a delicate scalloped edge or flower petal. The length of the cut purls will depend on the size of the loops you wish to form, so it is a good idea to experiment on a sample piece of fabric before you begin.

Cut the required number of purls to length following the steps for cutting purls on see page 91.

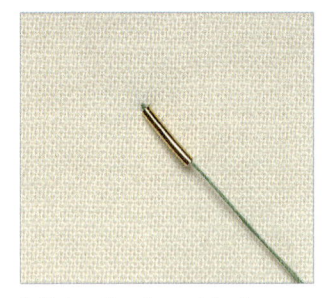

1 Bring the thread to the front. Thread a length of purl onto the needle and slide it to the base of the thread.

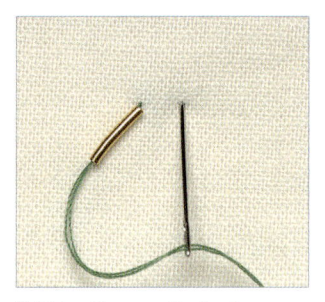

2 Take the needle to the back a short distance from where it emerged.

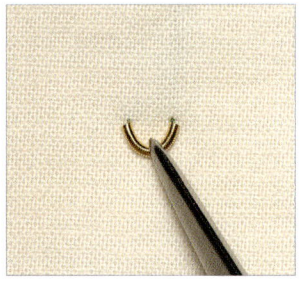

3 Gently pull the thread through, using a mellor or pointed tweezers to manipulate the loop without bruising the purl.

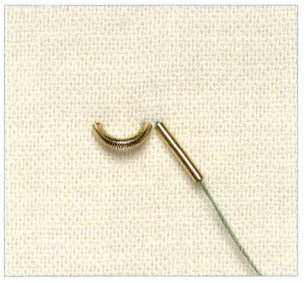

4 Bring the thread to the front next to the first looped purl and slide a second purl onto the thread.

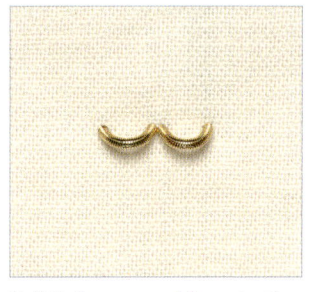

5 Stitch a second loop in the same way as before.

6 Continue in this manner.

7 The distance between the entry and exit points of the needle will vary the shape of the loops.

8 Loops worked in a circle can be used to form delicate petals.

98

LOOP ~ UPRIGHT

Short lengths of purl can be looped to 'stand' on the fabric. The upright loops can be spaced or packed closely together to create different textures.

Measure and cut the required number of purls to length following the instructions on page 91.

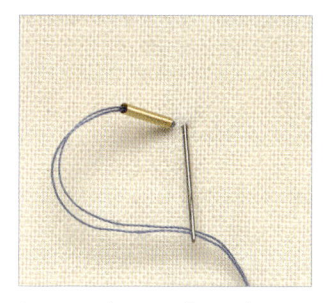

1 Bring the needle to the front and slide a length of purl onto the thread. Take the needle to the back next to where it emerged.

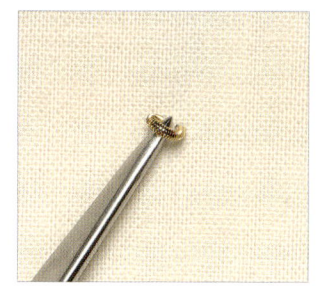

2 Gently pull the thread through, shaping the purl into a loop over the tip of a mellor or awl, without bruising the purl.

3 Work the second and subsequent loops in the same manner. Change the texture by working the loops close together or spaced further apart.

4 The texture can be varied by working the loops in neat rows.

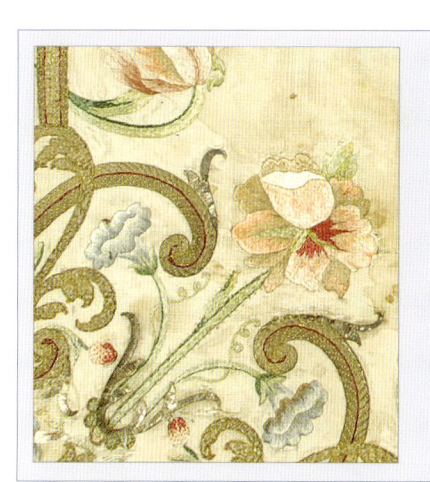

Chalice cover, Southern Europe. Late 18th century.

Created from beige silk with handmade metal thread lace edging.

The printed central medallion is of a saint holding an infant. The embroidery is worked in laid gold thread for the scrolls and the silk embroidery is worked in long and short stitch, satin stitch and French knots.

99

PURL OVER FELT PADDING

Cut the required number of purls following the instructions on page 91.

The purls should be slightly longer than the marked design to accommodate the padding. Stitch the felt padding in place following the instructions on page 29.

1 Bring the thread to the front halfway along or at the widest point of the shape. Slide the first purl onto the needle and check the length across the shape.

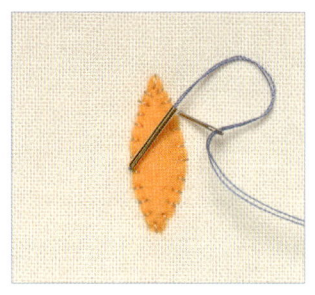

2 Slide the purl to rest on the fabric and place it at the correct angle across the felt. Take the needle to the back on the opposite side.

3 Pull the thread through while manipulating the purl into position. Keep a firm tension on the thread, but take care not to hold it so tight that it damages the purl.

4 Bring the thread to the front a purl's width below the first purl. Slide a second purl onto the thread and position it across the shape next to the first.

5 Take the needle to the back close to the first purl, angling it under the padding. Ensure the pieces sit snugly together.

6 Pull the thread through.

Tension

~ To keep a constant tension on the thread, work a tiny back stitch after every three to four purls.

~ The purls must be stitched firmly in place. If the stitches are too tight they will damage the purl and distort the padding.

~ The purls should sit snugly side by side. If they are too close, they will 'buckle' over one another and if too far apart the padding will show through.

Points

Bringing the thread to the front, close to the previous purl will slightly alter the angle of the purl, straightening them across the tip of the shape.

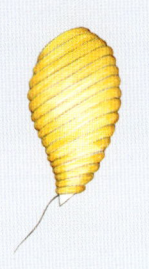

100

PURL OVER FELT PADDING – CONTINUED

7 Continue to stitch purls in place across the shape, maintaining the correct angle, see hint page 102. Check and adjust the length of each purl as you work.

8 As you near the tip of a tapered shape, straighten the angle of the purl to prevent it from sliding off the padding.

9 Turn the work around to maintain the same stitching direction. Complete the second half of the shape in the same manner.

PURLS OVER SOFT COTTON PADDING

This is an excellent method for creating strong raised lines.

Purls are traditionally placed at a 45° angle over string padding, but can also be placed at a right angle. To achieve a good finish it is important that all the pieces of purl are cut to exactly the same length and are long enough to accommodate the padding. Cut the required number of purls following the instructions on page 91. Stitch the cotton padding in place following the instructions on page 31.

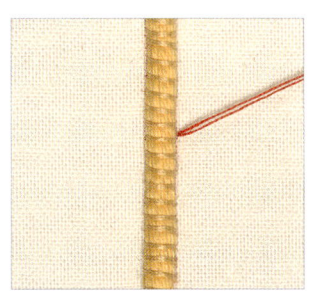

1 Bring the thread to the front halfway along the padding close to the right hand side.

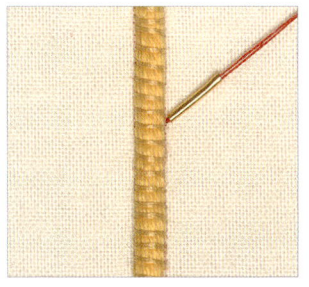

2 Thread a length of purl onto the needle and slide it onto the fabric.

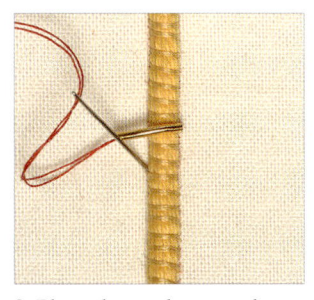

3 Place the purl across the padding at a 45° angle and take the needle to the back on the opposite side, angling it slightly under the padding.

101

PURLS OVER SOFT COTTON PADDING – CONTINUED

4 Bring the thread to the front, one purl's width above the first purl. Thread a second length of purl onto the needle. Slide it onto the fabric and lay it across the padding as before.

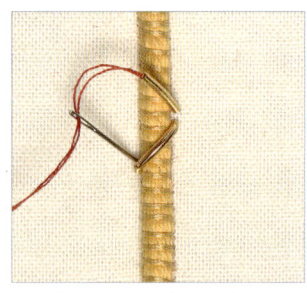

5 Take the needle to the back close to the first purl, angling it under the padding.

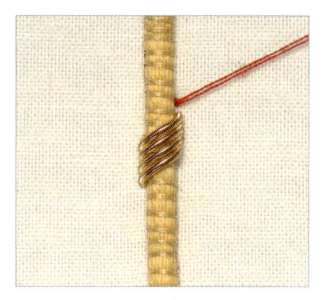

6 Continue in this manner, taking a tiny back stitch close to the padding after every three to four purls, to maintain a constant tension.

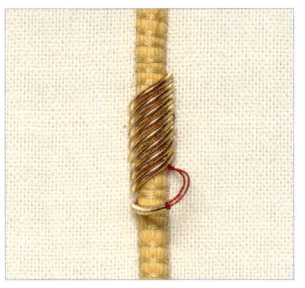

7 To work the second half, bring the needle to the front on the left hand side one purl's width below the previous purl. Take it to the back close to the purl on the right hand side.

8 Fabulous rope-like bands can be created by mixing different types of purl.

Always work all the padding and other embroidery before commencing the goldwork.

Achieving the correct angle

To maintain the correct angle, the stitches should be close together when the needle is taken to the back and spaced a purl's width away when it is brought to the front. The spacing of the stitches on the emerging side will be further apart than those on the entering side.

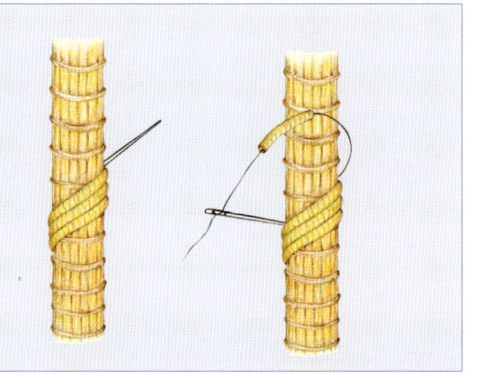

102

S-ING

This technique is similar to stem stitch worked in reverse with a cut purl threaded onto each stitch. It creates a rope-like twisted look and is used along straight or curved lines. S-ing is mainly worked using smooth or rough purl, but check purl can also be used. Cut all the purls to the same length, approximately 6mm (¼"), following the steps for cutting purl on page 91.

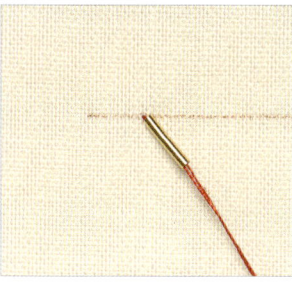

1 Bring the thread to the front one purl's length from the end of the line. Thread a cut purl onto the needle and slide it to the base of the thread.

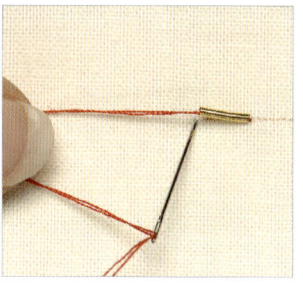

2 Place the cut purl back along the line to be covered and take the needle to the back at the end.

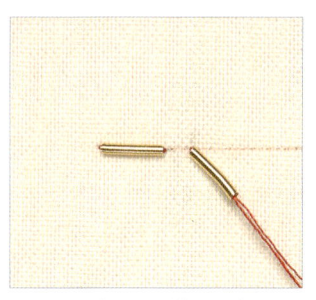

3 Bring the needle to the front, half a purl's length ahead of the first purl and slide a second length of purl onto the thread.

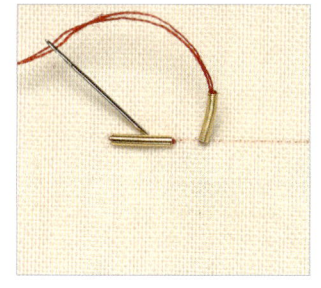

4 Take the needle to the back on the design line above and halfway along the first purl, angling it underneath.

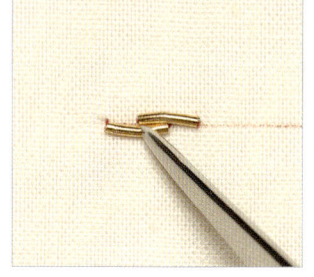

5 Use a mellor or pointed tweezers to gently manipulate the first purl aside while pulling the thread through.

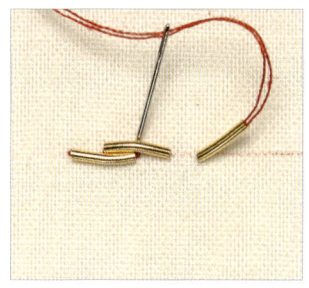

6 Repeat for the third purl, taking the needle to the back at an angle, above and halfway along, angling it under the previous purl.

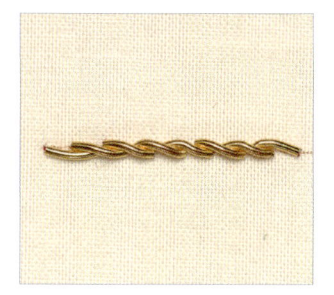

7 Continue in this way, taking the needle to the back above the previous purl, manipulating it into an s-shape.

8 Finishing. To even up the tapered ends on a row of s-ing, a half length of purl can be stitched in place alongside the first and last purl.

SEQUINS AND SPANGLES

Sequins and spangles can be used singly or in rows and groups. The following techniques can be worked using either sequins or spangles. They should be stitched in place using matching waxed sewing thread. We used contrasting thread for photographic purposes.

COUCHED THREADS OVER SEQUINS

Couching a metal or coloured thread over a row of sequins and spangles can form a strong line.

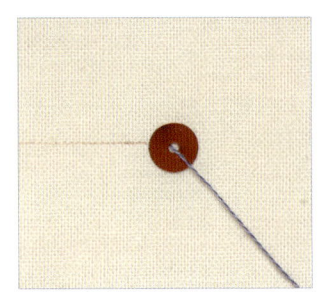

1 Bring the couching thread to the front through the centre of a sequin.

2 Leaving a 2.5cm (1") tail, lay the metal thread across the sequin and take the needle to the back on the opposite side, through the hole.

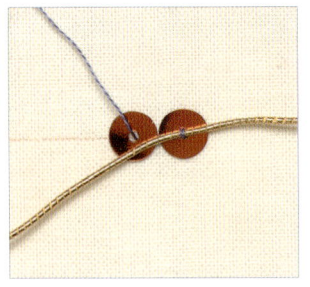

3 Position the second sequin next to the first and bring the thread to the front through the centre.

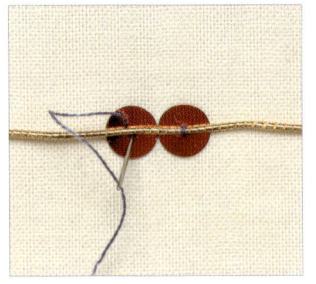

4 Lay the metal thread across the sequin and take the needle to the back on the opposite side, through the hole in the sequin.

5 Continue in this manner to the end of the row. Take the metal thread tails to the back over the edge of the first and last sequin and secure.

INDIVIDUAL SEQUIN WITH BACK STITCH

Back stitch can be used to attach individual sequins or spangles or for rows where the sequins lie edge to edge.

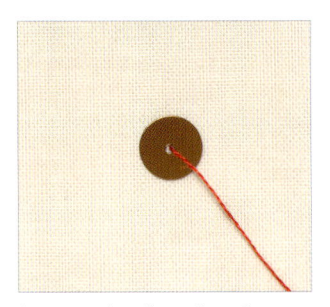

1 Bring the thread to the front and slide a sequin onto the fabric.

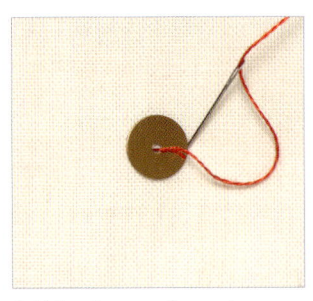

2 Take the needle to the back at the edge of the sequin.

INDIVIDUAL SEQUIN WITH BACK STITCH – CONTINUED

3 Bring the thread to the front at the opposite side and take the needle to the back through the centre of the sequin.

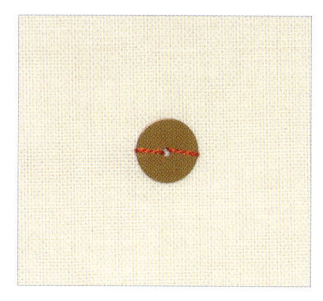

4 Pull the thread through. The sequin is secured with a stitch on each side of the hole.

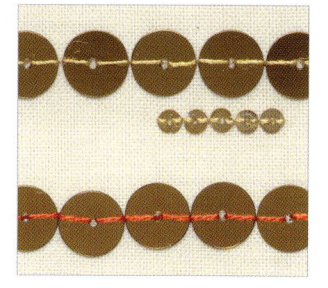

5 Rows of sequins and spangles stitched in place with back stitch, using matching thread and contrasting cotton.

INDIVIDUAL SEQUIN WITH BEAD

Sequins and spangles can be stitched in place individually using small beads or purl chips.

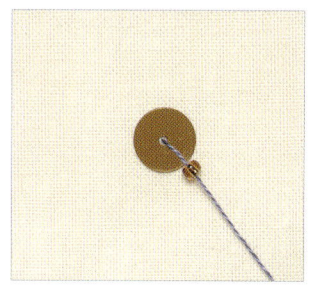

1 Bring the thread to the front and slide a sequin, followed by a bead, onto the fabric.

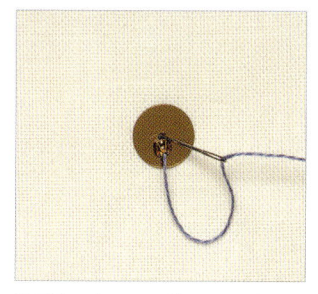

2 Take the needle over the bead and back through the centre of the sequin.

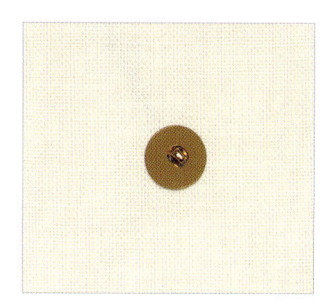

3 Pull the thread through. The bead locks the sequin in place.

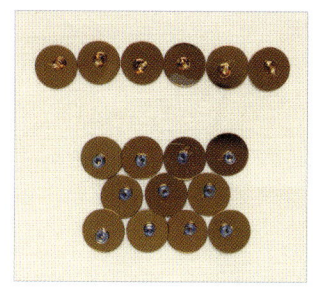

4 Sequins attached with beads placed side by side in rows or grouped to fill an area.

Detail of coat of arms. 1943, India.

The Coat of Arms of Sir Thomas Rutherford. The upper section is embroidered with spangles and cut purl and the unstitched areas cut away to create openwork. The lower section is embroidered onto red velvet.

From the collection of the Embroiderers' Guild of Victoria.

INDIVIDUAL SEQUIN WITH LOOPED PURL

Attaching sequins with looped purl creates an interesting texture and play of light caused by the shiny surface of the sequins and textured appearance of the purl. Cut the purl following the instructions on page 91.

1 Bring the thread to the front and slide a sequin, followed by a short length of purl, onto the fabric.

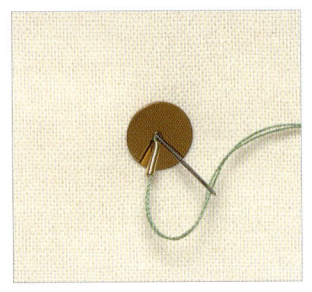

2 Take the needle over the purl and back through the centre of the sequin.

3 Carefully pull the thread through, taking care not to damage the purl, while shaping the loop over the tip of a mellor or pointed tweezers.

4 Groups or rows of sequins attached with looped purl.

OVERLAPPING SEQUINS WITH BACK STITCH

This technique allows rows or groups of sequins to be stitched in place while keeping the stitches concealed.

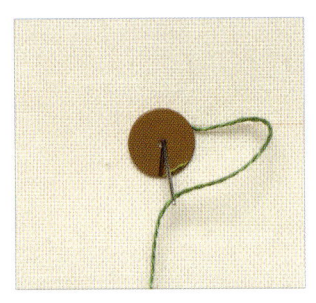

1 Hold the sequin in place and bring the thread to the front at the edge of the sequin. Take the needle to the back through the centre.

2 Bring the thread to the front, half a sequin's width from the first.

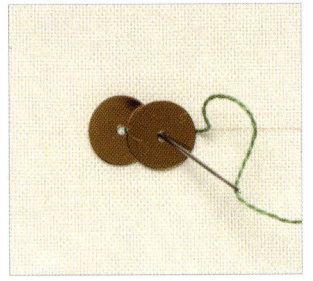

3 Position a second sequin over the first, aligning the hole with the edge. Take the needle to the back through the centre of the second sequin, at the edge of the first.

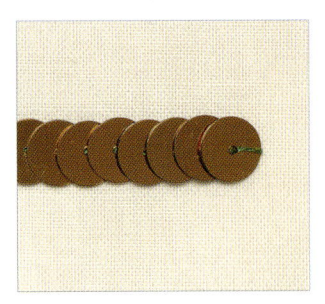

4 Continue in this manner to complete the row. Only the last stitch is visible.

OVERLAPPING SEQUINS WITH CUT PURL

Short lengths of cut purl can be added to the stitches when attaching a row of sequins. The length of the purl should be half the width of a sequin. Cut the purls following the instructions on page 91.

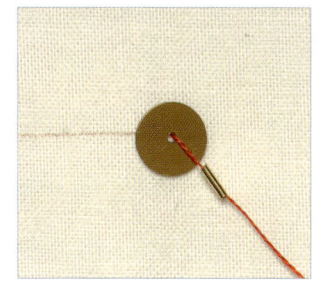

1 Bring the thread to the front and slide a sequin, followed by a cut purl, onto the fabric.

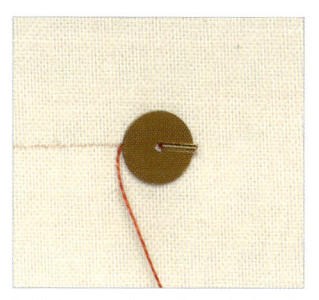

2 Take the thread to the back at the edge of the sequin and bring the needle to the front at the opposite side.

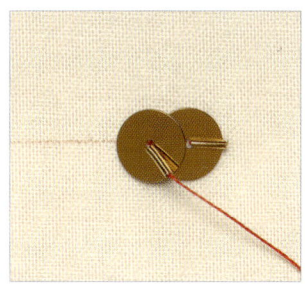

3 Slide a second sequin and purl onto the fabric. The second sequin will overlap the first.

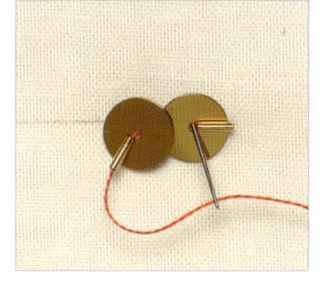

4 Take the needle to the back through the centre of the first sequin taking care not to damage the purl.

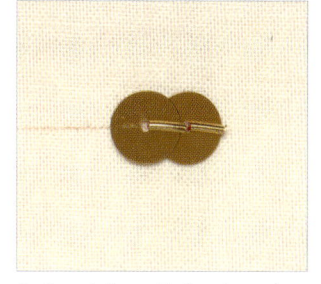

5 Carefully pull the thread through aligning the purls over the sequins.

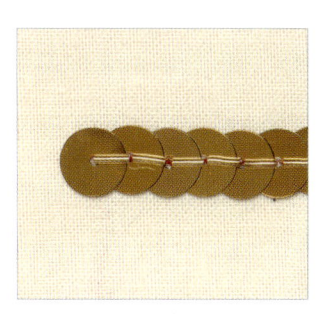

6 Continue in this manner to the end of the row.

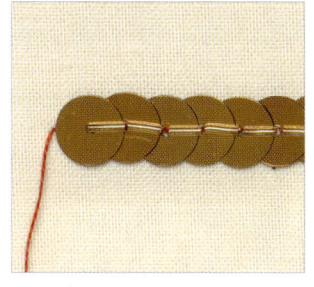

7 To finish, bring the thread to the front on the opposite side of the last sequin.

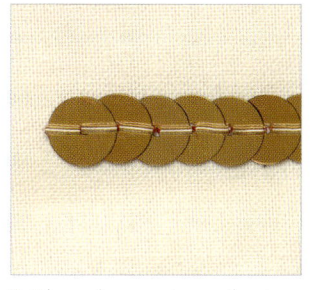

8 Thread on a piece of cut purl and take the needle to the back through the centre of the last sequin.

OVERLAPPING SEQUINS ~ FISH SCALES FILLING

This technique allows areas to be filled with sequins while keeping the stitches concealed.

1 Row one. Stitch the sequins in place side by side with a single stitch into each, angling the stitches to one side.

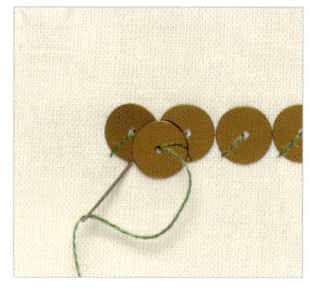

2 Row two. Bring the thread to the front between two sequins of the first row. Slide a sequin onto the fabric, partly overlapping the two above. Take the needle to the back directly below the hole of one sequin above.

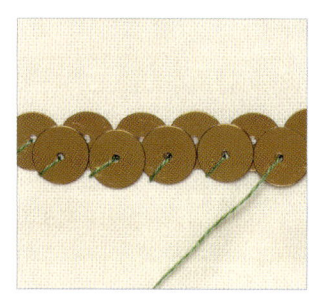

3 Continue to the end of the row, placing the sequins, halfway between the first sequins, concealing the stitches.

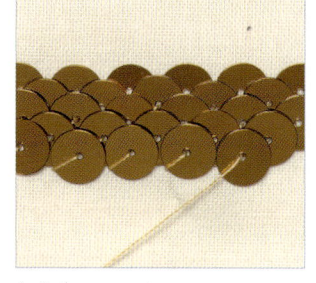

4 Subsequent rows. Continue in this manner, off-setting the sequins and covering the previous stitches.

Border. 19th century, India. Richly embroidered in a variety of purl, sequins and pearl-like beads. French knots worked in coloured silk is used for the birds' eyes. From the collection of the Embroiderers Guild of South Australia.

S-ING OVER SEQUINS

This is worked in a similar way to s-ing, with a sequin or spangle added under each cut purl. The length of the cut purl is dictated by the size of the sequins or spangles. We used contrasting sequins for photographic purposes.

1 Place purl over a sequin, aligning one end with the edge. Cut the purl to match the diameter of the sequin. Use this purl as a template to cut as many lengths as needed.

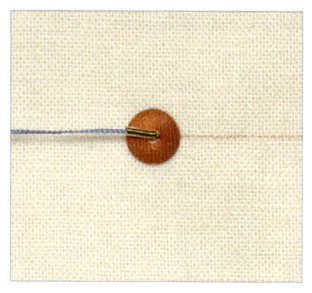

2 Cut one piece of purl in half. Bring the thread to the front, half a sequin's width from the end of the line. Thread a sequin followed by a half purl. Slide both to the base of the thread.

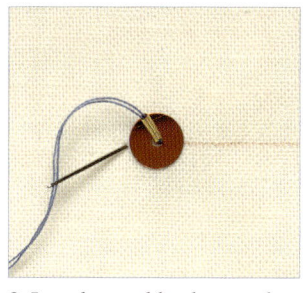

3 Lay the purl back over the edge of the sequin and take the needle to the back at the opposite end.

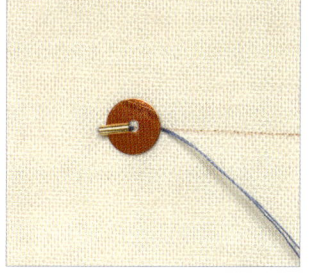

4 Bring the thread to the front at the opposite side of the sequin.

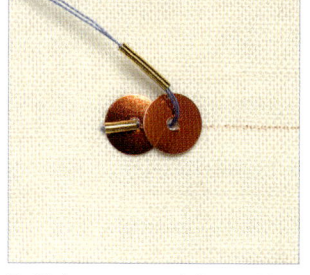

5 Slide a sequin followed by a purl to the base of the thread. The sequin should cover half of the first sequin.

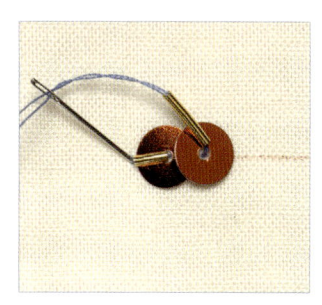

6 Lay the purl over the sequins above the first purl. Take the needle to the back on the opposite side, through the same hole in the fabric.

7 Use a mellor or pointed tweezers to manipulate the first purl a little to one side while pulling the thread through.

8 Bring the thread to the front on the opposite side of the second sequin. Thread on a sequin and purl as before.

109

S-ING OVER SEQUINS – CONTINUED

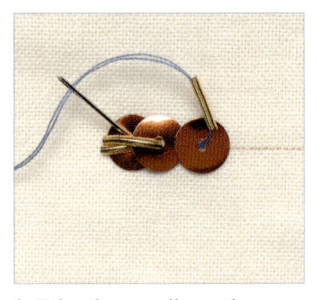

9 Take the needle to the back through the hole in the first sequin, above the previous purls.

10 Manipulate the second purl into an s-shape while pulling the thread through.

11 Continue in this manner, always taking the needle to the back above the previous purl.

12 To finish. Bring the thread to the front on the opposite side of the last sequin.

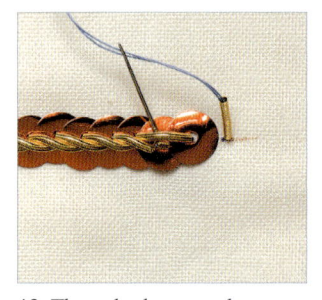

13 Thread a long purl onto the needle. Slide it onto the fabric and take the needle to the back through the second to last sequin.

14 Re-emerge outside the last sequin through the same hole in the fabric, above the last purl. Thread on a half-length of purl. Take the needle to the back through the last sequin.

Small panel, mid 20th century. China.

Silk satin pasted onto paper backing. Laid work embroidered in gold and silver threads with coloured detail in fine silk.

From the collection of the Embroiderers Guild of South Australia.

110

Silk embroidery

Silk embroidery is often used in combination with goldwork. The luster and colours of the silk threads and the reflection of the gold threads, complement one another extremely well.

The secret of silk

The use of silk is suggested to go back at least 4500 years and according to legend the princess Xi Ling Shi was the first to reel a silk yarn from a cocoon that had fallen into her cup of tea. The Chinese developed the production of silk and guarded their knowledge successfully for thousands of years.

It has been written that the secret eventually reached Tibet in 140BC, when silkworm eggs were smuggled in the headdress of a Chinese princess.

In around 550AD two Persian monks smuggled mulberry leaves and silkworm eggs inside their walking staffs as a present to the Emperor. Though the emperor tried to protect the secret but by the 9th century the knowledge of silk production had reached Europe.

Silk yarn

'A yarn reeled from the cocoons spun by the caterpillars of silk-producing insects'.

After the caterpillars have finished spinning their cocoons they are dried before they reach maturity and hatch. The cocoons are then cooked to soften the outer layers. Brushes are used to loosen and remove the short fibres on the outside of the cocoons after which the cocoons are ready to be reeled. They a placed in warm waterxand the thread from 4 to 12 cocoons are reeled together depending on the thickness of thread required. Up to 900m (984yd) can be reeled from each cocoon.

Women's striking and preparing silk, painting by Emperor Huizong of Song, early 12th century.

Rank badge. Chinese, late 19th century.

One of a pair of matching rank badges. Black silk ground fabric with surface embroidery in silk and metal threads, depicting a white bird among flowers and symbols with sun and key. Surrounded by a key border and backed in ice blue silk.

From the collection of the Embroiderers Guild of America.

SILK EMBROIDERY STITCHES

Most surface embroidery stitches can be worked in silk threads. The stitches included in the following pages are those most often used in combination with goldwork embroidery.

Because the fabric for goldwork embroidery is always held taut in a hoop or frame, the embroidery stitches must always be worked in a stabbing motion to avoid distorting the fabric.

Always complete the silk embroidery before commencing the goldwork.

BACK STITCH

This is primarily used as an outline stitch and for fine lines such as tendrils. Back stitch will follow a curved line well and the stitches should be kept small and even.

1 Bring the thread to the front a short distance from the end of the marked line.

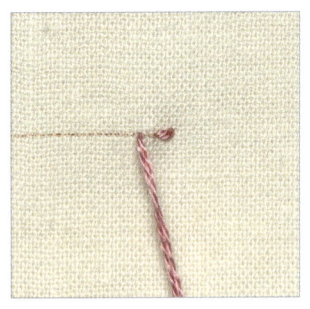

2 Take the thread to the back at the end of the line. Emerge a short distance from the first stitch. The distance should equal the length of the first stitch.

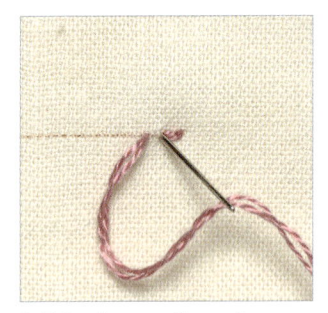

3 Take the needle to the back at the end of the first stitch, through the same hole in the fabric.

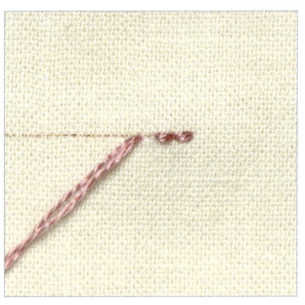

4 Pull the second stitch through and emerge an even distance from the second stitch.

Stitching with multiple strands

~ When working with more than one strand of thread, 'strip' the threads before use (ie separate the strands and then put them back together).

~ Keep re-stripping the thread as you work to ensure the fullest stitch coverage. To do this, slide the needle down the threads onto the fabric. Separate the strands, then take the needle back up the thread to resume stitching.

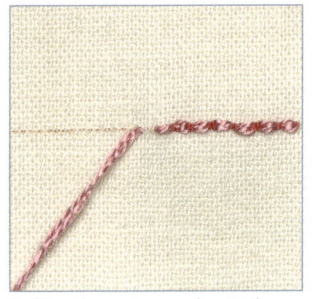

5 Continue to work stitches in this manner, keeping them all the same length.

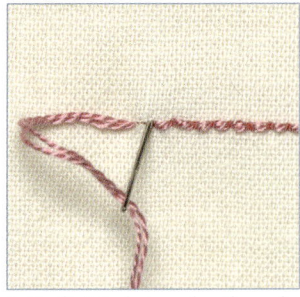

6 To finish, bring the thread to the front at the end of the line and take the needle to the back at the beginning of the previous stitch.

BULLION KNOT

When working this stitch combined with goldwork, the fabric is held taut, changing the usual working method slightly. Milliner's needles are the most suitable for working bullion knots as the shaft of the needle is the same from eye to the tapering point.

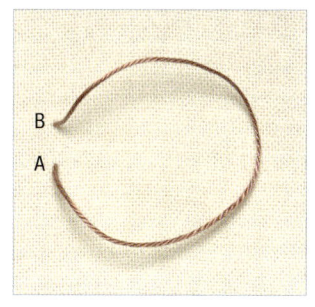

1 Bring the thread to the front at A and take it to the back at B, leaving a long loop on the front. The distance from A to B is the length of the finished knot.

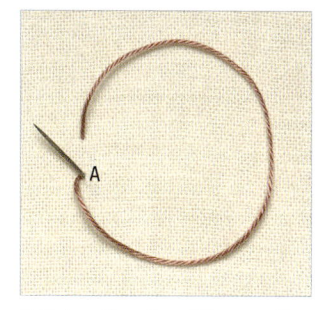

2 Bring the tip of the needle to the front at A, through the same hole in the fabric. Take care not to split the thread.

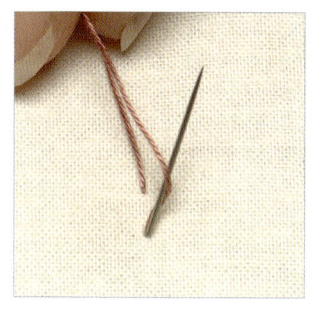

3 With one hand below the frame, hold the tip of the needle upright. Wrap the thread clockwise around the needle.

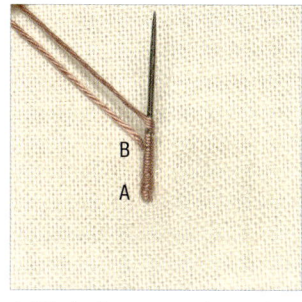

4 Work the required number of wraps around the needle, packing them down evenly. For a straight bullion knot, the number of wraps must cover the distance from A to B plus an extra 1–2 wraps.

5 Keeping tension on the wraps between the thumb and index finger of one hand, begin to ease the needle through the wraps.

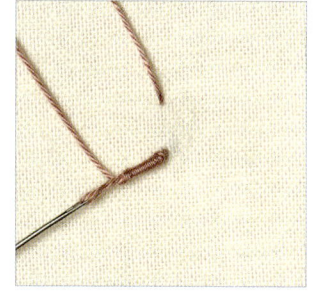

6 Hold the wraps between your fingers and maintain even tension on the wraps. Pull the needle and thread through in the direction away from the position of the knot.

7 As the thread loop tightens, lift the knot around into the correct position, while continuing to pull the remaining thread through the wraps.

8 To make sure the wraps are even, gently stroke and manipulate them with the needle while maintaining tension on the thread.

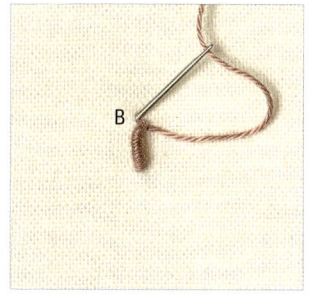

9 Take the needle to the back at the end of the knot at B, through the same hole in the fabric.

10 Pull the thread through and secure.

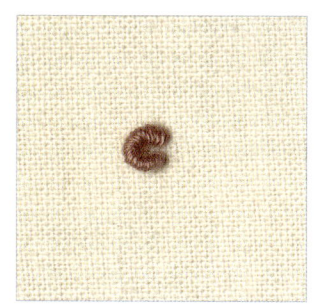

11 Bullion loop. This is formed in a similar manner, except that the distance between A and B is short and the number of wraps increased.

CHAIN STITCH

This very versatile stitch can be used as an outline, or in close rows as a filling stitch. Take care not to pull the stitches too tight as they will lose their rounded shape.

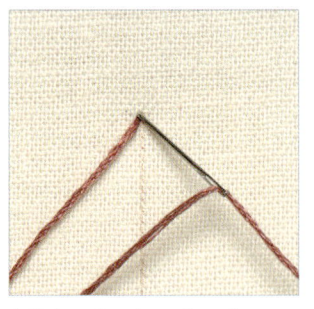

1 Bring the thread to the front. Hold the emerging thread and take the needle to the back through the same hole in the fabric.

2 Begin to pull the thread through, leaving a loop. Bring the needle to the front inside the loop.

3 Pulling away from the fabric, pull the thread through, anchoring the loop around the emerging thread.

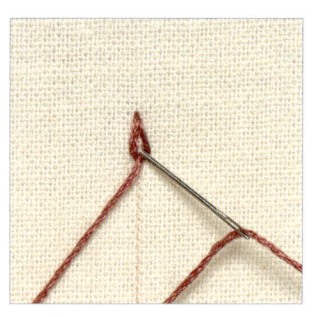

4 Holding the thread, take the needle to the back inside the thread loop, through the same hole in the fabric.

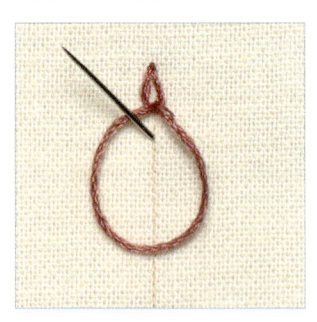

5 Repeat step 2 The distance from the first stitch to the emerging needle should equal the length of the first chain stitch.

6 Pull the thread through. Continue to stitch in this manner to the end of the line.

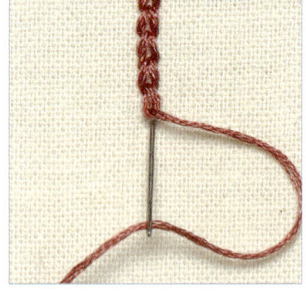

7 Finishing. Take the needle to the back just over the last loop. Pull the thread through to anchor the loop.

8 Turning a corner. Finish the row along one side following step 7. Re-emerge inside the last chain stitch.

9 Continue to stitch along the adjacent side.

10 Filling a shape. Take the needle through the fabric along the inside of the marked line, to accommodate the width of the stitches.

11 Stitch the subsequent rows taking the needle through the fabric a short distance from the previous row, to allow room for the stitches to fit snugly.

12 Shape filled with rows of chain stitch. Rows can be worked back and forth or all in the same direction.

CHAIN STITCH ~ REVERSE

This stitch is the most suitable method for working chain stitch with a metallic thread, as the thread is not 'dragged' through the fabric. Work the stitch from the top of the design line towards you. We used silk thread for photographic purposes.

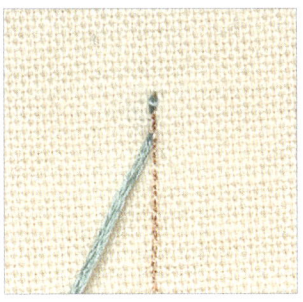

1 Work a small back stitch at the end of the line. Bring the thread to the front a short distance away, the required length of the chain stitch.

2 Slide the eye end of the needle under the back stitch. Do not pick up any fabric.

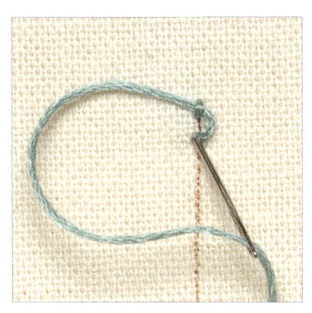

3 Pull the thread through but not taut. Take the needle to the back through the same hole in the fabric.

4 Pull the thread through, forming the first chain.

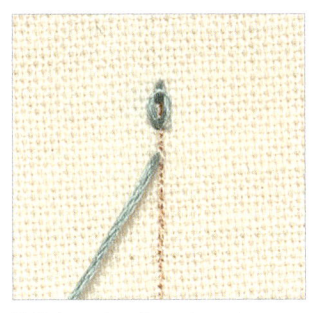

5 Bring the thread to the front one stitch length from the first stitch.

6 Slide the eye end of the needle under the first stitch. Do not pick up any fabric and avoid splitting the thread.

7 Pull the thread through. Take the thread to the back through the same hole in the fabric. Pull through to form the second chain stitch.

8 Continue to the end of the line in this manner.

9 Reverse chain stitch worked using metallic hand embroidery thread.

Coif (informal headwear), English c1600. Blackwork with stems worked in heavy chain stitch using gold thread.

CHAIN STITCH ~ HEAVY

Heavy chain stitch is a variation of reverse chain stitch. It gives a firm, slightly raised corded effect. It follows curves well and is useful for creating heavy textured lines.

For the best result, use a firm round thread such as perlé silk or cotton and keep the stitches small. Heavy chain stitch may also be worked using a pliable metallic thread. Work the stitch from the top of the design line towards you.

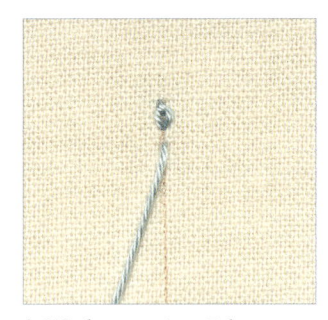

1 Work steps 1 to 5 for reverse chain stitch.

2 Slide the eye end of the needle under the straight stitch one more time in the same direction. Avoid catching the fabric and splitting the thread.

3 Pull the thread through, placing it along the first stitch. Take the needle to the back through the same hole in the fabric next to the emerging thread.

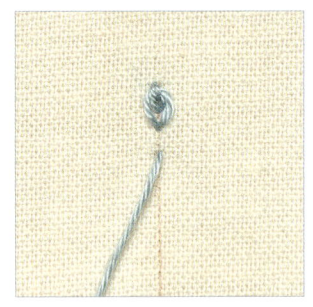

4 Pull the thread through. The second chain wraps around the first. Bring the thread to the front one stitch length from the second stitch.

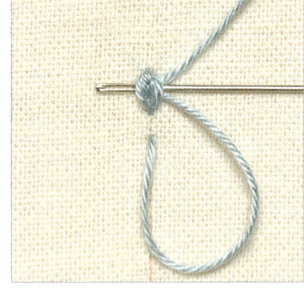

5 Slide the eye end of the needle under the first two chain stitches, taking care not to catch the fabric or split the threads.

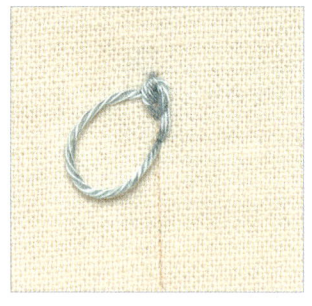

6 Pull the thread through. Take the thread to the back through the same hole in the fabric.

7 Bring the thread to the front one stitch length away and slide the eye end of the needle under the last two chain stitches.

8 Pull the thread through. Take the thread to the back through the same hole in the fabric.

9 Continue in this manner, sliding the needle under the previous two chain stitches for each stitch.

10 Heavy reverse chain stitch worked using metallic hand embroidery thread creates a heavy braided effect.

FRENCH KNOT

This is an adaptable stitch that can be used individually to form dots and accents or grouped closely together to create a textured surface. The traditional French knot is worked with only one or two wraps. Larger knots will look neater if worked with more strands of thread rather than too many wraps.

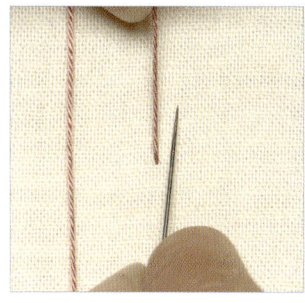

1 One wrap. Hold the thread firmly a short distance from the fabric. Hold the needle so it points in the direction of the thread.

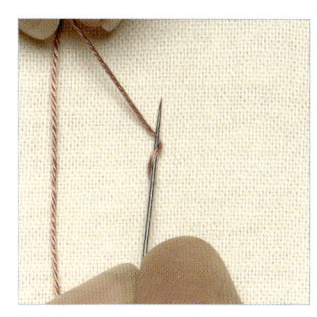

2 Wrap the thread over and around the needle with your other hand.

3 Insert the point of the needle 1–2 fabric threads from the emerging thread.

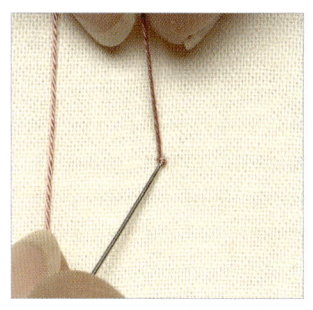

4 Slide the wrap down the needle onto the fabric. Pull the thread until the wrap is firm around the needle.

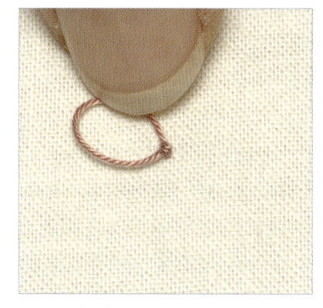

5 Push the needle through the fabric while holding the knot in place.

6 Pull the thread through.

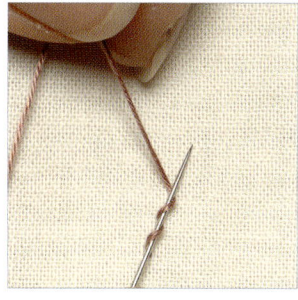

7 Two wraps. Begin the knot following steps 1 and 2. Wrap the thread twice around the needle.

8 Insert the tip of the needle close to where the thread emerges.

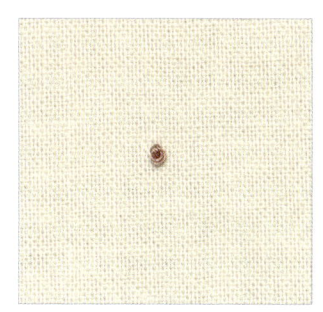

9 Complete the knot following steps 4–6.

Filling worked in close rows of French knots, using shades of silk.

LONG AND SHORT STITCH ~ DIRECTIONAL

Long and short stitch is also known as soft shading, needle or thread painting. To achieve a smooth finish it is important that the stitches are kept relatively long. Only the first row is made up of alternating long and short stitches. All subsequent rows are stitched with long stitches only, 8mm–12mm (5/16"–1/2") is a good length. Always begin with a long stitch halfway along one side of the shape. A split stitch outline can be worked first to achieve a smooth stable edge.

Stitch length

Keep the stitch length as varied as possible. This will help to blend the colours and create a smooth surface. Work the stitches well into the previous row of stitches to achieve a smooth blend.

Stitch direction

~ The aim of long and short stitch, or thread painting, is to create a natural looking object, one that has been painted with thread. It can be helpful to draw or stitch directional lines within the shape as a guide, before you commence the long and short stitch.

~ When embroidering an animal the stitching should follow the direction of the fur. For flowers and foliage the stitches should follow the direction of the veins, from tip to base.

Detail of chalice cover on page 99.

1 Outline the shape with split stitch worked along the inside edge of the marked design line. Begin a new thread and bring it to the front inside the shape.

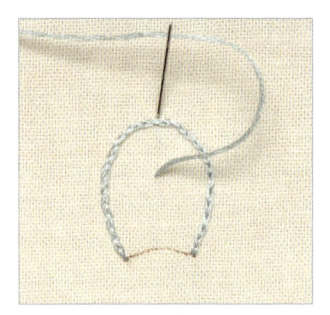

2 Take the needle to the back over the outline, keeping the stitch at a right angle to the design line.

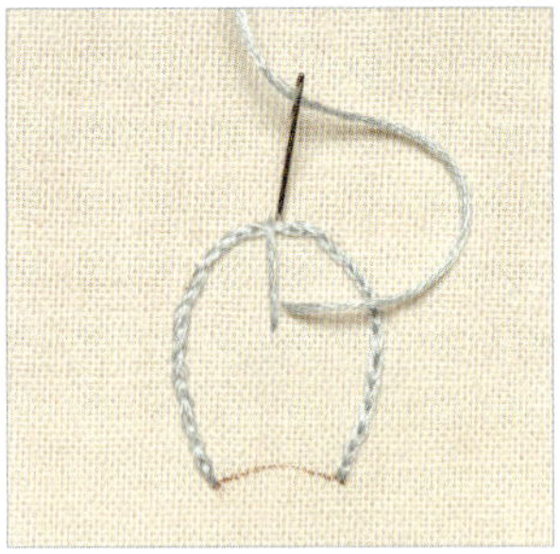

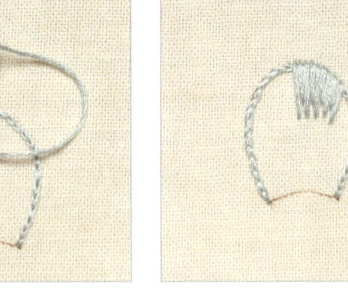

Second and subsequent rows

Begin each row halfway along the shape and work one side at a time. All the stitches are a similar length to the long stitches in the first row.

3 Bring the thread to the front alongside the first stitch. This stitch will measure ¾ the length of the first. Take the needle to the back over the outline.

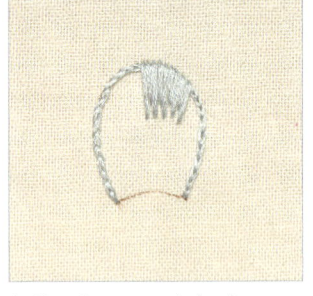

4 Continue to stitch along one side of the shape. Keep the stitches close together and alternate between long and short stitches.

5 Bring the thread to the front, splitting the end of a stitch in the previous row. Take the needle to the back inside the shape.

6 Continue to fill the shape in this manner. Stagger the stitches as you work to avoid creating stripes or ridges.

7 When stitching layered shapes, such as overlapping petals, begin with the shape furthest to the back and complete one layer at a time.

SATIN STITCH

Satin stitch is also known as Damask stitch. Split stitch can be used to outline the shape before the satin stitch is worked to achieve a smooth, stable edge. Angle the needle under the outline when bringing it to the front and taking it to the back.

Blending colour

When choosing colour, use as many shades as you can, even if they are similar. The result is more realistic. Try blending shades in the needle to create new colours.

STRAIGHT SHAPE

When filling a shape with straight sides, satin stitch is worked from one side of the shape to the other.

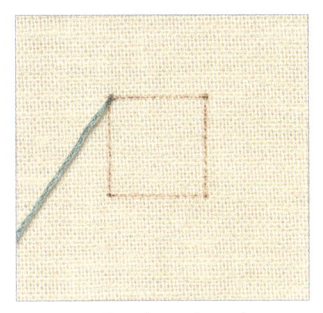

1 Bring the thread to the front at the left hand side on the upper edge of the outline.

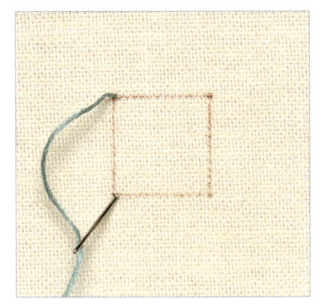

2 Take the needle to the back directly opposite from where the thread emerged.

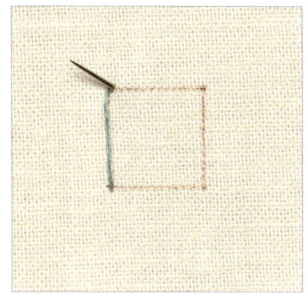

3 Emerge just next to the first stitch.

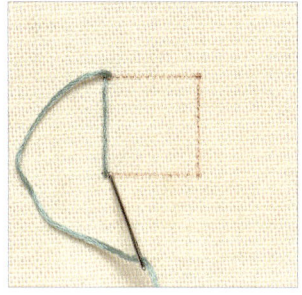

4 Take the needle to the back just next to the first stitch on the opposite side of the shape.

5 Continue working stitches in the same manner to cover the shape.

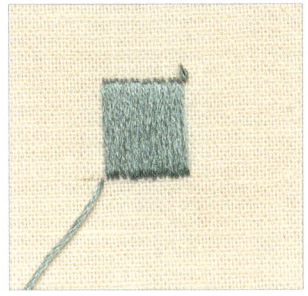

6 Back of work. The stitches are worked across the shape on the back of the work.

7 Satin stitch shape outlined with split stitch.

Stroking the stitches

To achieve even tension and high sheen on the threads, use a mellor, large darning needle or dressmaker's awl to smooth the stitches as you work.

1 Place the tip of the mellor under the thread and take the needle to the back on the opposite side of the shape.

2 Begin to pull the thread through. As the thread tightens over the mellor, slide it towards you, stroking the threads.

3 Ease the mellor out while pulling the stitch taut.

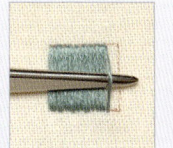

SATIN STITCH ~ BLOCK SHADING

Rows of satin stitch can be used to fill a shape. Shading is achieved by using various shades of thread, but unlike long and short stitch, the ridges formed between each row becomes part of the design.

This filling technique is more traditional to Asian embroidery styles and is not often seen in European work.

Block shading can be worked with or without split stitch outlines. The split stitch should always be worked against any previously stitched sections to define the individual shapes.

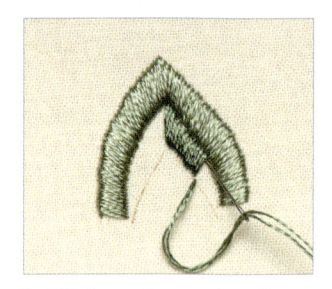

1 Fill the outermost section in satin stitch. Stitch the next section, bringing the thread to the front inside the design and to the back at the edge of the previous row.

2 Repeat for any remaining sections in the design.

3 Narrow voids, known as 'water roads' in Chinese embroidery, can be left between the rows of satin stitch.

SATIN STITCH ~ CURVED SHAPE

When covering a curved shape with satin stitch, the stitching is worked from the centre of the shape, filling one half at a time to maintain accurate stitch direction. The shape can be outlined with split stitch before the satin stitch is worked to achieve a crisp edge.

Where the shape curves steeply it may be necessary to add half stitches along the outer edge to avoid overcrowding the stitches along the inner edge.

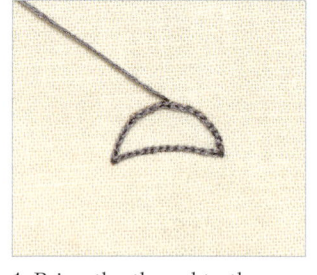

1 Bring the thread to the front halfway along the upper edge of the shape, angling the needle outside the outline stitching.

2 Take the needle to the back at an angle on the opposite side from where the thread emerged, on the outside of the outline.

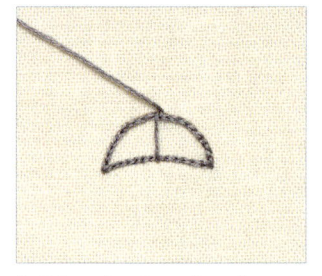

3 Bring the thread to the front on the outside, next to the first stitch.

4 Continue to cover one half of the shape. Work the stitches side by side along the outer edge and closer together on the inside edge to follow the curve.

5 Bring a new thread to the front next to the starting point.

6 Fill the remaining half of the shape in the same manner.

120

SATIN STITCH ~ SURFACE STITCH

This stitch has the same appearance on the front of the work as satin stitch. However the stitches are placed from side to side and therefore use far less thread, so it is useful when filling very large areas such as under laid work. Soft, flat threads should be used for the best result.

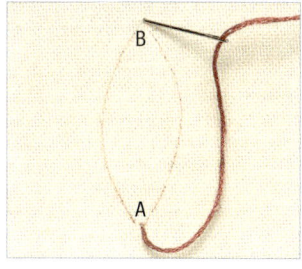

1 Bring the thread to the front at A and take the needle to the back at B on the opposite side.

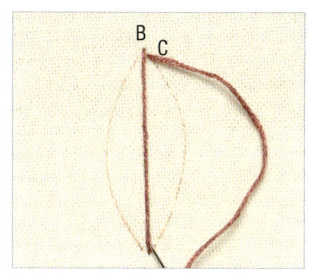

2 Bring the thread to the front at C, just next to B, catching only a few fabric threads. Take the needle to the back on the opposite side.

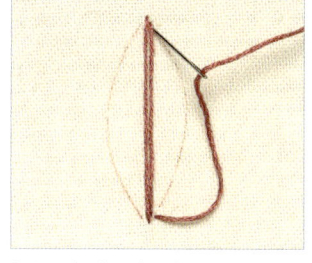

3 Work the third stitch in the same direction as the first, leaving just a tiny stitch on the back of the work at the edge of the design.

4 Continue in this manner, working the stitches from side to side and filling one half of the shape at a time.

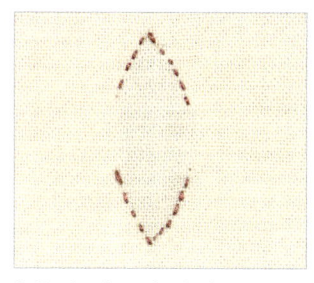

5 Back of work. Only tiny stitches are visible along the edge of the design.

SPLIT STITCH

Split stitch is most commonly used as an outline stitch under satin stitch or long and short stitch. Split stitch lends itself to fine detail and subtle shading, when worked in multiple rows to fill a shape. It was used extensively as a filling stitch in opus anglicanum for embroidering faces and robes.

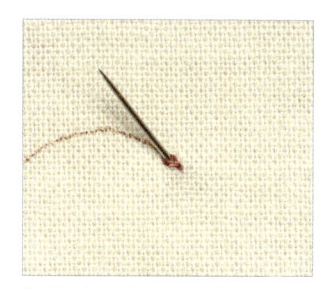

1 Work a short stitch. Bring the needle to the front halfway along the first stitch, splitting the thread.

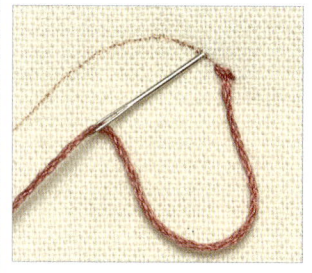

2 Pull the thread through. Take the needle to the back a short distance from the first stitch.

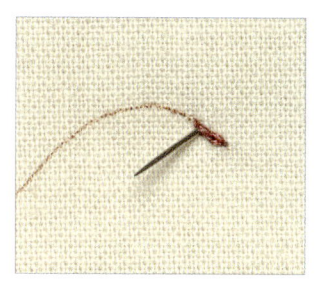

3 Pull the thread through. Bring the needle to the front through the centre of the previous stitch.

4 Continue working stitches in this manner to the end of the row.

5 Closely worked parallel rows of split stitch can be used to fill a shape. We used two shades of thread for photographic purposes.

Silk threads

Discard thread that becomes worn and start with a new piece as worn thread looses its sheen.

STEM STITCH

Viewing
Observing your work from a distance from time to time will reveal any problems not visible when viewed closely.

A very versatile stitch that will follow fine and curved lines perfectly. Worked in multiple close rows it makes an elegant filling stitch. Stem stitch can be worked from left to right keeping the thread below the needle, or from the base to the top, keeping the thread to the right of the needle.

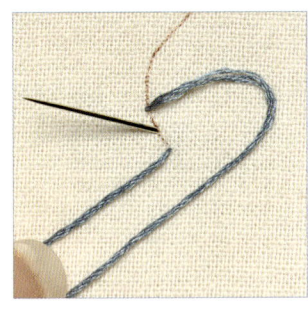

1 Bring the thread to the front at the end of the drawn line. Take the thread to the back, leaving a small loop. Bring the needle to the front halfway along the stitch.

2 Pull the thread through.

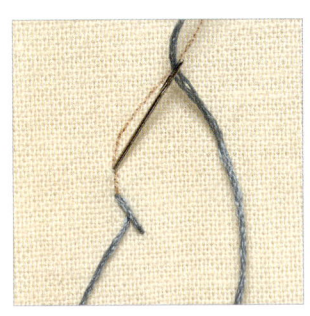

3 Take the thread to the back a short distance from the first stitch, leaving a loop.

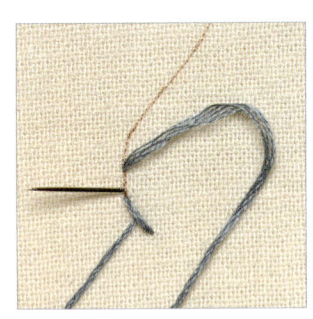

4 Bring the needle to the front at the end of the first stitch, sharing the same hole in the fabric.

5 Pull the thread through. Continue in this manner, keeping the length of the stitches even.

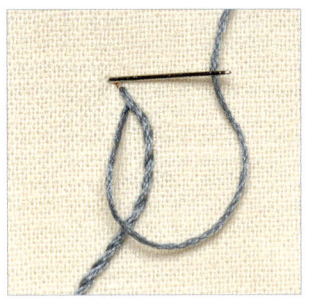

6 Take the needle to the back at the end of the row.

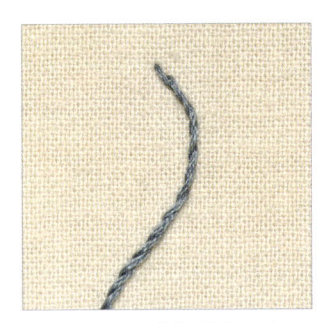

7 Starting and finishing the row of stem stitch with a full stitch creates tapered ends.

8 Flat end. Work a short stitch, at the beginning of the line and re-emerge at the starting point.

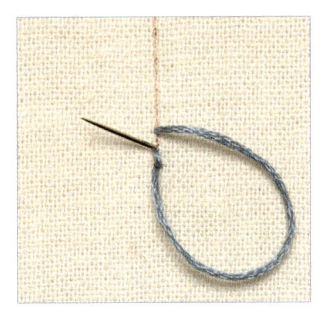

9 Take the thread to the back, a full stitch length away. Bring the needle to the front at the end of the first stitch.

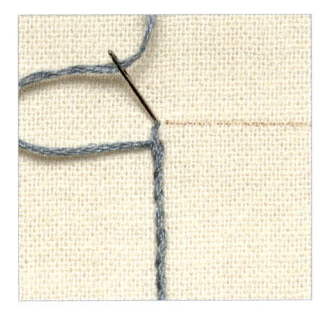

10 Work stem stitch to the end of the line. Finish with a short stitch.

122

STEM STITCH CORNERS

Because of the nature of the stitch, the thread is secured on the back at the corner points.

1 Work stem stitch until you reach the corner.

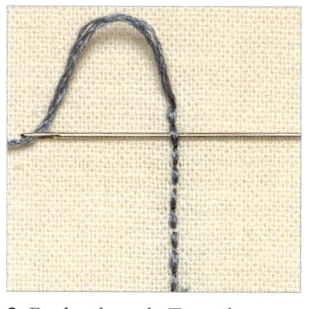

2 Back of work. Turn the work over. Slide the needle under the second to last stitch on the back to anchor the thread.

3 Re-emerge at the corner point through the same hole in the fabric.

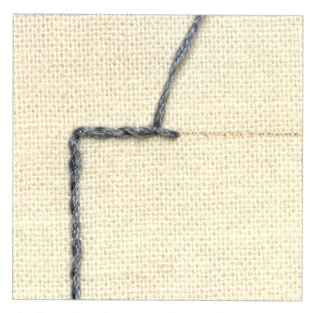

4 Beginning with a short stitch, work stem stitch along the adjacent side.

STEM STITCH FILLING

Rows of stem stitch worked close together are fantastic for filling shapes. This type of filling is usually worked from the edge of the design towards the centre of a shape. We used two shades of thread for photographic purposes.

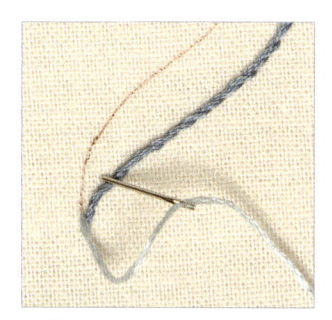

1 Work a row of stem stitch along the edge of the shape. Rotate the work. Bring the thread to the front on the design line and take the needle to the back next to the first row.

2 Leaving a loop, bring the needle to the front halfway along the first stitch. Pull the thread through. The stitch should lie snugly against the first row.

3 Continue to stitch alongside the first row, keeping the rows close together but not crowded.

4 Continue to fill the shape, rotating the work for each row and keeping the rows close together.

DESIGN GALLERY
BUTTERFLY

Goldwork techniques
Attaching purl
Attaching spangles
Chipwork
Cord padding
Couching pair of threads
Couching single thread
Couching twist
Felt padding
Kid leather over padding
Laid work
Purl over string padding

Embroidery stitches
Chain stitch
Whipped stem stitch

Requirements

Fabric
40cm × 35cm wide (16" × 13 ¾") piece of teal/mauve shot silk dupion
40cm × 35cm wide (16" × 13 ¾") piece of calico

Supplies
5cm (2") square of yellow felt
Size 1 cord
Gold coloured sewing thread
Pink sewing thread
Velvet covered board
Beeswax
Sharp metal thread scissors
Dressmaker's awl or mellor
Tweezers
Magic tape
30cm × 25cm wide (12" × 10") stretcher frame (or slate frame)
Thumbtacks for stretcher frame
Sling
Fine black pen
Tracing paper
Yellow dressmaker's carbon paper

Needles
No. 10 crewel
No. 11 sharp

Threads
Benton & Johnson metal threads
A = 9m (9yd 30 ¼") 371 gold couching thread
B = 70cm (27 ½") T69 gold imitation Japanese thread
C = 60cm (23 ½") gold rococo
D = 30cm (12") gold fine twist
E = 25cm (10") gold antique twist
F = 50cm (20") gold Grecian cord
G = gold metallic embroidery thread
H = 25cm (10") gold smooth purl
I = 15cm (6") gold check purl
J = 3 × 3mm (⅛") gold spangles

Preparation for embroidery
See page 150 for the embroidery design and padding template. The shaded areas indicate felt padding.

Transferring the design
Using the pen, trace the embroidery design onto the tracing paper. Centre the tracing over the silk, aligning the straight lines with the grain of the fabric. Transfer the design onto the silk using the dressmakers's carbon, following the instructions on page 17. Position the silk over the calico and mount both into the frame following the instructions on page 20.

Preparing the padding
See pages 27 and 29 for instructions on applying cord and felt padding.

Secure a length of cord padding along the length of the abdomen. Transfer and cut the felt padding for the abdomen. Stitch in place over the cord, bringing the needle to the front through the fabric and taking it to the back through the edge of the felt. Cut two pieces of felt padding for the thorax and stitch in place.

Embroidery
Use the sharp needle when attaching the spangles and purl and the crewel needle for all other embroidery.

Use the dressmaker's awl or mellor when sinking the metal thread tails to the back of the work.

Order of work
All couching is worked with gold coloured sewing thread, spacing the stitches 3mm (⅛") apart unless otherwise specified.

Flower

Petals
The petals are filled using a pair of A couched in place with pink sewing thread. Begin near the flower centre and couch the pair of threads in place along the outline of the petal. When you reach the opposite side of the petal, turn by cutting and rejoining the outer thread and turning the inner, following the instructions on page 54.

This design measures 18cm × 13cm wide (7" × 5⅛").

Continue couching and placing the couching stitches in a brick pattern, pushing the rows close together. When you reach the centre vein of the petal cut both threads at the end of each row, following the instructions on page 40 for acute corners. Sink and secure the thread tails at regular intervals.

Couch four to six rows following the outline until the turns at the top of the petal becomes tight. Smooth the turn on the following row, allowing the background fabric to show through (diag 1).

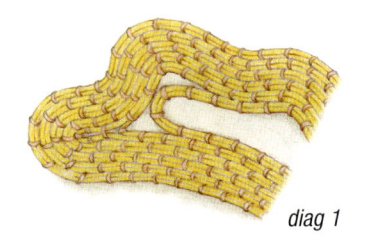

diag 1

Continue towards the centre and finish, allowing fabric to show through in the middle. Repeat for the remaining petals.

Centre
Cut very short lengths of H and I. Stitch the pieces in place, changing the direction of each piece and allowing the fabric to show between the pieces.

Butterfly

Upper wing
Beginning above the thorax, couch a pair of A along the outline of the upper wing, using tweezers to shape the threads at the tight turns along the upper edge.

Sink and secure the thread tails. Starting at the edge of the lower wing, begin to couch a pair of A threads along the marking on the upper wing.

When you reach the first dip, secure the couching thread with a small back stitch and separate the pair of laid threads. Leave the outer thread to one side.

Extend the inner thread to the base of the wing marking and fold it back on itself, using tweezers to shape the fold.

Using a second couching thread and beginning at the folded end, couch the doubled thread in place along the marked line (diag 2).

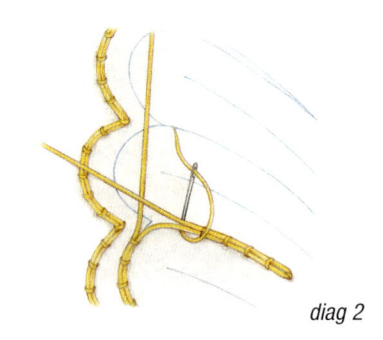

diag 2

When you reach the dip, rejoin the upper thread. Use tweezers to kink the upper thread into the point of the dip and couch in place. Couch the pair of threads in place along the second curve of the wing marking. Stitch the second wing marking in the same way as the first. Couch the pair of threads in place to the point where they merge with the outline.

Sink the thread tails, off-setting the points where you take them to the back to achieve a smooth join (diag 3).

diag 3

Cut a 20cm (8") length of C. Fold the piece in half matching the pattern in the thread and kink the fold closed with tweezers. Couch the folded end in place at the tip of the right hand line on the wing.

Couch the doubled thread in place along the marked line, placing a stitch across each 'crimp' in the thread (diag 4).

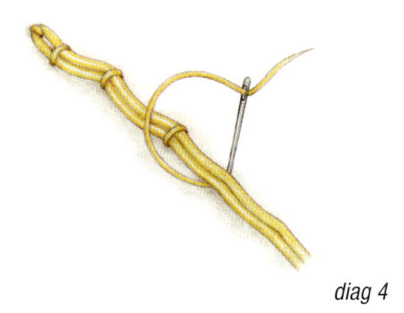

diag 4

Sink and secure the tails. Cut the remaining length of C in half. Fold and couch each piece along the remaining two marked lines on the upper wing, in the same manner as the first. Off-set the points where the tails are sunk to the back to achieve smooth joins to the first row.

Lower wing
Couch the length of E in place along the outline of the lower wing. Sink and secure the thread tails. Starting near the thorax, couch a pair of A threads in place along one line for the marking on the wing. Continue into the circle at the top. Couch three rounds, placing the stitches in a brick pattern and pushing the rounds close together. Sink and secure the tails, off-setting the threads along the inside edge of the circle. Repeat for the remaining two lines and circles on the wing. Stitch a spangle in place at the centre of each circle.

Abdomen
Cut seven lengths of I and twenty lengths of H to fit at a right hand angle over the padding, referring to the instructions on page 101. Beginning halfway along the abdomen, stitch the pieces in place over the padding, attaching one check purl for every two smooth purls. Towards the tip of the abdomen, use smooth purl only and adjust the length of the pieces to taper the shape slightly. To finish, stitch a shorter looped piece of smooth purl in place at the end of the padding (diag 5).

diag 5

Thorax
Cut the kid leather to fit. Place it over the padding and tack to hold it in place following the instructions on page 68. Stitch the leather in place with small stitches around the edge. Starting at the top of the abdomen, outline the thorax with a single row of D, couched in place along the edge of the leather.

Head
Starting at the tip of the proboscis, couch a single length of D in place along the marked line. Continue around the outline of the head and coil the thread to fill the head with close concentric circles of couching. Sink and secure the thread tails.

Legs
Starting at the tips, embroider the legs in reverse chain stitch using G.

Antennae
Using G, stitch the antennae in whipped stem stitch.

Border
Place a length of magic tape along the lower edge of the border. Cut a 21cm (8 ¼") and a 27cm (10⅝") length of F. Tape the ends to prevent them from unravelling while you work. Temporarily secure the end of the short piece with a few stitches 5cm (2") from the starting point, at the lower left hand side of the border. Stitch the cord in place, bringing the needle to the front at the edge of the tape and to the back through the cord referring to steps 3–7 on page 43.

Repeat for the longer piece along the right hand side. You will need to use a mellor or awl to prepare quite large holes in the fabrics so you can sink the tails to the back. Remove the temporary stitches. To maintain the twist in the cord, rotate the cord in the direction of the twist as you pull the tails through using a sling. Secure the tails on the back.

Couch a single thread of B in place along each side of the cord. Sink and secure the tails.

Embroidery key

All couching is worked with matching sewing thread unless otherwise specified.

Flower

Petals = A and pink sewing thread (couching)

Centre = H and I (chipwork)

Butterfly

Upper wing = A and C (couching)

Lower wing = A and E (couching)

J (attaching spangles)

Abdomen = H and I (attaching purl)

Thorax = (kid over padding)

D (couching)

Head = D (couching)

Legs = G (chain stitch)

Antennae = G (whipped stem stitch)

Border = F (couching twist)

B (couching)

STRAWBERRY PINCUSHION

Requirements

Fabric

15cm × 30cm wide (6" × 12") piece of pale gold silk dupion
20cm (8") square of calico

Supplies

Gold coloured and plum sewing thread
Pale gold no. 8 perlé cotton
10cm × 20cm wide (4" × 8") piece of red felt
12cm (4¾") square of medium weight wadding
Small amount of fibre-fill
Velvet covered board
Beeswax
Sharp metal thread scissors
Dressmaker's awl or mellor
10cm (4") embroidery hoop
6cm (2⅜") square of 3mm (⅛") foam core
6cm (2⅜") square of thin card
Sharp HB pencil

Needles

No. 9 crewel
No. 10 beading

Threads and beads

Benton & Johnson metal threads
A = 60cm (23⅝") no. 6 gold smooth purl
B = 10cm (4") no.1 gold pearl purl
C = 371 gold fine couching thread
Au Papillion fil d'or deluxe
D = antique gold
Mill Hill seed beads
E = 00557 gold

Goldwork techniques
Couching pearl purl
Couching threads
Felt padding
Looped purl

Embroidery stitches
Beading
Detached chain
Fly stitch
Needle weaving
Stem stitch
Straight stitch

The pincushion measures 6cm (2⅜") square excluding the tassel.

Preparation for embroidery

See page 151 for the embroidery design and strawberry tassel template. The shaded areas indicate padding.

Preparing the fabric

Cut the silk into two 15cm (6") squares. Neaten the edges of the silk by hand or machine to prevent the fabric from fraying.

Transferring the design

Mirror the embroidery design. Transfer the design and cutting lines onto the wrong side of the calico, using your chosen method. Centre the silk over the calico, making sure the grain of the fabrics is aligned. Place the layered fabrics in the hoop and adjust until tight. Using the gold coloured sewing thread, work small running stitches through both layers along all design lines to make the design visible on the front.

Preparing the felt padding

Trace and cut out three strawberry shapes from the felt; one the same size as the design and the remaining two decreasing in size.

Stitch the smallest piece in place at the centre of the strawberry shape. Stitch the medium piece over the first and the largest piece on top, keeping the stitches just inside the marked outline.

Embroidery

Use gold coloured sewing thread for the couching and attaching the beads. Pass the sewing thread over the beeswax to strengthen it. Use the beading needle for the beading and attaching the smooth purl, and the crewel needle for all other stitching.

Order of work

Strawberry outline

Gently pull the length of B to stretch it slightly. Starting at the top of the berry, stitch the pearl purl in place around the felt, pulling the stitches into the grooves. As you near the starting point, measure and trim the pearl purl to the correct length.

Seeds

Cut twenty-five, 1cm (⅜") lengths of A. Secure doubled sewing thread and bring it to the front through the felt padding. Thread a length of A onto the needle and slide it onto the felt. Take the needle to the back, close to where it emerged and gently pull the length of purl into a loop. Bring the thread to the front inside the loop and couch it in place without distorting the purl. Stitch a bead in place inside the loop. Continue to cover the felt with loops and beads, allowing some felt to show through.

Stem

Cut a 20cm (8") length of C and fold one third of the length back on itself. Couch the folded end at the top of the strawberry. Continue to couch the doubled thread in place to the top of the stem. Leave the short tail and fold the long tail back on itself. Couch it in place close to the first row, back to the top of the berry. Take the thread tails to the back and secure.

Using one strand of D, work a row of stem stitch along each side of the stem.

Leaves

Using one strand of D, work a fly stitch for each section of the leaf outline (diag 1).

diag 1

Embroider the centre veins in straight stitches.

Sepals

Using one strand of D, work a long detached chain. Re-emerge at the top of the strawberry, just next to the base of the detached chain (diag 2).

diag 2

Weave the thread from side to side, over and under, until the chain stitch is covered (diag 3).

diag 3

Take the thread to the back at the tip of the detached chain and secure. Work the remaining four sepals in the same manner.

Making the pincushion

Cut the wadding into three pieces measuring 6cm (2⅜"), 4cm (1½") and 2cm (¾") square.

Trim the embroidery along the marked cutting lines. Place the embroidery face down on a well padded surface. Centre the largest piece of padding over the wrong side of the fabric, followed by the medium and then the smallest piece. Centre the square of foam core over the wadding. Pull the fabric firmly over the foam core, ensuring that the embroidery is centred on the front. Hold in place with pins around the edges and lace the fabric in place (diag 4).

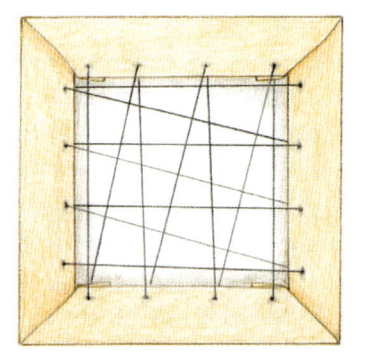

diag 4

Trim and lace the second piece of silk over the thin card. Place the two pieces with wrong sides together and join with ladder stitch around the edges.

Strawberry tassel

Using the strawberry template, cut the semi-circle from the red felt. Fold the felt in half along the straight edge. Stitch the straight edges together using matching sewing thread to form a cone. Secure the thread but do not cut (diag 5).

Using the same thread, work running stitch around the upper edge of the cone. Leave the thread tail hanging.

Make a 38cm (15") length of twisted cord from the perlé cotton. Fold in half and knot the ends together.

Place the knotted end of the cord inside the cone and fill the cone with fibre-fill. Pull the thread to draw in the upper edge tightly. Secure the thread through the cord.

diag 5

Beginning at the top, cover the strawberry with rows of looped purl and beads in a similar way to the pincushion. Cover the tip of the strawberry with beads only. As you stitch, take care not to pull the thread tight and distort the shape.

Work a round of six upright looped purls around the cord at the top of the strawberry for the hull.

Finishing

Place the large cord loop around the pincushion. Beginning at the centre top, stitch the cord in place along one half at a time, covering the join. Stitch the cord tails together at the centre base (diag 6).

diag 6

Embroidery key

All couching is worked with matching sewing thread unless otherwise specified.

Strawberry outline = B (couching)
Seeds = A (looped purl) E (beading)
Stem = C (couching)
D (stem stitch)
Leaves = D (fly stitch, straight stitch)
Calyx = D (detached chain needle weaving)

ROSEHIP

This design measures 8.5cm × 10cm wide (3⅜" × 4").

Requirements

Fabric
25cm (10") square of sage silk
25cm (10") square of calico

Supplies
Silver-grey sewing thread
Beeswax
Dressmaker's awl or mellor
Sharp metal thread scissors
Tweezers
25cm (10") square stretcher frame
Thumbtacks
Fine black pen
Carbon paper
Tracing paper

Needles
No. 10 crewel
No. 20 chenille

Threads
Benton & Johnson metal threads
A = 2.5m (2yd 26½") T71 silver imitation Japanese thread

Madeira stranded silk
B = 0801 lt lavender
C = 0815 buff
D = 1409 lt avocado
E = 1510 dk grey-green
F = 1701 vy lt jade
G = 1910 lt beige
H = 2013 vy lt old gold
I = 2209 lt mustard

Goldwork techniques
Couching single threads
Laid work

Embroidery stitches
Block shading
Long and short stitch
Satin stitch
Split stitch
Stem stitch

Preparation for embroidery

See page 151 for the embroidery design.

Transferring the design

Transfer the design onto the silk using the dressmaker's carbon, following the instructions on page 17.

Position the silk over the calico and mount both into the frame following the instructions on page 20.

Embroidery

Use the crewel needle for all stitching and the chenille needle for sinking the metal thread tails to the back of the work.

All couching is worked with matching sewing thread unless otherwise specified.

Silk embroidery

Seeds

Beginning at the base, work split stitch along the upper edge of the first seed using B. Cover the seed in satin stitch, working from the centre to the sides and covering the split stitch outline. Working in rows towards the top, embroider the remaining seeds in a similar manner, referring to the photograph for colour placement. Use the same colour thread for the split stitch outline and the satin stitch for each seed.

Cup

Embroider the large outer walls first. Using F and starting at the base, work stem stitch along the outer edge. Place the stitches along the inside edge of the marked line so the laid thread can be placed on the line later (diag 1).

diag 1

Anchor the last stitch at the tip. Recommence stitching along the inside of the outer walls, leaving a narrow void for the laid thread (diag 2).

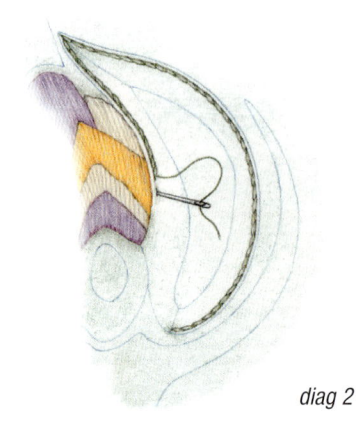

diag 2

Continue to fill the outer section of each wall with close rows of stem stitch. Fill the inner sections using C in a similar manner. Using F, fill the outer section of the three ovals at the base with stem stitch in a similar manner, leaving the inner sections free.

Sepals

Stitch the sepals in close rows of stem stitch, beginning each section at the outer edge and stitching towards the centre vein. Refer to the photograph for colour placement.

Leaves

Outline the leaves in split stich using E. Fill the leaves in long and short stitch, working from the outer edges towards the centre vein after the metal thread embroidery.

Metal thread embroidery

Cup

Fill the inner section of each oval at the base with a single silver thread couched in place using B. Begin each oval along the outer edge, coiling the laid thread towards the centre. Sink and secure the thread tails one at a time.

Outline the cup using a single silver thread, starting and finishing along the lower edge.

Stem

Cut and fold a 20cm (8") length of silver thread in half. Starting at the lower left side of the stem, couch the doubled thread in place, continuing partway around the side of the cup.

Fold and couch a second length of silver thread in place alongside the first. As the area narrows towards the tip, couch over the outer thread of the second pair and the inner thread of the first (diag 3).

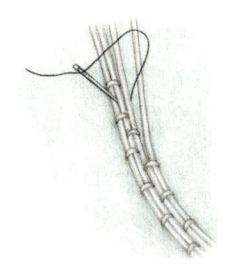

diag 3

Repeat for the right hand side of the stem. Continue to fill the stem, working towards the centre.

Once the laid threads meet at the base, begin the following rows at the upper edge, turning the threads at the base (diag 4).

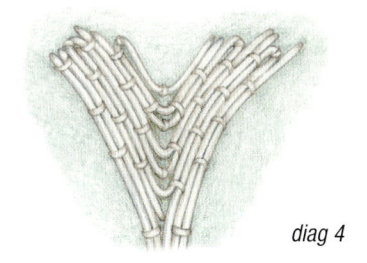

diag 4

To complete the stem, coil a single thread to fill the remaining area at the upper edge of the stem.

Veins

Fill the veins in a similar manner to the stem, working the couching stitches over one of the previously laid threads, where the shape narrows.

Embroidery key

The silk embroidery is worked with one strand of thread and all couching is worked with silver grey sewing thread unless otherwise specified.

Seeds = B, C, G, H and I (split stitch, satin stitch)
Cup
Filling = C and F (stem stitch)
A and F (couching)
Outline = A (couching)
Sepals = D, E and H (stem stitch)
Leaves = E (split stitch long and short stitch)
Stem and veins = A (couching)

Detail of large panel. Richly coloured silk embroidery worked in close rows of chain stitch. The goldwork is stitched with cut purl and heavily padded dots covered in guimped couching using silver thread.

133

FLOWER BORDER

This design measures 18.5cm (7 3/16") square.

Goldwork techniques
Attaching spangles with beads
Circular or nué
Couching single thread
Guimped couching variation
Looped purls

Embroidery stitches
Back stitch
Beading
Fly stitch
French knot
Padded satin stitch
Satin stitch
Split stitch

Or nué
In this design the couching stitches completely cover the gold thread in the shaded sections. Keep the stitches side by side. Over-crowding the stitches makes it difficult to keep the laid thread close together between the coloured sections.

Requirements

Fabric
45cm (17¾") square of cobalt blue silk dupion
45cm (17¾") square of calico

Supplies
5cm × 10cm wide (2" × 4") square of yellow felt
Gold coloured sewing thread
Yellow soft cotton
40cm (15¾") square stretcher frame (or slate frame)
Thumbtacks for stretcher frame
Velvet covered board
Beeswax
Dressmaker's awl or mellor
Sharp metal thread scissors
Sling
Tweezers
Tracing paper
Fine black pen
Yellow dressmaker's carbon
Fine acid free brown permanent pen, eg micron pen

Needles
No. 7 crewel
No. 10 crewel
No. 20 chenille

Threads and beads
Au Ver à Soie, Soie d'Alger
A = 4622 dusty rose
DMC stranded cotton
B = 3838 cobalt blue (colour to match silk fabric)
Gloriana variegated stranded silk
C = 096 summer foliage
Madeira stranded silk
D = 0504 rose pink
E = 0506 geranium
F = 0511 garnet
G = 0613 lt candy pink
H = 0815 vy lt dusky pink
Benton & Johnson metallic thread
I = 5m (5yd 17") 371 dk gold couching thread
J = 3m (3yd 10") gold fine rococo
K = 16m (17yd 17½") T71 gold imitation Japanese thread
L = 60cm (23½") no. 6 gold rough purl
M = 8 × 3mm (⅛") gold spangles
Mill Hill petite beads
N = 42012 royal plum

Preparation for embroidery
See page 152 for the embroidery design. The shaded areas on the design indicate padding.

Transferring the design
Transfer the solid design lines using the dressmaker's carbon, referring to the instructions on page 17. Carefully retrace the design lines with the permanent pen.

Transfer the padded shapes indicated in grey on the design, onto the felt.

Using the permanent pen, draw the centre vein onto each felt piece and cut out.

Position the silk over the calico and mount onto your frame following the instructions on page 20.

Preparing the felt padding
The centre leaf along each side of the design is padded with felt over soft cotton. Using the soft cotton in the no. 7 crewel needle, work a row of stem stitch along each side of the centre vein (diag 1).

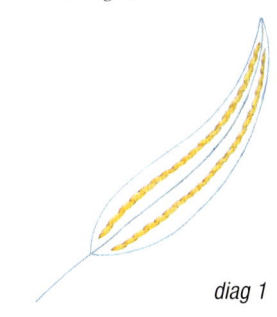

diag 1

Place the felt padding over the stitching on each leaf and stitch in place following the instructions on page 29. Work running stitch along the centre vein, pulling the felt into the groove between the rows of stem stitch.

Embroidery
Use the chenille needle for sinking the metal threads to the back and the no. 10 crewel needle for all embroidery.

Silk embroidery

Or nué flower
Work a padded satin stitch dot at the centre of each flower, using E.

Green leaves
Using B and working from the centre vein, fill each section of the leaves with satin stitch. Keep the stitches parallel to the centre vein and leave a narrow void between each section to accommodate the thread to be laid later.

Red buds
Using F, stitch a row of French knots along the outline of each bud. Place the knots close together without crushing them. Change to A and work a row of French knots next to the first. Using G, fill the remaining area with French knots.

Pink flowers
Using D, outline the oval shape at the tip of each petal in split stitch. Fill the shape with three layers of padding stitches, placing the final layer along the length.

Cover with satin stitch, working the stitches diagonally across the shape and covering the split stitch outline (diag 2).

Fill the remaining section of each petal in long and short stitch, using H. Work a fly stitch over the long and short stitches for the veins, using G.

Metal thread embroidery

The gold threads are couched in place using matching sewing thread unless otherwise specified.

Gold leaves
The gold leaves are worked as a variation of guimped couching described on page 66. Use I for the laid thread and A for the couching.

Leave a 2.5cm (1") tail at the base of the leaf and place the thread along one side. Couch the fold in place at the edge of the felt. Using tweezers form a kink in the thread at the centre vein. Work a couching stitch on the centre vein and place the laid thread along the edge of the second half of the leaf, forming a V-shape (diag 3).

Continue to lay the thread back and forth in a V-shape across the leaf, couching at each side and along the centre vein. Pull the laid thread firmly into the groove along the centre. Sink and secure the tails.

Or nué flowers
The flowers are worked in circular or nué over a single thread from the centre. Use I for the laid thread and B for the couching. The colour of the couching thread should be the same as the background fabric.

Sink one end of the gold thread to the back, just next to the flower centre. Keeping the thread tail out of the way, begin to couch the gold thread around the centre, placing the couching stitches close together in the sections between the petals. Continue to couch, spiralling the laid thread and filling the coloured sections with closely worked couching stitches. Keep the rows of laid thread close together.

Sink and secure the gold thread tail at the outer edge.

diag 2

diag 3

Green leaves

Couch short lengths of K in a V-shape in the voids to form the veins (diag 4).

diag 4

Sink and secure the thread tails for each leaf as you work. Using K to outline the leaf, leave a 2.5cm (2) tail at the base and couch along the inside edge (diag 5).

diag 5

Kink the thread to form the tip. Couch along the other side, continuing along the stem to the base. Starting at the tip of the leaf, couch a length of J along the centre vein, rotating the thread so the 'crimps' in the thread fits neatly over the gold thread veins. Continue to couch along the inside of the previously laid thread to the base of the stem.

Red buds – stems, sepals and leaves

Using K and beginning above the green leaf, couch a single thread along the stem to the base of the inner bud. Continue couching the thread, coiling it to fill the middle sepal. Fill the remaining two sepals in a similar manner. Sink and secure the thread tails. Repeat for the remaining two buds. Work the small leaves along the stem in the same manner as the sepals.

Couch a short length of thread along the remaining section of the stem between the leaves and the outer bud.

Couch a length of J along the inside of each stem in the same manner as the green leaves.

Stems and tendrils

Using K, couch along the remaining stems, starting each section at the base of the stem and working to the tip of each tendril where required. Cut and restart the thread at the crossover point. Couch J along the inside of the stems, cutting the thread as before. Finish with the four larger tendrils using K.

Pink flowers

Starting at the base of a petal, place a pair of I threads along one side and couch in place. When you reach the oval section, separate the threads. Kink the inner thread at the corner point and couch it in place in the void below the oval (diag 6).

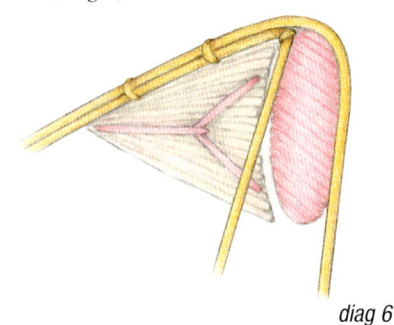

diag 6

Leave the thread at the opposite side. Couch the outer thread around the top of the petal. Rejoin the threads at the opposite side and couch the pair along the remaining side of the petal. Sink and secure the thread tails.

Bring a doubled thread to the front at the centre of the flower. Thread on a spangle and stitch it in place with a seed bead. Cut five 12mm (½") lengths of purl. Bring the thread to the front at the edge of the spangle. Slide a length of purl onto the fabric. Take the needle to the back close to where the thread emerged, allowing enough space for the purl to fit. Pull the thread through, gently shaping the purl into a loop. Repeat for the remaining four purls around the centre.

Embroidery key

All silk embroidery is worked with one strand of thread. All couching is worked with matching sewing thread unless otherwise specified.

Pink flowers = D (padded satin stitch), H (long and short stitch) G (fly stitch), I (couching) M and N (attaching spangle with bead), L (looped purl)

Green leaves = B (satin stitch) J and K (couching)

Buds = A, F and G (French knot) J and K (couching)

Gold leaves = B and I (guimped couching)

Gold flowers = E (padded satin stitch), B and K (circular or nué)

Stems and tendrils = J and K (couching)

GOLDEN RETICELLA

Requirements

Fabric
Panel
25cm (10") square of plum velvet
25cm (10") square of calico
Scissor fob
15cm × 25cm wide (6" × 10") piece of plum velvet
15cm × 25cm wide (6" × 10") piece of calico

Supplies
Gold coloured and plum sewing threads
1 ball no. 8 perlé cotton to match velvet
Velvet covered board
Beeswax
Dressmaker's awl or mellor
Sharp metal thread scissors
10cm (4") embroidery hoop
15cm (6") embroidery hoop
4cm × 8cm wide (1½" × 3⅛") stiff card
Sharp HB pencil

Needles
No. 1 milliner's
No. 9 crewel
No. 10 beading

Threads and beads
Benton & Johnson metal threads
A = 15m (16yd 15") 371 gold couching thread
B = 55cm (21⅜") no.6 gold bright check
Beads
C = 5gms (1.76oz) 3mm (⅛") pearls
D = 3 × 4mm (³⁄₁₆") red cut crystals

Goldwork techniques
Attaching purl
Couching loops
Couching pair of threads
Couching right angled corner
Couching sharp corner
Looped border

Embroidery stitches
Beading

Embroidery key
All couching is worked with matching sewing thread.

Grid = A (couching)

Centre intersections = C and D (beading), B (attaching purl)

Intersections = C (beading), B (attaching purl)

Loops = A (couched loop)

Loop border = A (looped border)

The panel measures 10cm × 7cm wide (4" × 2¾").

The scissor fob measures 4cm (1½") square excluding the tassel.

Preparation for embroidery

See pages 149 and 151 for the embroidery designs.

Preparing the fabrics

Cutting out ~ scissor fob

Cut one piece each of velvet and calico, measuring 15cm (6") square for the front. Cut one piece each of velvet and calico, 7cm (2¾") square for the back.

Transferring the designs

Using a ruler, transfer the embroidery design and scissor fob cutting lines onto the wrong side of a corresponding piece of calico using your chosen method. Aligning the grain of the fabrics, centre the velvet over the calico. Place the layered fabrics in a suitable size hoop.

Using the gold coloured sewing thread, work small running stitches through both layers along all design lines, making the design visible on the right side of the velvet.

Embroidery

Use waxed sewing thread for the couching and attaching the beads.

Use the crewel needle for the couching, the beading needle for attaching the beads and the milliner's needle for taking the metal threads to the back.

The embroidery design on the panel and scissor fob is worked in a similar manner.

Order of work

Grid ~ panel

Cut a 1.5m (1yd 23") length of A and fold in half. Beginning at one corner, couch the doubled thread in place around the outline of the design. At the corners, turn the threads one at a time to achieve sharp corner points. When you reach the starting point, turn the threads sharply and couch along the diagonal lines referring to the diagram (diag 1).

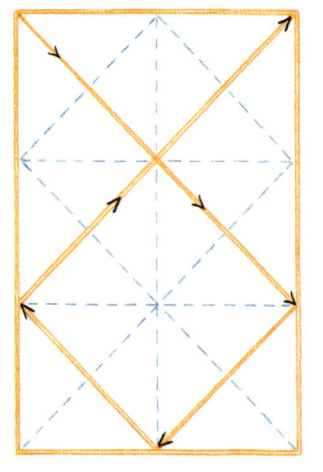

diag 1

Take the threads to the back one at a time and secure. Cut a 75cm (27½") length of gold thread and repeat for the remaining diagonal lines in the opposite direction.

Couch doubled lengths of gold thread along the remaining lines, securing the thread tails on the back as you work.

Scissor fob

Cut a 50cm (20") length of A and fold in half. Beginning at one corner, couch the folded end in place. Continue couching along one side, spacing the stitches 4mm (³⁄₁₆") apart. At the corner, turn and couch the threads one at a time to achieve a sharp corner point. Couch along the adjacent side. At the next corner, turn the threads sharply and couch along one diagonal. Continue along the remaining two sides of the square. Thread the gold threads, one at a time, into the milliner's needle. Take each thread to the back at the corner and carry across the back of the work. Bring it to the front at the opposite corner. Couch the pair of threads along the second diagonal line. Sink and carry the threads to couch the centre lines in the same manner.

Beading

Using doubled thread, stitch a red crystal in place at the centre of the fob design. For the panel, stitch a red crystal in place at the two central intersections.

Stitch eight pearls in place closely around each crystal, placing a pearl in each section of the gold grid.

Attach a pair of pearls at each corner and at the end of each straight line on the fob design. On the panel, stitch four pearls in place at all remaining intersections and a pair of pearls at each corner.

Take the thread to the back on the opposite side of the laid threads leaving a 5mm (³⁄₁₆") loop.

Emerge at the next grid line and rest the thread. Using sewing thread, couch the first loop in place with four evenly spaced couching stitches (diag 2).

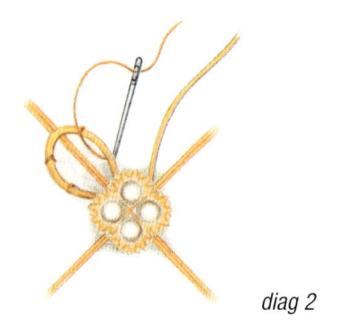

diag 2

Work a second loop in the same manner and couch in place. Continue in this manner, placing couched loops around each group of pearls, over each line in the grid.

Looped border
Beginning halfway along the lower edge, lay a single A thread along the outline. Twist the thread into a small loop and couch the loop in place at the crossover point and at the top. Continue along all sides in this manner, spacing the loops 6mm (¼") apart on the panel and 4mm (³⁄₁₆") on the scissor fob. Adjust the spacing to make sure a loop is placed at each corner.

Attaching check purl
Measure and cut B into short lengths to fit into the sections, curving around the pearls. Use doubled waxed sewing thread in the beading needle. Stitch each length of check purl carefully in place between the sections, curving it gently to follow the shape of the pearl.

Loops
Thread a 30cm (12") length of A into the milliner's needle. Secure the thread on the wrong side at one group of pearls. Bring the thread to the front next to the couched threads, just above the check purl.

Making the scissor fob
Rule and cut the card into two 4cm (1½") squares. Trim and lace the velvet for the back of the fob over one piece and the embroidered front over the second piece of card, following the instructions on page 23.

Place the front and back with wrong sides together. Using matching sewing thread, join the pieces with ladder stitch around all sides.

Cut six 1m (40") lengths of perlé cotton and make a twisted cord. Fold the cord in half and knot the ends. Cut a 5cm (2") wide piece of card and wrap enough perlé thread around it to form a small tassel. Cut the threads along one side and remove the card. Loop the threads over the knot on the twisted cord. Secure by wrapping a short length of thread tightly around the threads below the knot, to form the neck of the tassel (diag 3).

Diag 3

Position the tassel at the base of the fob and stitch the cord in place along two sides. Secure at the top. Beginning at the tassel, stitch the cord along the remaining two sides. Stitch the two cords securely together at the top, leaving a loop.

140

AUTUMN GOLD

Goldwork techniques
Attaching spangles with beads
Couching pair of threads
Couching pearl purl
Looped border
Looped purl
Open laid filling

Embroidery stitches
Cross stitch
Detached chain
Fly stitch
Surface satin stitch

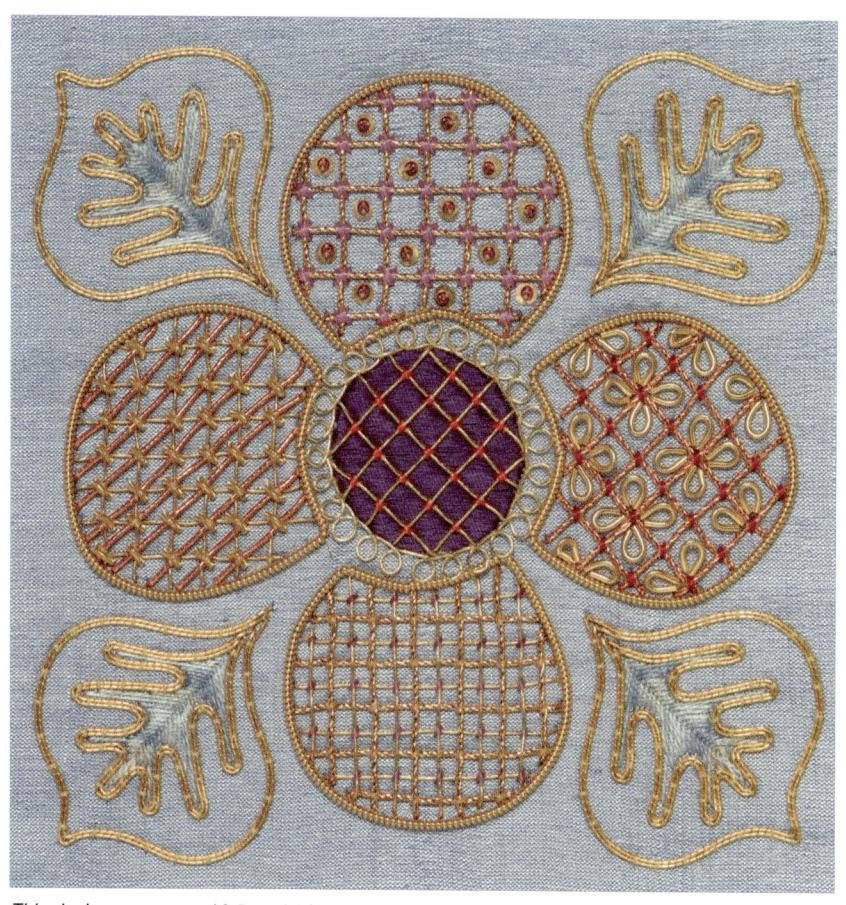

This design measures 10.5cm (4⅛") square.

Requirements

Fabric

30cm (12") square of dusky blue silk dupion
30cm (12") square of calico

Supplies

Gold coloured sewing thread
30cm (12") square stretcher frame
Thumbtacks
Velvet covered board
Beeswax
Sharp metal thread scissors
Sling
Dressmaker's awl or mellor
Tweezers
Tracing paper
Small piece of tissue paper
Orange dressmaker's carbon
Fine black pen

Needles

No. 10 crewel
No. 20 tapestry

Threads and beads

Benton & Johnson metallic thread
A = 3.5m (3yd 29¾") T71 gold imitation Japanese thread
B = 2.2m (2yd 14⅝") 371 gold fine couching thread
C = 75cm (29½") 3 ply gold twist
D = 40cm (16") no. 6 gold passing thread
E = 60cm (23½") no. 2 gold pearl purl
F = 70cm (27½") no. 6 gold smooth purl
G = 14 × 3mm (⅛") gold spangles
H = 50cm (31½") T69 copper imitation Japanese thread
I = 1m (40") 3 ply copper twist

Gloriana variegated stranded silk
J = 071 winter brook

Madeira stranded silk
K = 0511 garnet
L = 0701 lt raspberry

Pipers silk
M = flame
N = lt purple

Mill Hill petite beads
O = 42012 royal plum

Transferring the design

See page 149 for the embroidery design. The grey lines are placement guides only.

Trace the black design lines onto the tracing paper.

141

Centre the tracing over the silk. Using a ruler for the straight lines, transfer the design using the dressmaker's carbon, following the instructions on page 17.

Trace the centre circle and gridlines onto the tissue paper.

Preparation for embroidery

Position the silk over the calico and mount onto the frame following the instructions on page 20.

Embroidery

Use doubled waxed sewing thread for attaching the purls and spangles and a single thread for all couching.

Couch the intersections of the laid threads in place using matching sewing thread before adding the decorative coloured stitches.

Use the tapestry needle for the secondary grid of laid threads in petal three and the crewel needle for all other embroidery.

Centre

Fill the circle with satin stitch using N. Using the tissue paper tracing, tack the gridlines over the satin stitch following the instructions on page 79. Lay and couch the B thread over the satin stitch. Gently remove the tacking. Using M, work a cross stitch over each intersection.

Work the looped border outline using D, after all other embroidery is complete.

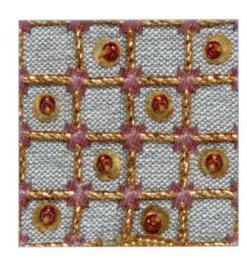

Petal one

Work the laid thread grid using C. Sink and secure the metal thread tails. Using L, work two cross stitches, one on top of the other, at each intersection (diag 1).

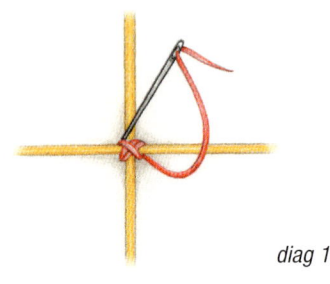

diag 1

Stitch a spangle in place with a bead in every second square of the grid.

Petal two

Stitch the laid grid using I. Sink and secure the metal thread tails. Using K, work two couching stitches over the previous stitches at each intersection. Cut short lengths of F, each approximately 14mm (⅝") long. Stitch each purl in place as a loop, grouping the loops around the intersections in the grid.

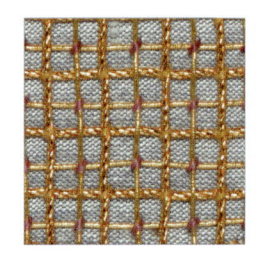

Petal three

Work and couch the main grid using C. Sink and secure the metal thread tails. Thread the tip of an 8cm (3¼") length of B into the tapestry needle. Slide the needle under one row of vertical threads in the main grid.

Gently pull the thread through to place it midway between the previous horizontal rows (diag 2).

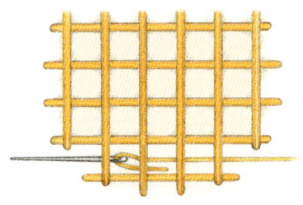

diag 2

Repeat for every row in the first grid, leaving the thread tails. Beginning at one side, place lengths of B halfway between the vertical rows of the first grid and couch the intersections of B threads in place with L. Continue couching the secondary grid in this manner (diag 3). Sink and secure the tails.

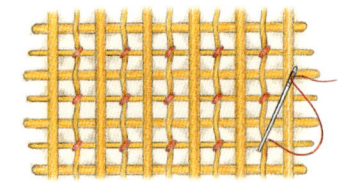

diag 3

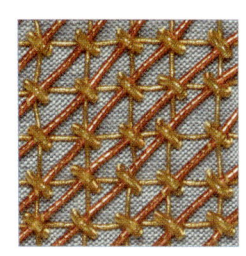

Petal four

Stitch the main grid using B. Sink and secure the metal thread tails.

Couch I diagonally across each row in the grid. Cut short lengths of smooth purl, each approximately 6mm (¼"). Bring a doubled thread to the front at one intersection, to one side of the copper thread. Slide a purl onto the fabric and take the needle to the back on the opposite side of the intersection. Pull the thread through carefully, using the mellor or awl to gently help shape the purl over the other threads (diag 4).

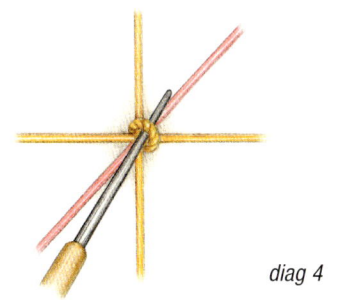

diag 4

Stitch a cut purl over each remaining intersection.

Petal outlines

Cut the pearl purl into four even lengths. Starting halfway along the base, outline each petal, using tweezers to shape the pearl purl at the corners. As you near the starting point, trim to the exact length and couch in place.

Leaves

Outline the main section of each leaf with a pair of A threads, using tweezers to kink the threads at the tip. Leave the tails on the surface. Couch a pair of threads along the outline of the inner section of each leaf. Take the eight thread tails to the back alternating from side to side, following steps 4–6 on page 40. Secure the tails.

Using J, work a long detached chain at the tip of the inner section of each leaf. Fill the inner leaf with closely worked fly stitches (diag 5).

diag 5

Embroidery key

All couching is worked with matching sewing thread.

Centre = N (satin stitch) B (open laid filling) M (cross stitch) D (looped border)

Petal one = C (open laid filling) L (cross stitch) G and O (attaching spangle)

Petal two = I (open laid filling) K (couching) F (looped purl)

Petal three = C (open laid filling) B and L (open laid filling)

Petal four = B (open laid filling) I (laid thread) F (attaching purl)

Petal outlines = E (couched pearl purl)

Leaves = A (couching) J (detached chain, fly stitch)

"Gold symbolizes perfection in everything, the very height of achievement. It is used to aid worship, to convey status and to portray wealth, and so it is with goldwork embroidery."

Sally Saunders

Royal School of Needlework Embroidery Techniques

FLEUR DE LYS

Requirements

Fabric

30cm (12") square of raw silk
30cm (12") square of calico

Supplies

4m (4yd 14") yellow soft cotton thread
Gold coloured sewing thread
Velvet covered board
Beeswax
Sharp metal thread scissors
Dressmaker's awl or mellor
Tweezers
25cm (10") square stretcher frame
Thumbtacks
Fine black pen
Tracing paper
Pricker and pounce

Needle

No. 10 crewel

Threads

Benton & Johnson metal threads
A = 65cm (25½") no. 6 gold birght check purl
B = 50cm (20") no. 6 gold rough purl
C = 2.25m (90") no. 6 gold smooth purl
Au Ver à Soie, Soie d'Alger
D = 916 red

This design measures 9.5cm × 7.5cm wide (3¾" × 3").

Goldwork techniques
Attaching purl
Soft cotton padding

Embroidery stitches
Long and short stitch

Embroidery key

All stitching is worked with doubled sewing thread unless otherwise specified.

Silk embroidery = D (1 strand, long and short stitch)

Goldwork

Upper sections = C (purl over string padding)
Lower sections = A (purl over string padding)
Centre bars = A and C (purl over string padding)
Arms = B and C (purl over string padding)

Preparation for embroidery

See page 150 for the embroidery design. The shaded areas indicate padding and the number of threads required in each section.

Transferring the design

Using the pen, trace the embroidery design and placement marks onto the tracing paper. Transfer the design onto the silk using prick and pounce referring to the instructions on page 8. Ensure the tracing is centred over the silk and the placement mark aligns with the straight grain of the fabric.

Place the fabrics onto the frame one at a time, following the instructions on page 20.

Padding

Referring to the numbers given on the embroidery design, apply soft cotton padding to the upper sections and arms of the fleur de lys, tapering to the number of threads at the points. Pad the small central sections with a single strand of cotton. The lower section is divided along the centre, and it is important to leave a small void in the padding. Pad each side of the lower section by couching a single length of cotton in place, beginning at the outermost point (a) and working towards the centre top (b) (diag 1).

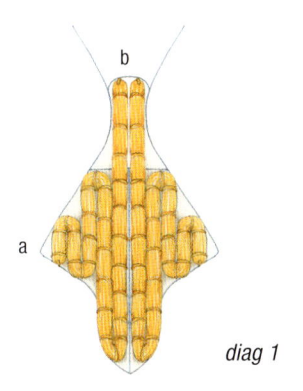

Embroidery

Use double waxed sewing thread for attaching the cut purl.

Silk embroidery

Starting at the top of the design, fill the unpadded areas with long and short stitch, using D. Keep the stitches approximately 1cm (⅜") long to achieve a smooth finish.

Goldwork

Use the velvet board when cutting the purl to achieve accurate cutting.

Upper sections

Cut C into the required lengths following the instructions on page 91 for cutting purl.

Bring the thread to the front on the left hand side and halfway along the centre band. Place the purl at a 45° angle across the section and take the needle to the back on the opposite side. Continue to stitch purls in place close together over the padding, working towards the top. Turn the frame 180°. Cover the lower half of the section in the same manner.

Cut and stitch lengths of C in place over the two outer bands in the same way.

Lower sections

The lower section is divided into three areas, each covered with purls separately to create defined lines within the section.

Using A, measure and cut the first purl from the outermost point on the left hand side to the centre, placing it at a 45° angle. Stitch in place. Place two more purls in place above the first. Measure and cut the fourth purl to fit across the entire section and stitch in place (diag 2).

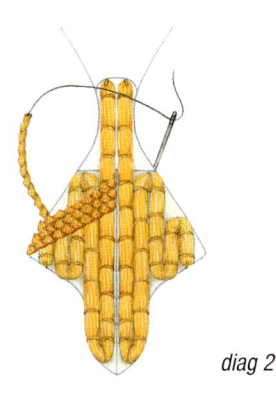

diag 2

Continue to stitch purls in place to the top of the section. Cover the lower part of the left hand side, bringing the needle to the front on the left edge and to the back on the centre line.

Beginning at the outermost point on the right hand side, place a purl at a 45° angle across the right half, matching the corresponding purl at the centre. Cover the right hand side, bringing the thread to the front on the right edge and taking it to the back through the centre. Make sure that the lengths of purl match along the centre.

diag 1

145

LYRE

Centre bars
For the two vertical bars, cut and stitch short lengths of C in place over the string padding, placing the purls at a 45° angle across the shape.

Cover the horizontal bar with short lengths of A placed at a 45° angle across the padding.

Arms
The upper scroll of each arm is worked with C and the lower scrolls using B.

Begin each section halfway along the scroll. Cut and stitch the purls in place over the padding at a 45° angle. Working from the upper left to the lower right on the left hand arm and from the upper top right to the lower left on the right hand arm.

To maintain the 45° angle around the curve, it is necessary to space the purls slightly, along the outer edge (diag 1).

To avoid any fabric or string showing between the purls, cut these pieces a little longer.

diag 1

This design measures 9.5cm × 7.5cm wide (3¾" × 3").

Embroidery key

All stitching is worked with doubled sewing thread unless otherwise specified.

Silk embroidery = D (1 strand, long and short stitch)

Goldwork

Outlines = B (couching)

Plate = C (attaching plate)

Twist = D (couching)

Spangles = A and E (attaching spangles)

146

Requirements

Fabric
30cm (12") square of raw silk
30cm (12") square of calico

Supplies
8cm × 10cm wide (3¼" × 4") piece of yellow felt
Gold coloured sewing thread
Velvet covered board
Beeswax
Sharp metal thread scissors
Dressmaker's awl or mellor
Tweezers
25cm (10") square stretcher frame
Thumbtacks
Fine black pen
Tracing paper
Pricker and pounce

Needles
No. 10 crewel
No. 18 chenille

Threads
Benton & Johnson metal threads
A = 20cm (8") no. 6 gold smooth purl
B = 55cm (22") gold milliary wire
C = 1.5m (60") no. 6 gold broad plate
D = 3.25m (3½ yd) no. 1 gold twist
E = 100 × 2.5mm (1/16") gold spangles

Au Ver à Soie, Soie d'Alger
F = 916 red

Goldwork techniques
Attaching plate
Attaching spangles with looped purl
Couching milliary wire
Couching pearl purl
Couching twist
Felt padding
Reverse felt padding

Embroidery stitches
Long and short stitch

Preparation for embroidery
See page 149 for the embroidery design. The shaded areas indicate felt padding and the number of layers required.

Transferring the design
Using the pen, trace the embroidery design and placement marks onto the tracing paper. Transfer the design onto the silk using prick and pounce, referring to the instruction on pages 8. Ensure the tracing is centred over the silk and the placement marks aligned with the straight grain of the fabric.

Place the fabrics onto the frame one at a time, following the instructions on page 20.

Preparing the felt padding
Using the pricked design, transfer the centre section, the base and the five circles onto the felt. Using a fine permanent pen, draw the design lines onto the felt to mark the shapes within the centre section and base and cut out (diag 2).

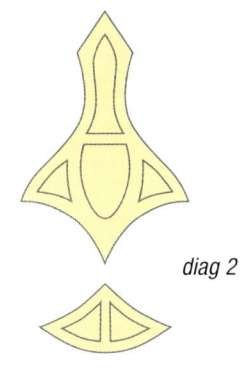

diag 2

Cut a second base piece, decreasing it by 2mm (1/16") around all sides.

Stitch the smallest base piece in place on the fabric, followed by the larger. Stitch the five circles and the large centre section in place at the marked positions.

Using the pricked design, transfer the smaller shapes within the centre section and the base and cut out. Cut another two pieces for the half oval, decreasing the size of each by 2mm (1/16") around all edges.

Stitch the smaller shapes in place at the marked positions over the larger pieces. For the half oval stitch the smallest piece in place first, followed by the medium and large piece (diag 3).

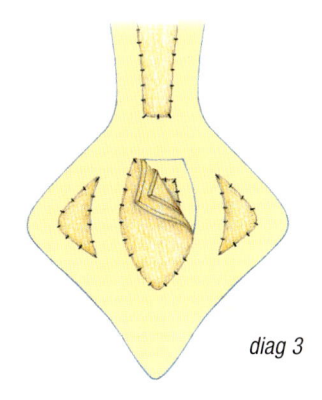

diag 3

Embroidery
Use the crewel needle for all stitching and the chenille needle for sinking the metal thread tails to the back of the work.

Silk embroidery

Starting at the top of the design, fill each arm with long and short stitch, using F. Keep the stitches approximately 1cm (⅜") long to achieve a smooth finish.

Plate

Centre section

Beginning at the tip of the half oval shape, cover the shape with plate, zig-zagging back and forth across the area.

Stitch the plate in place over the two triangular shapes and the narrow top area in the same way, making sure you begin each section at the narrowest point.

Base

Cover each triangle with plate, stitched in place from the outer point towards the centre, in a similar way to the centre areas.

Twist

Centre section

Fill the areas between the plate and outline with D, couched in place in close rows. Leaving a tail, begin each section close to the plate and couch towards the outline in a spiralling fashion. Place the couching stitches to follow the grooves in the twist. Sink the tails to the back and secure.

Base

Fill the area between the plate and the outline in the same way at the centre section.

Outlines

Base

Measure and cut a 7.5cm (3") length of B. Secure the end of the wire at the left hand point with a few stitches.

Couch the wire in place along the edge of the shape, placing the stitches at a right angle over the wire 3mm (⅛") apart. Use tweezers to shape the wire at the points. As you near the starting point, measure and trim the wire to fit. Couch securely in place.

Centre section

Cut a 18cm (7") length of B. Beginning at the base of the shape, couch the wire in place along the edge of the felt around the shape in a similar way to the base.

Arms

Cut a 25cm (6") length of B for each arm. Begin at the base and stitch the wire in place around the edge of silk embroidery a similar way as the base.

Spangles

Circles

Cut A into 5mm (3/16") lengths. Bring the thread to the front at the edge of the felt.

Stitch at spangle in place with a looped purl, following the instructions on page 106.

Bring the needle to the front at the edge of the felt at the position of the next spangle. Stitch the second and subsequent spangles in place in the same manner around the edge of the felt. Fill the centre of the circle with spangles stitched in place in the same manner.

Arms

Stitch eighteen spangles evenly spaced, in place with looped purls along the centre of each arm.

Centre and base

Stitch a spangle in place with a looped purl at the top and bottom of the centre section and at the top of the base area.

Sampler: Fil d'or *by Tanja Berlin.*

Patterns

Autumn gold
Embroidery design

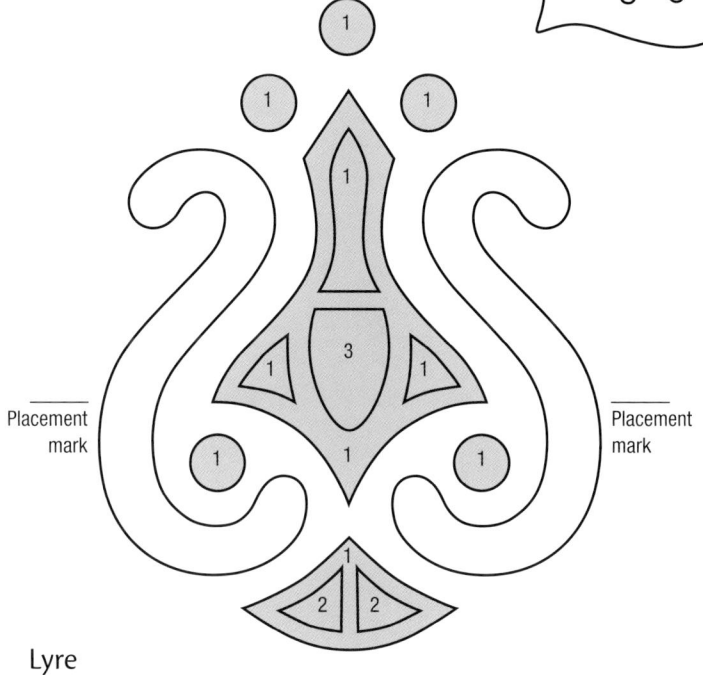

Lyre
Embroidery design and padding diagram

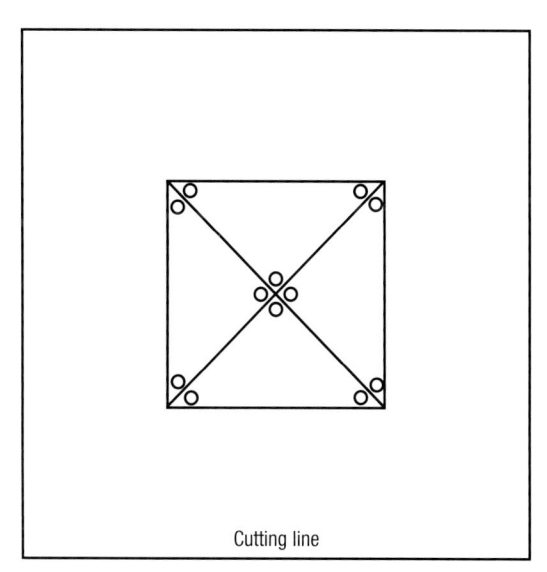

Placement mark

Placement mark

Golden reticella
Scissor fob embroidery design and pattern

Cutting line

Fleur de lys

Embroidery design and padding diagram

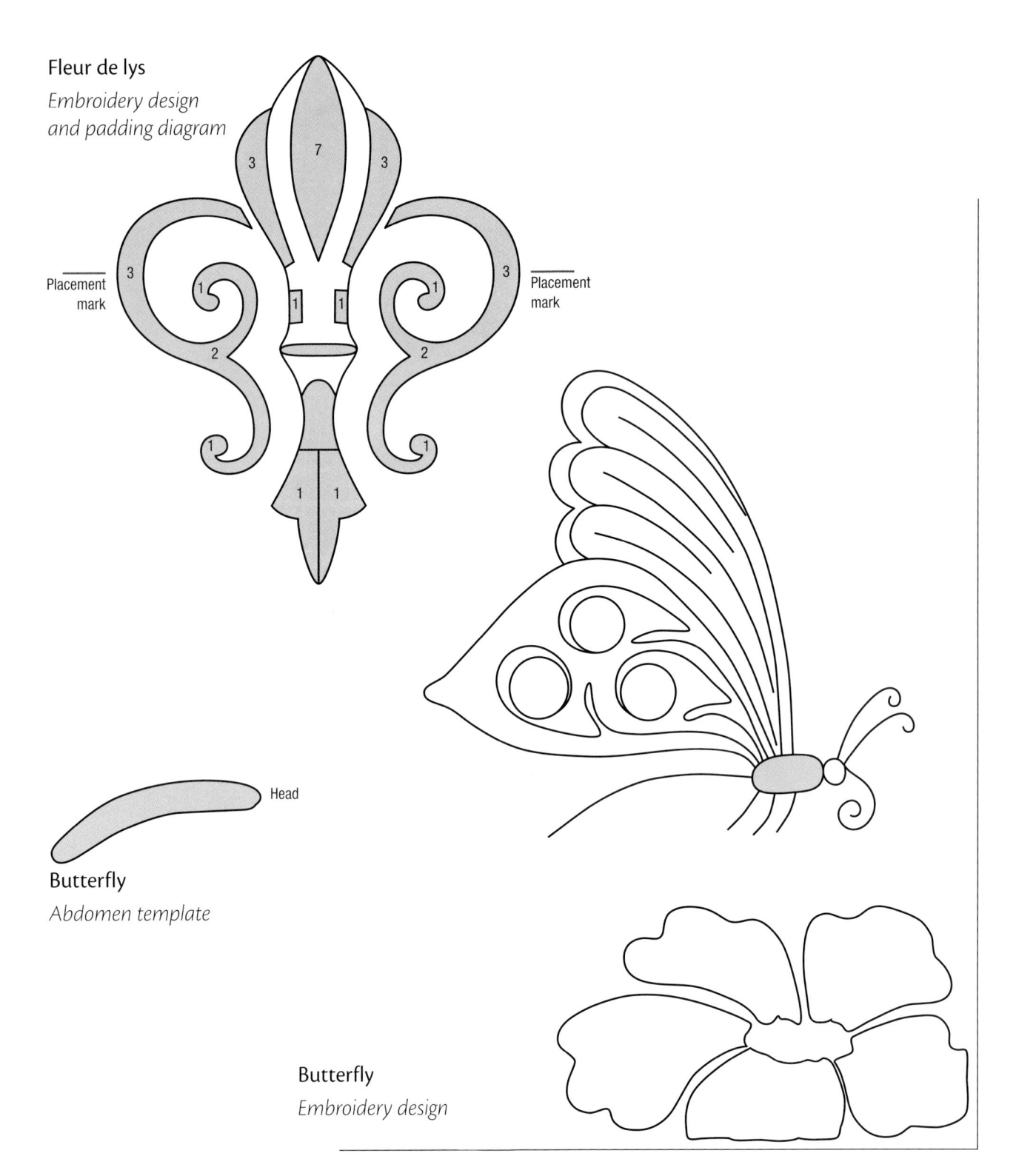

Placement mark

Placement mark

Butterfly

Abdomen template

Head

Butterfly

Embroidery design

Golden reticella panel

Embroidery design

Strawberry pincushion

Embroidery design and pattern

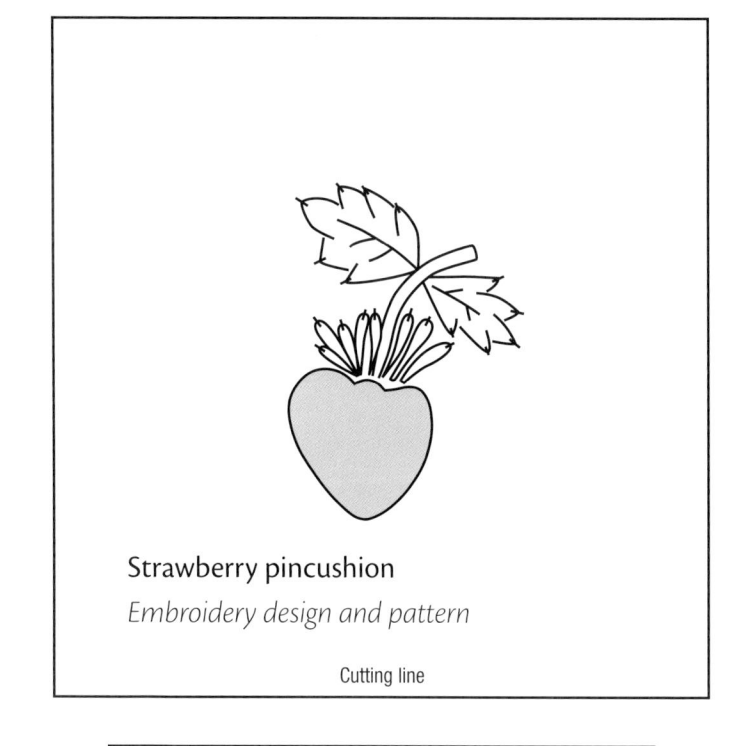

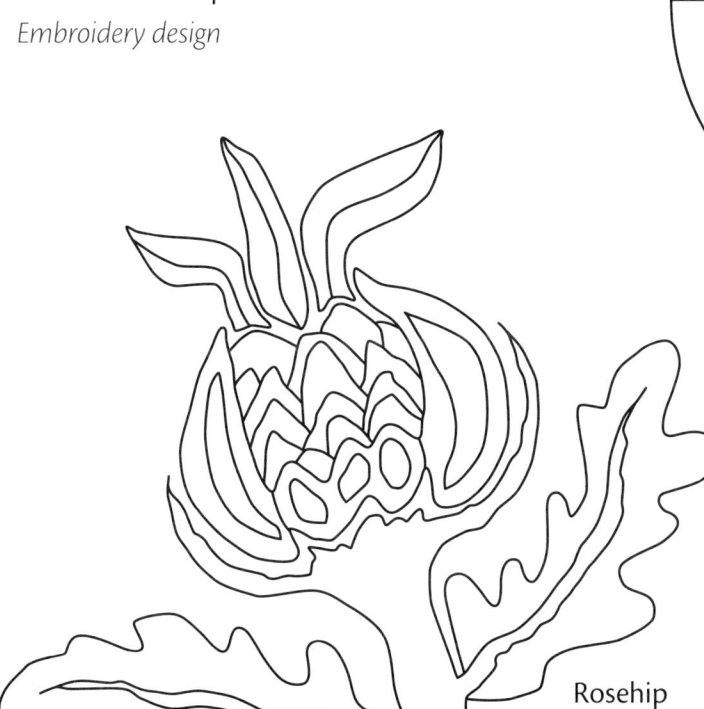

Cutting line

Strawberry tassel

Template

Red felt cut one

Rosehip

Embroidery design

Flower border

Stitch direction diagrams

Flower border

Embroidery design

Acknowledgements

A sincere thank you to the following individuals, museums and organisations who have generously shared items from their collections.

Antonia Lomney

Benton & Johnson, UK

Embroiderers Guild of America

Embroiderers Guild of South Australia

Embroiderers Guild of Victoria

Greve Museum, Denmark

National Czech and Slovak Museum and Library, Cedar Rapids, Iowa, USA

Society of Ecclesiastical Art and Craft, Copenhagen, Denmark

A special thank you to Tanja Berlin for kindly sharing her knowledge.

Designer index
Anna Scott
Butterfly, page 124
Rosehip, page 131
Flower border, page 135
Autumn gold, page 141

Christine Bishop
Strawberry pincushion, page 129
Golden reticella, page 138

Tanja Berlin
Fleur de lys, page 144
Lyre, page 146

Index

A

Acid free card and paper, 12
Acknowledgements, 153
Acute corner, 40
Angular shapes, couching 48
Appliqué, 24–26
  ~ securing large shapes, 25
Applying padding, 27–32
Autumn gold, 141
Awl, 8

B

Back stitch, 112
  ~ over sequin, 104, 106
Backing fabric, 11, 12, 19
Basic couching, 36
Basket stitch filling, 64
Beads, 16
  ~ over sequins, 105
Beeswax, 8, 31
Beetle wings, 16
Bobbin, 8
Border, looped purl, 95
Braid, 13
Bricking, 57
Broad plate, 13
Brooch, 71
Bullion knot, 113
Bullion thread, 15
Burden stitch
  ~ coloured couching, 72
  ~ cut purl, 74
Butting cord ends, 29
Butterfly, 124

C

Carbon tracing, 17
Card, 12
  ~ padding, 27, 66, 69
  ~ tacking, 27

Caring for old embroidery, 23
Chain stitch, 114
  ~ heavy, 116
  ~ reverse, 115
  ~ with cut purl, 92
Chalk, 8
Charcoal, 8
Check purl, 14, 15, 90
Chequered filling, 94
Chip work, 90
Circle 50, 51, 60
Clamps, 8
Cleaning, 22
Coiled filling, 76
Contents, 2
Cord, 12, 13
  ~ fine, 28
  ~ intersection, 29
  ~ padding, 27, 64, 70
  ~ tension, 29
  ~ wrapping, 28
Corners, 40–42
Cotton sewing thread, 19
Couching
  ~ circle, 50, 51
  ~ corners 40–42
  ~ doubled laid thread, 36, 37
  ~ embellished, 46
  ~ hints, 36, 37, 38, 54
  ~ loop purl, 96
  ~ milliary wire, 81
  ~ outline, 24, 39, 44
  ~ pearl purl, 80
  ~ plate, 86
  ~ rococo, 38
  ~ rows, 52–55
  ~ single thread, 38
  ~ thread over sequins, 104
  ~ twist, 43–45
  ~ underside, 62

Couching over padding, 64–71
Couching thread, 8, 13
  ~ securing, 32
Couching twisted threads, 43–45
Cutting purl, 91

D

Damascening, 77
Design gallery, 124–148
Detached chain, cut purl, 93
Direct tracing, 17

E

Embellishment, 16
Embellished couching, 46
Embroidered letters, 75
Embroidery designs, 149–152
Embroidery hoop, 9, 20
Embroidery threads, 15
Embroidery stitches, 92, 112–123
English work, 4
Equipment, 8–11

F

Fabrics, 11
Feather stitch, cut purl, 93
Felt, 12
  ~ padding, 29, 68, 71
Felt bobbin, 8
Filling shapes, 48–63, 72–79, 86, 90, 94, 108
Fine twist, 14, 43
Finishing embroidery, 22
Fish scale filling, 108
Fleur de lys, 144
Flower border, 134
Fly stitch, cut purl, 93
Framing up, 20

Frames and hoops, 9
French knot, 117

G

Geometric patterns, 57
Golden reticella, 138
Guimped couching, 66

H

Heavy chain stitch, 116
Heavy twist, 14, 15, 44
Herringbone stitch, cut purl, 93
History of goldwork, 3–7

I–J

Imitation Japanese thread, 13, 15
Indirect tracing, 18
Joining ends, pearl purl, 82

K–L

Kid leather, 12
  ~ applying, 68, 69
Lacing embroidery, 23
Laid work, 47–57
  ~ circle, 50–51
  ~ couching patterns, 57
  ~ fillings, 48
  ~ on velvet, 56
  ~ over padding, 69–71
  ~ sinking thread tails, 52
  ~ stitch direction, 47, 48
  ~ rows, 52–55
Leather, 12, 68, 69
Long and short stitch, 118
  ~ blending colour, 119
Looped purl, 95–99
Lyre, 146

M

Main fabric, 11
Materials, 12
Measuring purl, 91, 94
Mellor, 9
~ stroking silk stitches, 119
Metal threads, 13–15
~ securing, 35
~ sinking, 33, 34
Milliary wire, 14, 81

N–O

Needles, 9
~ sinking thread tails, 33
Open laid filling, 78
~ over satin stitch, 79
~ patterns, 79
Opus anglicanum, 4, 62
Or nué, 5, 58, 60, 134
Other metallic threads, 15
Outline, 24, 39, 44, 65, 69
Overstretched pearl purl, 83
~ coloured, 84, 85

P

Padding, 27–32, 64–71
Passing thread, 14, 15, 62, 76
Pearls, 16
Pearl purl, 14
~ couching, 80
~ coloured, 84, 85
~ joining ends, 82
~ overstretched, 83
~ turning corner, 82
Plate, 13, 15, 86–88
Pliers, 10
Pounce, 8
Pounce pad, 10
Preparing fabrics, 19
Preparing for embroidery, 17–22

Pressing, 23
Prick and pounce, 18
Pricking tool, 10
Purl, 14, 15, 89–103
~ chequered filling, 94
~ chip work, 90
~ cutting, 91
~ embroidery stitches, 92
~ looped, 95 – 99, 106
~ measuring, 91, 94
~ over padding, 100–102
~ over sequins, 106, 107, 109
~ removing, 89
~ s-ing, 103, 109
~ tension, 100

R

Removing purl, 89
Reverse chain stitch, 115
Reverse felt padding, 30, 71
Rhinestones, 16
Right angled corner, 41
Rococo, 14, 15, 38
Rough purl, 14, 15
Rosehip, 131

S

S-ing, 103
~ over sequins, 109
Satin stitch, 119
~ block shading, 120
~ curved, 120
~ surface stitch, 121
Scallops, purl, 98
Scissors, 10
Securing threads, 32, 35, 44, 52
Semi-precious stones, 16
Sequins, 15, 16

Sequins and spangles, 104–110
~ couched thread, 104
~ filling, 108
~ individual, 104–106
~ overlapping, 106–110
~ with s-ing, 109
Sewing thread, 10
Silk embroidery, 111–123
~ multiple strands, 112
~ stroking stitches, 119
Sinking metal thread tails, 33, 34, 52
Shaded gold, 5, 58
Sharp corner, 42
Slate frame, 9, 21
Sling, 10, 34
Slip, 24
Smooth purl, 14, 15
Soft cotton, 12
~ padding, 31, 101
Spangles, 15, 16
Split stitch, 121
Stabilising, laid threads, 36, 37, 38, 54
Starting and finishing, 24–35
Stem stitch, 122
~ corners, 123
~ filling, 123
Stiletto, 8
Stitch direction, 43, 47, 48, 118
Storing metal threads, 33
Strawberry pincushion, 128
Stretcher frame, 9, 20, 21
String, 12
~ padding, 27, 31, 64, 70, 101

T

Tacking, 19, 20
~ card, 27
~ kid leather, 68
~ layered fabrics, 20, 21
~ without tissue paper, 19
Tension, 29, 53, 54, 100
Thimble, 10
Thumbtacks, 11, 20
Tissue paper, 12, 19, 79
Tracing paper, 12, 17, 18
Transfer methods, 17–19
Turning corners, 40–42, 82
Turning rows, 52–55
Tweezers, 11
Twist, 14, 15
~ couching, 43–45

U

Underside couching, 62
Upright purl loop, 99

V–W

Velvet covered board, 11, 91
Velvet, laid work, 56
Vermicelli, 77
Weights, 11
Wrapping, 28, 44

First published in Great Britain 2015

Search Press Limited
Wellwood, North Farm Road,
Tunbridge Wells, Kent TN2 3DR

Reprinted 2020

First published in Australia by Inspirations Studios
© Inspirations Studios

Illustrations and patterns by Kathleen Barac

Photography by Andrew Dunbar Photography

All rights reserved. No part of this book, text, photographs or illustrations may be reproduced or transmitted in any form or by any means by print, photoprint, microfilm, microfiche, photocopier, internet or in any way known or as yet unknown, or stored in a retrieval system, without written permission obtained beforehand from Search Press. Printed in China

ISBN: 978-1-78221-170-9

The Publishers and author can accept no responsibility for any consequences arising from the information, advice or instructions given in this publication.

Readers are permitted to reproduce any of the items/patterns in this book for their personal use, or for the purposes of selling for charity, free of charge and without the prior permission of the Publishers. Any use of the items/patterns for commercial purposes is not permitted without the prior permission of the Publishers.

Suppliers
If you have difficulty in obtaining any of the materials and equipment mentioned in this book, then please visit the Search Press website for details of suppliers: www.searchpress.com